Sharper Axes, Lower Taxes: Big Steps to a Smaller State

Sharper Axes, Lower Taxes: Big Steps to a Smaller State

EDITED BY PHILIP BOOTH

WITH CONTRIBUTIONS FROM

SAM COLLINS

NIGEL HAWKINS

PATRICK MINFORD

JULIAN MORRIS

KRISTIAN NIEMIETZ

PAUL ROBINSON

J. R. SHACKLETON

DAVID B. SMITH

CORIN TAYLOR

JIANG WANG

RICHARD WELLINGS

The Institute of Economic Affairs

First published in Great Britain in 2011 by
The Institute of Economic Affairs
2 Lord North Street
Westminster
London SW1P 3LB
in association with Profile Books Ltd

The mission of the Institute of Economic Affairs is to improve public understanding of
the fundamental institutions of a free society, by analysing and expounding the role of
markets in solving economic and social problems.

A CIP catalogue record for this book is available from the British Library.

ISBN 978 0 255 36648 9

Many IEA publications are translated into languages other than English or are reprinted.
Permission to translate or to reprint should be sought from the Director General at the
address above.

Typeset in Stone by MacGuru Ltd
info@macguru.org.uk

Printed and bound in Great Britain by Hobbs the Printers

CONTENTS

AUTHORS

Philip Booth

Philip Booth is Editorial and Programme Director of the Institute of Economic Affairs and Professor of Insurance and Risk Management at the Sir John Cass Business School, City University. He has written extensively on regulation, social insurance and Catholic social teaching. He is a fellow of the Institute of Actuaries and of the Royal Statistical Society and associate editor of *Annals of Actuarial Science* and the *British Actuarial Journal*. He has also advised the Bank of England on financial stability issues (1998–2002).

Sam Collins

Sam Collins is a political specialist who has worked for a number of politicians, lobby groups and think tanks in New Zealand, London and Washington. He worked for the Institute of Economic Affairs from 2010 until 2011 and aided a number of Conservative Party campaigns during the 2010 general election. He has previously co-authored 'Regulating the labour market can be bad for your health' (in *International Labour and Social Policy Review*, 2008), and 'Green Monitor' (pamphlet, Progressive Vision, 2009). Sam is currently a candidate for the National Party in the 2011 New Zealand general election.

Nigel Hawkins

Nigel Hawkins is an investment analyst who specialises primarily in the electricity, gas, water and telecoms sectors. He has worked in the City since 1988. He is a regular features writer for *Utility Week* and *Cleantech* magazines and frequently contributes to the financial media. Prior to joining the City, he worked in politics, including for three years as Political Correspondence Secretary to Lady Thatcher at 10 Downing Street. In 1987, he stood in the general election as Conservative Party candidate in Sedgefield against Tony Blair.

Patrick Minford

Patrick Minford is Professor of Applied Economics at Cardiff University, where he directs the Julian Hodge Institute of Applied Macroeconomics. Between 1967 and 1976 he held a variety of economic positions, including spells in East Africa, industry and HM Treasury. From 1976 to 1997, he was the Edward Gonner Professor of Applied Economics at Liverpool University. He was a member of the Monopolies and Mergers Commission from 1990 to 1996, and one of HM Treasury's Panel of Forecasters (the 'Six Wise Men') from 1993 to 1996. He was made a CBE in 1996. He has written widely on macroeconomics and related policy issues.

Julian Morris

Julian Morris is vice-president of research at Reason Foundation, a non-profit think tank advancing free minds and free markets. Julian has degrees in economics and law and is the author of dozens of scholarly articles on issues ranging from the morality of free trade to the regulation of the Internet. He has also edited several books and co-edits, with Indur Goklany, the *Electronic Journal of Sustainable Development*. Julian is a visiting professor in the Department of International Studies at the University of Buckingham (UK). Before joining Reason, he was executive director of International Policy Network, a London-based think tank which he co-founded. Before that, he ran the environment and technology programme at the IEA.

Kristian Niemietz

Kristian Niemietz is the IEA's Poverty Research Fellow. He is also a PhD student, and a tutor in economics, at King's College London. Kristian studied economics at the Humboldt Universität zu Berlin and the Universidad de Salamanca, graduating as *Diplom-Volkswirt* (MSc in Economics) in 2007. After graduating, he went on to work for the Berlin-based Institute for Free Enterprise (IUF).

Paul Robinson

Paul Robinson is a professor in the Graduate School of Public and International Affairs at the University of Ottawa. He is the author of numerous books and articles on military history, international security and defence policy, including *Doing Less with Less: Making Britain More Secure* (Imprint Academic, 2005) and *Dictionary of International Security* (Polity, 2008).

J. R. Shackleton

J. R. Shackleton is Professor of Economics at the University of East London and an IEA Economics Fellow. He has been dean of two business schools, taught at four universities and has worked in the Government Economic Service. He has written extensively in academic journals and policy publications, has given evidence to parliamentary committees and has appeared many times on TV and radio. For the IEA he has written *Training Too Much?*, *Trouble in Store?* (with Terry Burke), *Employment Tribunals* and *Should We Mind the Gap?*

David B. Smith

David B. Smith studied at Trinity College, Cambridge, and the University of Essex in the 1960s. He then worked as an economist, mainly in banks and the securities industry, from 1968 to 2006. David is currently a visiting professor at the University of Derby, has been chairman of the IEA's Shadow Monetary Policy Committee since 2003, is an occasional lecturer at Cardiff University Business School and the chief economist on the TaxPayers' Alliance/Institute of Directors 2020 Tax Commission. He maintains his own econometric forecasting model of the international and UK economies at Beacon Economic Forecasting.

Corin Taylor

Corin Taylor is a freelance political consultant and a senior fellow at the Economic Policy Centre. He was formerly a senior policy adviser at the Institute of Directors, secretary to the Public Sector Pensions Commission and a member of the Social Return on Investment Working Group at the Centre for Social Justice (CSJ). Previously, he was a member of the Economic Dependency Working Group at the CSJ, Research Director at the TaxPayers' Alliance, Political Secretary at the Tax Reform Commission and Economics Research Officer at the think tank Reform. He has also written for the Centre for Policy Studies, Civitas and Policy Exchange think tanks on a freelance basis.

Jiang Wang

Jiang Wang obtained his PhD in economics from Cardiff University in 2007. His thesis was entitled 'Growth and relative living standards: testing barriers to riches on post-war panel data'. He is the co-author of several research papers examining the relationship between levels of public spending and economic growth.

Richard Wellings

Richard Wellings is Deputy Editorial Director at the IEA. He was educated at Oxford and the London School of Economics, completing a PhD on transport and environmental policy at the latter in 2004. He joined the IEA in 2006 to work on the production of its monograph series and the journal *Economic Affairs*. Richard is the author or editor of several papers, books and reports, including *Towards Better Transport* (Policy Exchange, 2008) and *A Beginner's Guide to Liberty* (Adam Smith Institute, 2009). He is a senior fellow of the Cobden Centre, the Economic Policy Centre and the Libertarian Alliance.

FOREWORD

In October 2010, the coalition government unveiled its Comprehensive Spending Review. Perhaps the most obvious characteristic of the review was that it was piecemeal and anything but comprehensive. Many benefits and government functions remained untouched and unreformed and there was a definite air of 'salami slicing'. For example, there were tweaks to housing benefit that will save a little money but do nothing to improve incentives, labour mobility and the efficient allocation of housing space.

In many areas a policy decision was taken to avoid reductions in spending altogether. Ironically, these decisions were taken in the area of health (which government figures suggest has been dogged by increasing inefficiency as real spending has increased) and overseas aid (which the evidence suggests does little, if any, good). Areas within other departments have also been protected from spending reductions. For example, many benefits for the elderly will be 'over-indexed' in the coming years.

This piecemeal approach to the Comprehensive Spending Review (CSR) has two disadvantages. The first is that government spending will not reduce significantly. There will be cuts in anticipated increases in government spending rather than actual cuts in nominal spending. It is true that there will be cuts in real spending of 0.4 per cent per year but, as a proportion of national income, spending will merely fall back to the levels we experienced in 2007. Secondly, the CSR has been a missed opportunity to reform large areas of economic life and reduce and simplify taxes. In his 2010 budget, the Chancellor of the Exchequer pointed out that the government has never been able to raise more than 40 per cent of national income in taxation. This is the level of spending to which the CSR will return the UK government. It appears that the limit of the ambition of the government is to reduce spending to the maximum it is possible to tax its citizens. An alternative approach would lead the government to ask which functions it should no longer be carrying out because the money would be best left to 'fructify in the pockets of the people'.

The authors of this monograph were asked to make radical proposals for cuts in government spending that the coalition has avoided. They were told to ignore the politically possible, though most of the proposals are, indeed, well within the realms of the politically possible. An important aspect of our authors' proposals is that they are designed to lead to much better economic outcomes – or achieve given outcomes much more efficiently than current policies. As such, the proposals would be equally welcome if the government's coffers were overflowing and the exchequer were in surplus.

Why a smaller state?

There are several reasons why the government should seek to spend less. First, the taxes necessary to finance government spending damage economic growth, as is shown in the chapter by Jiang Wang and Patrick Minford. Taxes damage economic growth, it would appear, to a much greater extent than government spending in areas such as research and development, education and investment subsidies benefit economic growth. Indeed, the sort of tax cuts proposed by this monograph might, according to the work of Wang and Minford, raise the sustainable growth rate by nearly 1 per cent. This damage to economic growth from high taxation comes from a number of sources, such as disincentives to save and work, the discouragement of enterprise and the 'deadweight costs' of taxes on work, savings and consumption. Indeed, as the chapter by Richard Wellings on climate change policy and related fields shows, in many areas the state has become incoherent and is almost tripping over itself. It therefore levies taxes in ways that greatly damage economic growth while offering subsidies that directly counter the effects of the taxes it levies. For example, in the UK we have 'climate change' taxes yet also have an exemption from VAT for domestic fuel consumption. We subsidise carbon-intensive agriculture and also subsidise renewable energy production. The elimination of various subsidies and tax expenditures in this area promises a 'win-win' outcome.

As the chapter by David Smith demonstrates, a large state feeds on itself and encourages further growth in the size of the state by supporting the interest groups that benefit from increased public spending. Three observations are apparent from Smith's chapter. The first is that, in all major countries, government spending has grown rapidly in the twentieth century – from about 10 per cent of national income in many countries to between 40 and 50 per cent of national income. Secondly, it is possible to have a state that provides extensive protection for the poor and which fulfils its most important functions while spending less than 30 per cent of national income. Thirdly, David Smith shows how small the proposed spending cuts are in the context of the rapid growth in spending that took place under Gordon Brown.

The UK also has a welfare system that strongly discourages work, family formation and saving – the three things necessary not just for economic prosperity but for economic fulfilment. State welfare has encouraged dependency and economic inactivity – again contributing to the reduction in economic growth as well as to social breakdown. The chapter by Kristian Niemietz demonstrates how this can be changed. We can have a simpler welfare system that does not tax the middle class in order to provide 'middle-class welfare' and which does not discriminate against work and family formation to nearly the same extent as current arrangements. Such welfare reform would also finance a considerable reduction in taxes. The chapter by Philip Booth and Corin Taylor applies this logic to benefits provided to the elderly and suggests 'voluntary privatisation' of the state pension system.

There are several areas where the authors show how much better economic outcomes could be achieved if the government withdrew from the provision of services and made consumers at least partially responsible for the finance of services. The central planning of health, education and transport discussed by Sam Collins, J. R. Shackleton and Richard Wellings respectively not only reduces efficiency but prevents the operation of the process of competition which can allow us to find new ways of meeting consumers' needs. As Austrian economics teaches us, the knowledge that is inherently dispersed among economic actors cannot be centralised. Education, health and transport cannot be rationally planned and coordinated by politicians and bureaucrats because they do not have the knowledge to use economic resources to meet consumers' preferences. In education, for example, we need individual schools – or chains of schools – to innovate with new ways of providing education. If such innovation improves educational outcomes then parents will respond by demanding places for their children in the schools that innovate successfully. Other schools will then copy successful innovations and unsuccessful innovations will wither. Under the current mechanisms of providing for health, education and transport, administrators and professionals are literally guessing how to increase the welfare of consumers – all the information signals that communicate the costs of different approaches and their benefits to the users of services have been removed from the system.

It is for this reason – and also because of the appalling productivity record of state provision – that our authors have proposed that the state substantially scales back its operations in providing health, education and transport services. As well as private provision, however, at least some degree of personal financial contribution to health and education is needed too – voucher systems with public finance and private provision are not enough. For example, Shackleton suggests a parental contribution for education (though not one which would be higher than the average cost of a nursery place) and Collins proposes health savings accounts to meet most health needs.

The proposals in this monograph would increase personal disposable income by about 20 per cent compared with the government's own plans. This ignores any effects on economic growth, work incentives and other dynamic effects of tax decreases. Different people in different situations may wish to choose to spend different amounts of their budget on health, education, insurance against contingencies, housing and so on. They will have increased freedom to do so under the proposals outlined in this monograph while provision for basic needs will be assured. Substantial improvements in economic welfare will arise from households being allowed to allocate their own budgets. For the first time for many decades it will be possible for the less well off to actually choose to spend more on health or education or on some of the 'hotel services' that often come with health provision. Privileges that have been reserved for the rich owing to our high level of state provision and high level of taxation will be extended to all.

A 'bottom-up' strategic review, not 'salami slicing'

Our authors were asked to do precisely what the government did not do – build up from the bottom a picture of the economic role the state should play and suggest reforms that would ultimately take us to that point. Perhaps this is best illustrated in the chapter on defence by Paul Robinson and that on aid by Julian Morris. Defence has undergone a 'strategic review' which, as Robinson points out, is anything but strategic. Paul Robinson conducts a genuinely strategic review of defence and concludes that much lower spending would be possible. Julian Morris looks at the economic purpose and record of aid and finds that development aid simply does not do the job it is intended to do. As such, we should no longer provide aid.

A strategic review also requires a long-term approach, again something that was missing from the CSR. Many of the reforms proposed by our authors are very long-term (for example, those to health and pensions). It cannot be expected, for example, that somebody who is 85 should suddenly develop funded health provision for later in their life. To deal with such situations, a pragmatic path towards the long-term goal has been proposed. This means that our authors' proposals should ensure that the size of the state is likely to decline further rather than creep back up again as the reforms evolve over future generations – although the reduction in government spending gets an initial 'one-off boost' from privatisations proposed in the chapter by Nigel Hawkins. One of the problems with the government starting from where we are and cutting back a little is that the size of the state is likely to grow back rapidly as soon as the emergency squeeze is over. If we redefine the functions of the state this is less likely to happen. The CSR has taken the approach of a gardener who lightly prunes a vigorous weed growing in a bed of perennials. Our authors have dug the weeds out and tidied up the bed, leaving what is necessary and desirable.

It should be noted that the proposals would not necessarily take us back to those functions of government that would be undertaken by a 'minimal state'. The state would still ensure that all citizens could access healthcare, education and pensions. Some economic liberals might question whether these are legitimate roles for government, and these are issues for debate in more philosophical and radical IEA publications. Our authors have taken big steps to a smaller state, not one step to a minimal state. Where our authors do propose a role for government, they were asked to suggest how that role could be most efficiently fulfilled. For example, in the case of health provision, government would assist the poor to save through health savings accounts rather than creating a national health service run and financed by the state for all citizens as happens at the moment.

Limitations of this spending review

The proposals in this monograph have not covered every possible area of public spending. Areas such as policing, justice and local government are not covered – though some services provided by local government are included implicitly. Most of the areas where the government's spending review has been least comprehensive have been covered in this monograph, with the possible exception of policing. In calculating

the total level of government spending after the review we have implicitly assumed that the government's plans will be implemented in those
public spending areas not covered by our authors. This is a relatively
conservative assumption as further savings would be possible in many
areas – such as EU contributions and policing. We have also assumed
that the trajectory for reducing the relative value of the national debt is
the same as that assumed by the government. In other words, it has been
assumed that all the spending cuts proposed in this monograph will be
used to finance tax cuts and that the level of the fiscal deficit will be close
to zero by 2015.

Overall, the spending cuts proposed by the authors would take
government spending back below 30 per cent of national income. This
level of spending could be financed by a simple tax system which was not
nearly as intrusive or complex as our current system. Indeed, the benefits
to economic growth would be so great under the proposals in this monograph that not only would people have more money to spend themselves
immediately but, if government spending remained at less than 30 per
cent of national income for a generation, real tax receipts would rise back
to current levels. In other words, after one generation taxes would be at
the same proportion of a much higher national income. Of course, the
poverty reductions that would arise from faster economic growth might
allow much greater spending reductions in future years.

Structure of the monograph

The first part of this monograph deals with taxation and the size of the
state. The first chapter examines the relationship between taxation and
economic growth. The second chapter looks at the size of the state in
an international and historical context. The third chapter in Part One
summarises the cuts in public spending proposed in the later chapters
and suggests a general shape for a tax system that would feasibly raise
just under 30 per cent of national income.

Parts Two to Five of this study take each major area of public spending in turn and propose radical policy reform and reductions in public spending. The authors do not, of course, have access to the detailed models that the Treasury might use to forecast public spending. As best they can, however, our authors have quantified the level of spending cuts that are possible in the areas that they are studying using a base date of 2015. It is assumed that the implementation date for all these reforms is 2015 – some could be phased in earlier and many of the reforms that began in 2015 would be the first stage in a long process: they would thus yield further savings in later years.

It should be pointed out that all the chapters have been written independently. For that reason, each chapter may not be entirely consistent with every other chapter. For example, the author proposing privatisation did not collaborate explicitly with the author who worked on transport. However, the proposals in this monograph are more or less compatible with each other. Individually, the chapters present important proposals for reducing the role of the state and increasing the role of the individual and the community in economic life. Taken together, they represent a radical general programme to dramatically reduce public spending and taxation and also reduce the distortions imposed on our economy by government intervention. They provide a fully comprehensive spending review.

Overall, this monograph is an important contribution to the discussion of the role that the state should play in economic life. In line with the mission of the IEA, it proposes a much greater role for markets in solving economic and social problems. The views expressed in this monograph are, as in all IEA publications, those of the authors and not those of the Institute (which has no corporate view), its managing trustees, Academic Advisory Council members or senior staff.

PHILIP BOOTH

Editorial and Programme Director,

Institute of Economic Affairs

Professor of Insurance and Risk Management,

Cass Business School, City University

June 2011

SUMMARY

- Government spending is over 50 per cent of national income. Spending grew steadily in the twentieth century and then experienced very rapid growth from the beginning of the 21st century.
- Much government spending discourages economic activity and prevents innovation and competition in crucial sectors such as health and education. Furthermore, government intervention is incoherent. For example, government spending and implicit subsidies strongly encourage certain carbon-intensive activities; other forms of government spending are then used to try to reduce carbon-intensive energy generation.
- The recent Comprehensive Spending Review was anything but comprehensive. Certain departments were omitted from the review altogether. Most other areas of spending were 'salami sliced'. No coherent, bottom-up analysis of government functions has taken place. The government could achieve its main public policy objectives at much lower levels of spending if there were to be a radical review of all aspects of spending.
- Even if the coalition achieves its objectives, there will be only modest reductions in government spending. Nominal spending will rise, real spending will be cut by less than 1 per cent per annum and spending as a proportion of national income will fall back only to 2007 levels.
- A complete review of government functions could, as a first step, lead to cuts in underlying government spending of £242 billion in addition to the government's proposed cuts. Using the

government's definitions of government spending and national income this would amount to a cut of £215 billion to around 29 per cent of national income.

- Government spending – even in areas such as research and development, investment and education – has little or no beneficial effect on economic growth. The taxation necessary to fund government spending, however, seriously and adversely affects economic growth. A reduction in government spending of the order suggested by our authors would lead to economic growth increasing by more than 0.75 per cent per annum: this would mean that national income would grow by an extra 20 per cent every 25 years.

- The current welfare system discriminates strongly against work, family formation and saving. Welfare should be completely reformed to provide income supplements through a negative income tax with household tax allowances. Furthermore, welfare claimants without jobs and who are of working age should be required to undertake work as a condition of receiving benefits. Reforming welfare and related changes to pensions would save £46.5 billion a year.

- The National Health Service should be replaced by health savings accounts with insurance for catastrophic risks. Experience from other countries suggests that this can lead to better outcomes, lower costs and much stronger incentives for health promotion. This reform would save £44 billion a year. More radical reform of education to save over £15 billion is required: reforms should include parents making some contribution to the cost of their children's education.

- Policy in areas such as defence and foreign aid should be strategically reviewed. Foreign aid should be cut entirely except for emergency aid: the evidence suggests that growth in poor countries will come about only as a result of the adoption of market economies and through private investment. Aid probably hinders growth in the poorest countries. Reforms to defence and foreign aid should lead to spending reductions of £29 billion a year.

- Much government-owned infrastructure can be privatised; market-based solutions to transport urgently need to be adopted with a consequent elimination of government subsidies; and climate change policy is currently incoherent. Huge savings in government spending are possible in the field of climate change policy even if the government wishes to retain incentives to reduce carbon emissions. Over £80 billion a year could be available for tax decreases from the proposals made in these areas.

TABLES AND FIGURES

PART ONE: ECONOMIC GROWTH, GOVERNMENT SPENDING AND TAXATION

1 PUBLIC SPENDING, TAXATION AND ECONOMIC GROWTH – THE EVIDENCE[1]

Patrick Minford and Jiang Wang

Introduction

There is now a huge and rapidly expanding literature on 'endogenous growth'. In this literature certain ingredients 'enter the production function' – that is contribute to the generation of output – which are themselves enhanced in their effects by the extra output. Hence growth may enter a 'self-feeding' phase when these elements are present or increased beyond a certain threshold. Such elements are said to include education or personal knowledge ('human capital'), public infrastructure and research and development (R&D).

This view is often found to be associated with the advocacy of policies to increase public spending in ways that add to these elements. It seems fairly obvious after all that public spending can directly finance education, infrastructure and R&D. If so, it is natural to argue that this will add to the stock of these desirable elements and so promote growth. On this view, to pay for this spending the tax rate will need to rise somewhat but the extra growth will itself raise revenue. The higher tax rates will not affect growth. We will call this the 'activist theory of development'.

An alternative policy approach would not necessarily dispute the importance of the elements identified in the endogenous growth literature as mechanisms of growth transmission. Rather it would question whether these elements would have their effect in the absence of strong incentives for people to engage in entrepreneurial activity. Thus it is people who invest in their own (or their children's) education and

---

1   This chapter is adapted from a working paper which includes the details of the statistical models. See: http://www.irefeurope.org/en/sites/default/files/Minford.pdf.

knowledge who make use of infrastructure to produce goods and services, and who use research and development to innovate. It follows that the level of taxation – which is the main ingredient affecting personal incentives – will be the key determinant of growth. When it is high, however much is spent on education, etc., it will not fructify in enterprise and growth; when it is low, moderate public spending on these elements can have a strong effect on growth. In this approach, it is not denied that basic public sector provision of 'public goods' is necessary; rather it is argued that it should be restrained efficiently to enable the tax rate to remain low. We will call this policy approach 'the incentivist theory of development'.

How might one test these two policy approaches to growth? The key idea that separates them is the effect of incentives on 'dynamic activity' – that is, on entrepreneurial decisions to invest and innovate. In the activist approach this effect is absent; taxation has incentive effects on *allocation* (the standard welfare effects on productive efficiency and consumer choice) but not on dynamism and not therefore on the production function or its contributing elements (beyond these allocation effects, e.g. on labour supply). In the incentivist approach, the dynamic effect is all-important (beyond a certain low threshold of taxation below which government barely functions); with it growth occurs, without it growth does not occur – regardless of how much public spending is directed at education, infrastructure and R&D.

Consider therefore the nature of causality and exogeneity in each view. In the activist case, growth is caused by public spending on desirable elements, with no effects from taxation. Public spending on these variables, being a choice resulting from the political process, can be regarded as exogenous. There may be feedback from the economy's behaviour to these variables, but it is uncertain in direction and takes a long time.

In the incentivist view, growth is caused by incentives and thus by taxation. The level of public spending on desirable elements is now irrelevant. The level of taxation is generated by public choices and it is now exogenous for the same reasons as above. Taxation is usually a side effect of choices to spend public money on publicly chosen objectives; it is no less the result of policy choice.

In effect, therefore, our rival theories imply rival sets of exogenous variables. We can test them against each other straightforwardly on this basis.

Notice that a whole set of *other* variables – such as human capital and R&D – are *endogenous* on *both* views. Therefore, they cannot enter our tests except as endogenous results of the two rival sets of exogenous variables. Showing that education, for example, affects output does not discriminate between the two views. Much of the empirical literature on endogenous growth investigates mechanisms of this sort but cannot shed light therefore on our empirical choice between the two policy approaches.

In what follows we compare these views empirically using available post-war data. We develop two simple 'exemplar' models representing each approach and test them. Throughout we assume that spending and taxes must be matched to satisfy the budget constraint on government. While plainly the pattern of taxes can be deferred or hastened, the real present value of taxation must equal the real present value of spending plus present real public debt. Taxation here includes the 'inflation tax' if that is chosen by the authorities (i.e. if they choose to print money as a financing mechanism). We assume that citizens anticipate the tax effects of policies and react to the present value of taxation. A more transparent way of representing this is as the 'permanent tax rate' it implies (i.e. the constant tax rate that has the same present value). It follows from our assumptions that this permanent tax rate is equal to public spending as a share of GDP plus an adjustment for real debt interest.

Two simple models of growth

In our incentivist model, we assume that output is produced by labour of different efficiency; there is a (uniform) distribution of efficiency across people. People can choose to become more efficient (by unspecified actions such as investment in human and physical capital, via learning and borrowing) but to do so they run risks: they cannot be sure how successful their attempt will be – they could either be a lot more efficient or hardly better at all at the two extremes. Against this, they will lose their existing (certain) income/efficiency level, incur costs of changing their situation and pay a marginal tax rate on their increased income. Weighing these elements, people at lower income levels will decide to train in return for a lower marginal increment to income the lower is the tax rate; this, in turn, helps determine the growth rate.

In our activist model, we follow Aghion and Howitt (1998), who set out an economy in which R&D determines growth and public subsidy to capital investment and to R&D in turn determines R&D. This model is large and complicated in detail. But the basic ideas are simple enough. Final goods are produced by an imperfectly competitive inputs industry in which innovation occurs because of R&D. R&D is created by diverting output from final production; as an innovation occurs it is universally adopted in the input industry, causing existing producers to lose profit. Thus a wedge is driven between the private gain from innovation and the social gain, in the sense that an innovator will appropriate the gain from the innovation only until the next innovation comes along, whereas society will gain for ever the full improvement on each innovation. There is therefore a case for subsidy of R&D. The extent to which a country innovates and therefore grows will depend critically on this subsidy. The argument for subsidising not merely R&D itself but also investment generally is that new investment increases the adoption speed of innovation because new capital embodies the new technology.

Before we investigate these two models of growth, we will look at the existing empirical literature on tax and economic growth.

Is there a negative relationship between tax and economic growth?

We have drawn extensively on two surveys, Leach (2003) and OECD (Leibfritz et al., 1997), which document a rapidly expanding empirical literature on the effects of taxation on growth and output levels. Table 1 sets out a selection of the major studies, noting their data set, the explanatory variables used and the main tax effects found. All use reduced-form equations on panel data and control for various other supposedly exogenous factors (usually different across different studies).

Barro (1991) considers the positive role of education for human capital formation and finds a significant negative correlation between the level of government distortions (as measured by real government consumption purchases less spending on education and defence as a percentage of real GDP over the period 1970–85) and both real economic growth (averaged over the period 1960–85) and private investment.

Most of the studies also take human capital as exogenous and include proxies for it in their regressions; most also include some measure of capital/GDP as a regressor. One exception is Koester and Kormendi (1989). They leave most such variables out and include measures of marginal and average tax, as well as population and labour force growth. They find in a cross-country analysis for the 1970s a significant negative effect of marginal tax rates on the level of real GDP per capita, but not on the rate of growth when the latter is controlled for the initial level of income. They suggest that holding average rates constant, a 10 percentage point decrease in marginal tax rates would increase per capita income in an average industrial country by more than 7 per cent (and in an average developing country by more than 15 per cent). Thus, a revenue-neutral tax reform which reduces tax progressivity would raise income and lead to an upward shift in the whole growth path.

Alesina et al. (2002) are another exception. They focus on the extent of government spending of various sorts on the investment/GDP ratio (and hence by implication growth), in a reduced-form approach similar to our 'incentivist' model. They conclude that, via their effect in raising private sector labour costs, a 1 percentage point increase in government spending relative to GDP resulted in a decrease in the investment-to-GDP ratio of 0.15 percentage points and a cumulative fall of 0.74 percentage points after five years.

In general these studies, with their varying methodologies, find that there is a measurable effect of higher tax rates on growth, of the order of 0.5–1 per cent for a 10 per cent rise in the overall tax ratio to GDP. The OECD's own conclusion from its survey was that:

> A number of studies, influenced by the new growth theories, have taken a top-down approach to assess the impact of taxes on per capita income and growth at the macro level. Several of them purport to demonstrate a significant negative relationship between the level of the tax/GDP ratio (or the government expenditure ratio) and the growth rate of GDP per capita, implying that high tax rates reduce economic growth ... our estimates [using a top-down cross-country regression] suggest that the increase in the average (weighted) tax rate of about 10 percentage points over the past 35 years, may have reduced OECD annual growth rates by about 0.5 percentage points.

The OECD believe, as we do, that such a 'top-down' approach should be complemented by a full structural endogenous growth model detailing the tax transmission channels. They report that a 10 percentage point cut in the tax-to-GDP ratio could increase economic growth by 0.5 to 1.0 percentage points. Thus they also say that: '... up to one third of the growth deceleration in the OECD [over the 1965–95 period] would be explained by higher taxes. In some European countries, tax burdens increased much more dramatically than the OECD average, which would imply correspondingly larger effects on their growth rates'.

Table 1 **The negative impact of taxation on economic growth**

Author	Data coverage	Main explanatory variables	Comment
Barro (1991)	98 countries in the period 1960–85	Human capital, government consumption, political instability indicator, price distortion.	1% point of GDP increase in tax-to-GDP ratio lowers output per worker by 0.12%.
Koester and Kormendi (1989)	63 countries for which at least five years of continuous data exist for the 1970s.	Marginal tax rates, average tax rate, mean growth in labour force and population.	10% decrease in marginal tax rates would increase per capita income in an average industrial country by more than 7%.
Hansson and Henrekson (1994)	Industry-level data for 14 OECD countries	Government transfers, consumption, total outlays; education expenditure; government investment.	Government transfers, consumption and total outlays have a negative impact on growth while government investment is not significant.
Cashin (1995)	23 OECD countries over the 1971–88 period	Ratio of public investment to GDP, ratio of current taxation revenue to GDP, ratio of expenditure on transfers to GDP.	1% point of GDP increase in tax-to-GDP ratio lowers output per worker by 2%.
Engen and Skinner (1996)	US modelling together with a sample of OECD countries	Marginal tax rates, human capital, investment.	2.5% point increase in tax-to-GDP ratio reduces GDP growth by 0.2% to 0.3%.
OECD – Leibfritz et al. (1997)	OECD countries over the 1965–95 period	Tax-to-GDP ratio, physical and human capital formation and labour supply.	10% point increase in tax-to-GDP ratio reduces GDP growth by 0.5% to 1%.

Author	Data coverage	Main explanatory variables	Comment
Alesina et al. (2002)	18 OECD countries over the 1960–96 period	Primary spending, transfers, labour taxes, taxes on business, indirect taxes, government wage consumption (all in share of GDP).	1% increase in government spending relative to GDP lowers the investment-to-GDP ratio by 0.15%; cumulative fall of 0.74% after five years.
Bleaney et al. (2000)	17 OECD countries over the 1970–94 period	Distortionary tax, productive expenditure, net lending, labour force growth, investment ratio.	1% point of GDP increase in distortionary tax revenue reduces GDP growth by 0.4% points.
Folster and Henrekson (2000)	Sample of rich OECD/non-OECD countries over the 1970–95 period	Tax-to-GDP, government expenditure-to-GDP, investment-to-GDP, labour force growth, human capital growth.	10% point increase in tax-to-GDP ratio reduces GDP growth by 1%.
Bassanini and Scarpetta (2001)	21 OECD countries over the 1971–98 period	Indicators of government size and financing, physical capital, human capital, population growth.	1% point increase in tax/GDP ratio reduces per capita output levels by 0.3% to 0.6%.

Our basic results from testing the two policy approaches

As noted in our introductory remarks, growth is seen in the incentivist approach as depending on the tax rate, which we interpret as the marginal costs levied by the state on firm closure *plus* firm set-up *plus* the marginal tax rate (which we take to be approximated by the average overall share of public spending in GDP). Thus to test this a panel regression has been run using growth and this tax rate.

In the activist approach, as exemplified by Aghion and Howitt

(1998), growth is seen as depending on government subsidies to investment and to R&D specifically. To approximate the investment subsidy we took the difference between the world real interest rate and the national real interest rate; while this difference will be cyclical, as the real interest differential and the expected real exchange rate change respond to shocks, over the decadal averages we use in the data such effects should be minimal, leaving the systematic effect of government policy in protecting industry against world real capital costs. Government subsidy for investment will increase the capital intensity of an economy unless it substitutes for private sector investment; this, in turn, will reduce the marginal rate of return to capital and this will reduce the national real interest rate below the international real interest rate. While data on subsidies to R&D are not readily available we have found data on the amount of government spending on R&D and we use this as a measure of the subsidy to R&D (of course government R&D spending is not charged for and can be considered 100 per cent subsidised).

The results we find are shown below. Because it is hard to know whether country and time effects are random or fixed, we run both regressions on both assumptions. The assumption that these effects are 'fixed' amounts to saying that each country, for example, has a specific set of differences that endure through time and can be attributed to detailed causes. The assumption that they are 'random' asserts instead that each country varies around the basic relationship randomly; sometimes omitted factors will drive it towards more growth, sometimes towards less, and there is no systematic effect always pushing that country up or down. In theory it is hard to support the idea that country effects are fixed, in the sense that growth does not seem to be associated with countries as of right (e.g. because of their ethnic characteristics or their geography). Neither of our two theories asserts that; rather they suggest that it is underlying policies which cause growth. Hence it is attractive to think of country effects as being random. Time effects, however, are a different matter. Here it seems reasonable to argue that in a particular decade events were either favourable or unfavourable to growth, independently of the fundamental determinants of growth. Such reasons would be the behaviour of technological change at the world level, which one would expect to have particular effects on particular decades. Hence our preferred regressions treat country effects as random and time effects as fixed. But, in fact, the direction of the results is robust to the choice of these assumptions.

Results for the incentivist approach

Here we look at the relationship between the growth rate of GDP per capita, the tax rate, a dummy variable specific to each time period, and a dummy variable specific to each country. Panel data were used that were averaged over consecutive decades from 1970 to 2000 for 100 countries. Data on growth rate in real GDP per capita and tax rate originate from the *Penn World Table Version 6.1* (Heston et al., 2002).

Overall, there is an overwhelmingly strong negative relationship between tax and growth, with some models showing a stronger relationship than others. Specifically in our preferred model there is an elasticity of growth to tax of approximately –1.4 at the mean of the growth rate (1.6 per cent). The effects are not expected to be linear in the tax rate but, if they were, then a fall in the tax rate by 25 per cent of its existing value (from 40 to 30 per cent) would lead to a rise in the growth rate to 2.7 per cent if the initial growth rate were 2 per cent.

Some would argue that there are other exogenous variables that affect growth. These could include: initial GDP per capita (which should control for a country's potential to 'catch up'; the lower GDP the greater the growth); human capital; physical capital stock; and the rate of investment/GDP. We would argue that these are not exogenous because they are, in fact, at least partially determined by the level of taxation. In fact, testing the model we find that the basic result is immune to including these variables, singly or in combination.

Figure 1   **Correlation between GDP growth rate (per cent) and the subsidy rate to investment**

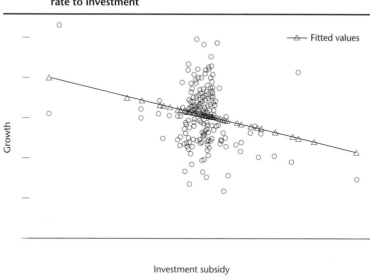

Investment subsidy

Results for the activist approach

In looking at the activist approach we examine the relationship between the growth rate and government subsidies to investment and to R&D (as defined above). We find that there is no statistically significant relationship between R&D and growth. Perhaps more surprisingly, we find that insofar as there is any relationship at all it is a negative relationship between growth and both investment and R&D, which would appear to deny the proposition of Aghion and Howitt (1998) that the growth rate depends positively upon the two subsidy rates. In particular, a 1 per cent increase in government subsidy rates to investment is associated with a reduction of the growth rate of 0.03–0.06 per cent while a 1 per cent increase in government subsidy rates to R&D reduces GDP growth by roughly 0.007 per cent. It is not, however, the negative relationship but the absence of a positive relationship which is most interesting. Figure

1, which shows the relevant data points with the subsidy rate to investment on the horizontal axis and growth on the vertical axis, is especially revealing.

Again we add the control variables used above to this activist case to test for sensitivity; again they do not change the insignificance of these subsidy effects.

Conclusion

In this chapter we have looked at two rival models of the effects of public spending: the 'activist', according to which spending raises growth via its effects in subsidising R&D, and the 'incentivist', according to which it reduces it by penalising incentives through higher taxes. We have sketched out the rival models and estimated the relationships using sophisticated statistical techniques. We have found that there appears to be no identifiable effect of R&D and other capital subsidies on growth but that there is an effect of taxation depressing growth – in this we join a growing literature that finds similar negative tax effects on growth. Only if we assume that growth differences between countries are 'fixed' in nature – that is, we assume that owing to climate or inherent ethnic characteristics some countries grow faster than others, an assumption that we would reject – does this effect become poorly determined and insignificant. Even in these circumstances, the effect remains, if somewhat reduced in size. Our theories suggest that no control variables should be added (for initial GDP per capita, education per head, capital/ GDP or investment/GDP) to either the activist or the incentivist model, but even if we do add such control variables they do not undermine the basic results.

Given the models that we have used, there is strong evidence of a negative effect of tax on growth. A 10 per cent reduction in the tax take as a percentage of national income from the rate proposed by the coalition at the end of the Comprehensive Spending Review period of 40 per cent of national income might add around 0.7 per cent to the annual growth rate if the current sustainable growth rate is 2 per cent per annum.[2] Increasing public spending on investment and R&D, on the other hand, would have a minimal effect on the growth rate. It would appear that the surest way to increase economic growth is to reduce government spending and taxation.

References

Agell, J., P. Englund and J. Södersten (1995), 'The Swedish tax reform: an introduction', *Swedish Economic Policy Review*, 2: 219–28.

Aghion, P. and P. Howitt (1998), *Endogenous Growth Theory*, Cambridge, MA: MIT Press.

Alesina, A., S. Ardagna, R. Perotti and F. Schiantarelli (2002), 'Fiscal policy, profits, and investment', *American Economic Review*, 92(3): 571–89.

Barro, R. J. (1991), 'Economic growth in a cross-section of countries', *Quarterly Journal of Economics*, 106(2): 407–33.

Barro, R. J. and J. W. Lee (2000), 'International data on educational attainment: updates and implications', Manuscript, Harvard University, February.

Bassanini, A. and S. Scarpettta (2001), 'Does human capital matter for growth in OECD countries? Evidence from PMG estimates', OECD Economics Department Working Papers no. 282.

Becsi, Z. (1996), 'Do state and local taxes affect relative state growth?', *Economic Review*, 81(2): 18–36.

Bleaney, M., N. Gemmell and R. Kneller (2000), 'Testing the endogenous growth model: public expenditure, taxation and growth over the long run', *Canadian Journal of Economics*, 34(1): 36–57.

Cashin, P. (1995), 'Government spending, taxes and economic growth', *IMF Staff Papers*, 42(2): 237–69.

---

2   Ignoring the likely non-linearity of the effect – this should be regarded very much as an order of magnitude.

Dar, A. and S. AmirKhalkhali (2002), 'Government size, factor accumulation, and economic growth: evidence from OECD countries', *Journal of Policy Modeling*, 24(7/8): 679–92.

Engen, E. M. and J. Skinner (1996), 'Taxation and economic growth', NBER Working Papers 5826, National Bureau of Economic Research, Inc.

Folster, S. and M. Henrekson (2000), 'Growth effects of government expenditure and taxation in rich countries', Stockholm School of Economics Working Paper no. 391, June.

Grossman, P. (1988), 'Government and economic growth: a non-linear relationship', *Public Choice*, 56: 193–200.

Hansson, P. and M. Henrekson (1994), 'A new framework for testing the effect of government spending on growth and productivity', *Public Choice*, 81: 381–401.

Heston, A., R. Summers and B. Aten (2002), Penn World Table Version 6.1, Center for International Comparisons at the University of Pennsylvania (CICUP), October.

Koester, R. and R. Kormendi (1989), 'Taxation, aggregate activity and economic growth: cross-country evidence on some supply-side hypotheses', *Economic Inquiry*, 27(3): 367–86.

Leach, G. (2003) 'The negative impact of taxation on economic growth', London: Reform, September.

Leibfritz, W., J. Thornton and A. Bibbee (1997), 'Taxation and economic performance', OECD Working Paper no. 176.

Mackness, W. (1999), *Canadian Public Spending: The Case for Smaller, More Efficient Government*, Public Policy Source 13, Vancouver, BC: Fraser Institute.

Peden, E. (1991), 'Productivity in the United States and its relationship to government activity: an analysis of 57 years, 1929–1986', *Public Choice*, 69: 153–73.

Vedder, R. K. (1993), *Economic Impact of Government Spending: A 50-State Analysis*, Policy Report 178, Dallas, TX: National Center for Policy Analysis.

2 THE CHANGING ECONOMIC ROLE OF GOVERNMENT: PAST, PRESENT AND PROSPECTIVE
David B. Smith

Introduction

This chapter begins by examining the expansion of the government sector internationally since the late nineteenth century, before looking in more detail at the British experience. Following an analysis of where the UK state's money comes from and where it goes, the latest official projections for the nation's public finances are compared with independently derived ones generated using the author's macroeconomic model. It is suggested that there are analytical flaws in the official methodology for projecting future tax receipts and public borrowing and that these flaws have led to misguided policy advice. Three conclusions stand out:

- The coalition inherited an almost unprecedented fiscal mess in 2010; a major cause being Labour's feckless spending before the 2008 global financial crash.
- The coalition's measures to rein back government spending have been too timid and its borrowing targets are unlikely to be achieved.
- The coalition's misplaced tax-raising measures have made public borrowing worse, not better.

Expansion of government 1870 to 2000

Arguably, the growing role of government has been the most significant single economic development of the past one and a half centuries in the 'Old West' (defined also to include Japan). Thus, the average government spending burden in the twelve economies for which continuous data exist increased from 10.7 per cent in 1870 to 47 per cent in 2010 (see Table 2). This more than fourfold increase in the government's share of national output proceeded in a series of fits and starts and was often driven by political events or changes in intellectual fashion. Both world wars, for example, were followed by a permanent rise in the government spending ratio. Despite the efforts of leaders, such as US President Reagan and Lady Thatcher, there was little net movement in the mean spending ratio between 1980 and 2000, although there were pronounced cyclical swings and marked changes within countries. In particular, the government spending ratio dropped by 17.6 percentage points between 1980 and 2000 in Ireland, 11 percentage points in the Netherlands and 9.4 percentage points in Belgium. Such figures suggest that the current UK 'cuts' are not particularly bold, despite the outcry that they have provoked.[1] There seems to be great gain, and little pain, from aggressive fiscal retrenchment once public spending exceeds around one half of national output (see Tanzi and Schuknecht, 2005).

Government spending in the 21st century

The 21st century has seen possibly the largest peacetime rise in the aggregate socialisation ratio since the heyday of Keynesian interventionism in the 1960s and 1970s. The mean twelve-country spending ratio rose by 3.8 percentage points between 2000 and 2010, while there was an increase of 5.7 percentage points in the Organisation for Economic Development and Co-operation (OECD) area as a whole, where the figures cover 30 countries but are not available so far back. The 14.4 percentage point rise in the share of government expenditure in Britain in the first decade of the present century, however, was the largest increase in the OECD – if one ignores Ireland's badly distorted 34.8 per cent increase (see note

---

[1]   The March 2011 Budget revealed that the cash value of UK general government expenditure is officially intended to rise from £685 billion in 2010/11 to £763 billion in 2015/16, so these are not 'cuts' as this term would be understood by a private sector manager facing a normal cash-constrained budget.

to Table 2) – and was also one of the largest peacetime rises recorded anywhere during one decade. In contrast, the Slovak republic managed a cutback from 52.2 to 40.9 per cent over the same ten years. This shows what could potentially be achieved in Britain given the correct policies of supply-side-oriented reform.

Table 2 **Ratios of general government expenditure, including transfers, to money GDP at market prices (per cent)**

	1870	1913	1920	1937	1960	1980	2000	2010
Australia	18.3	16.5	19.3	14.8	21.2	34.1	34.8	35.0
Austria	10.5	17.0	14.7	20.6	35.7	48.1	52.2	52.9
Belgium	–	13.8	–	21.8	30.3	58.6	49.1	53.9
Canada	–	–	16.7	25.0	28.6	38.8	41.1	43.5
France	12.6	17.0	27.6	29.0	34.6	46.1	51.6	56.2
Germany	10.0	14.8	25.0	34.1	32.4	47.9	45.1	46.8
Italy	13.7	17.1	30.1	31.1	30.1	42.1	46.1	51.4
Ireland	–	–	–	–	28.0	48.9	31.3	66.1
Japan	8.8	8.3	14.8	25.4	17.5	32.0	39.0	40.6
Netherlands	9.1	9.0	13.5	19.0	33.7	55.2	44.2	51.2
NZ	–	–	24.6	25.3	26.9	38.1	38.8	44.2
Norway	5.9	9.3	16.0	11.8	29.9	43.8	42.3	46.6
Spain	–	8.3	9.3	18.4	18.8	32.2	39.1	45.1
Sweden	5.7	10.4	10.9	16.5	31.0	60.1	55.1	54.5
Switzerland	16.5	14.0	17.0	24.1	17.2	32.8	35.1	33.6
UK	9.4	12.7	26.2	30.0	32.2	43.0	36.6	51.0
USA	7.3	7.5	12.1	19.4	27.0	31.4	33.9	42.2
Average	10.7	12.8	19.9	23.0	28.5	43.1	43.0	46.8

Sources: Tanzi and Schuknecht (2000); IMF, including May 2000 *World Economic Outlook* (see especially Table 5.4, p. 172); and *OECD Economic Outlook* (December 2010, Annex Table 25). Unfortunately, there are some substantial discrepancies between the Tanzi and Schuknecht and OECD data for the overlap year of 1996, and the figures should be regarded as illustrative only. The 2010 figure for Ireland is heavily distorted by the Irish bank bailout. The OECD forecast for 2011 is 55.5 per cent.

Despite the attempt of the current Labour opposition to blame the fiscal crisis on irresponsible bankers, much of the rise in the UK public spending burden had occurred before the financial crash. Britain's spending ratio was already 7.5 percentage points higher in 2007 than

Table 3 **Ratios of general government cyclically adjusted financial balances to money GDP at market prices and non-socialised GDP at market prices in 2010 (per cent)**

	Ratio of surplus (+) or deficit (−) to nominal GDP at market prices (%)	Ratio of surplus (+) or deficit (−) to private sector GDP at market prices (%)	Ratio of non-socialised economy to nominal GDP at market prices (%)
Australia	−2.5	−3.8	65.0
Belgium	−1.9	−4.1	46.1
Canada	−3.2	−5.7	56.5
France	−5.4	−12.3	43.8
Germany	−3.0	−5.6	53.2
Greece	−5.4	−10.4	51.7
Italy	−2.1	−4.3	48.6
Ireland	−26.1	−77.0	33.9
Japan	−6.7	−11.3	59.4
Portugal	−6.1	−11.7	52.2
Poland	−7.3	−13.3	54.7
Spain	−5.9	−10.7	54.9
Sweden	1.1	2.4	45.5
Switzerland	−0.1	−0.2	66.4
United Kingdom	−7.2	−14.7	49.0
United States	−8.8	−15.2	57.8
Euro-zone	−4.2	−8.5	49.3
Total OECD	−6.3	−11.4	55.4

Source: OECD Economic Outlook, December 2010, Annex Tables 25 & 28, and author's calculations. Again, the 2010 figures for Ireland are heavily distorted by the Irish bank bailout.

it had been in 2000 using OECD definitions. Furthermore, reputable international bodies such as the OECD, the European Commission and the International Monetary Fund (IMF) were concerned by the UK's spending policies and credit boom from the mid-2000s onwards but were cajoled into silence (see IMF/ Independent Evaluation Office, 2011). Nevertheless, Labour had presided over a 4 percentage point reduction between 1997 and 2000, during its 'Prudence' period, and the increase during Labour's entire period of office was a more modest 10.4 percentage points. This left Britain with the sixth-highest spending ratio out of the 30 OECD countries in 2010 – it had ranked number 23 in 1997 – and the third-worst budget deficit after Ireland and the USA. The funding strains caused by deficits on this scale become particularly apparent once it is understood that only the private sector and foreign investors can absorb government debt (Table 3). It is also noteworthy that Britain's underlying position on this and several other fiscal indicators is worse than that of countries such as Greece, Portugal and Spain, where the fears of sovereign (i.e. government) default have been most marked.

Failure of cost control

Even more damning, almost the entire UK structural deficit has resulted from Labour's failure to control its costs and match private sector productivity between 1997 and 2010. This means that taxpayers have enjoyed very little return on the money extracted from them, while future generations will have to service high debt interest payments without seeing any of the benefits. The national accounts can be manipulated to reveal that current government expenditure in 2010 would have been some £74 billion (21.8 per cent) lower than it turned out to be if its cost had risen in line with the household consumption deflator. The nation could have saved a further £19.7 billion if government productivity had matched that of the non-oil economy since 1997. The OECD's estimate that Britain's structural deficit was 7.2 per cent of GDP (i.e. approximately £105 billion) in 2010 implies that the bulk of the structural budget deficit bequeathed to the coalition reflected Labour's appalling failure to deliver value for money during its thirteen years in office.

Measurement issues and where the money goes

One problem facing endeavours to quantify Britain's government spending ratio is that there are several competing measures of spending and national output. These can make a difference of 5 to 7 percentage points to the estimated spending and tax burdens (see Smith, 2006, 2009). This is one reason why the concept of 'general government' used in Tables 2 and 3 should often be the preferred expenditure measure. General government includes central government and local authorities. It excludes, however, public corporations and bailed-out financial institutions, such as the Royal Bank of Scotland, which are included in the 'public sector'. Until now, the international convention of using gross domestic product (GDP) measured at market prices – that is gross of indirect taxes – has also been employed. Market-price GDP is raised whenever indirect taxes go up, however, and it is inconsistent over time and between countries. As a consequence, Table 4 displays figures using both the officially preferred market-price GDP and the conceptually superior factor-cost measure of GDP as the denominator.

One point to emerge from Table 4 is what a small share of public spending is accounted for by the two 'primary' government functions of external defence and the maintenance of law and order. Even adding in debt interest brings the primary total only to 9.2 per cent of factor-cost GDP. Some 82.7 per cent of government spending, and 43.7 per cent of GDP at factor cost, consists of secondary functions of government. In total, the budgets for social protection, personal social services, health and education sum to 62.9 per cent of government spending and 33.3 per cent of factor-cost GDP. This is why the decision to ring-fence huge blocks of expenditure, such as the health budget, was totally misguided.

For official budgetary control purposes, Table 4's Total Managed Expenditure (TME) is further split into Departmental Expenditure Limits (DELs), which were set for three years ahead in the November 2010 Comprehensive Spending Review (CSR), and so-called Annually Managed Expenditures (AMEs), which are considered predominantly demand-determined. Social security benefits are the main element in AMEs. The March 2011 Budget showed that combined current and capital DELs are intended to amount to £386.8 billion in 2011/12, and AME's to £323.6 billion (ibid.: Table 2.3). It is often claimed that the 45.5 per cent of TME made up of AMEs makes it difficult to control public spending. This partly reflects politics, custom and procedure, however. If the welfare bill were cash-limited, for example, more claimants would imply reduced benefits, not increased spending.

Table 4 **Official forecasts for public spending by function and government receipts in 2011/12**

	£bn	%	Ratio to GDP at market prices (%)	Ratio to GDP at factor cost, (%)
Total Managed Expenditure (TME)				
Social protection	200	28.1	13.0	14.9
Personal social services	32	4.5	2.1	2.4
Health	126	17.7	8.2	9.4
Transport	23	3.2	1.5	1.7
Education	89	12.5	5.8	6.6
Defence	40	5.6	2.6	3.0
Debt interest	50	7.0	3.2	3.7
Industry, agriculture and employment	20	2.8	1.3	1.5
Public order and safety	33	4.6	2.1	2.5
Housing and environment	24	3.4	1.6	1.8
Other	74	10.4	4.8	5.5
TME Expenditure	710	100	46.0	52.9
Government receipts				
Income tax	158	26.8	10.2	11.8
National Insurance	101	17.1	6.5	7.5
Excise duties	46	7.8	3.0	3.4
Corporation tax	48	8.1	3.1	3.6
VAT	100	17.0	6.5	7.4
Business rates	25	4.2	1.6	1.9
Council tax	26	4.4	1.7	1.9
Other	85	14.4	5.5	6.3
Total receipts	589	100.0	38.1	43.8

Source: HM Treasury, *Budget Report*, 23 March 2011

Departmental spending plans

Table 5 sets out a consolidated version of the more detailed official projections for total DELs which appeared in the November 2010 Comprehensive Spending Review (CSR). For presentational purposes, the cash figures provided in the CSR have been expressed as shares of factor-cost GDP, since this is the best measure of the resource costs that the programmes concerned place on the wider economy. The absence of AMEs from the official projections, however, represents a significant distortion because the spending of some departments is almost entirely composed of AMEs, whereas the AME content of other departments is close to zero. In addition, the figures for the cash DEL totals were revised upwards between the November 2010 CSR and the March 2011 Budget, while some offsetting reductions were made in welfare payments that count as AMEs. Perhaps the most striking feature of Table 5 is the contrast between the broad stability of the international development budget as a share of national output and the reductions elsewhere.

Table 5 **Official forecasts for total departmental expenditure limits expressed as a share of GDP at factor cost**

	2010/11	2011/12	2012/13	2013/14	2014/15
Education	4.5	4.2	4.0	3.8	3.6
NHS (health)	8.0	7.9	7.7	7.5	7.2
Communities and local government	2.9	2.3	2.0	1.9	1.7
Law and order	1.5	1.4	1.2	1.1	1.0
Defence	2.6	2.5	2.4	2.3	2.1
Scotland, Wales and Northern Ireland	4.2	3.9	3.7	3.5	3.3
International development	0.6	0.6	0.6	0.8	0.7
Other	5.0	4.7	4.5	3.9	3.8
Total	29.3	27.5	26.1	24.8	23.4

Source: HM Treasury Comprehensive Spending Review, Table A.9, p. 85

Alternative presentation of the government accounts

While the distinction between DELs and AMEs is important for budgetary control purposes, such administrative distinctions do not correlate well with the requirements of economic analysis, where it is more meaningful to analyse government receipts and expenditure by subsector and economic category (see Table 6). International organisations have generally concluded that government capital formation is growth-enhancing while paying means-tested benefits to the population of working age reduces labour supply and national output. The main issue with the other categories of expenditure is that they have to be paid for. In theory, this can be through higher taxes, borrowing in the government bond market, or by 'printing money'. All such funding methods, however, have adverse second-round effects on growth, employment, and inflation (see Chapter 1).

Table 6 **Official forecasts for general government transactions by sub-sector and economic category in 2011/12**

	£bn	%	Ratio to GDP at market prices (%)	Ratio to GDP at factor cost (%)
Current expenditure				
Current consumption of goods and services	350.3	50.4	22.7	26.1
Subsidies	10.2	1.4	0.7	0.8
Net social benefits	203.1	28.3	13.2	15.1
Net current grants overseas	2.4	0.3	0.2	0.2
Other current grants	41.0	5.9	2.7	3.1
Debt interest	48.9	6.3	3.2	3.6
Capital expenditure				
Fixed investment	32.3	5.1	2.1	2.4
Stocks	0.0	0.0	0.0	0.0
Capital grants	12.7	2.4	0.8	0.9
Total expenditure	700.9	100.0	45.4	52.2
Receipts				
Non-oil taxes	542.8	94.2	35.2	40.4
Rent, interest and dividends	23.0	4.0	1.5	1.7
North Sea taxes	13.4	1.7	0.9	1.0
Total receipts	579.2	100.0	37.5	43.1
Net borrowing	121.7	n/a	7.9	9.1

Source: Office for Budget Responsibility (OBR), *Economic and Fiscal Outlook – Supplementary Material*, Table 2.25, March 2011

An additional advantage of the Table 6 format is that it makes it possible to back-cast the current figures to the late nineteenth century

Table 7 **Ratios of main categories of UK general government expenditure to money GDP at factor cost at ten-year intervals (%)**

	Government final current expenditure	Grants to persons	Subsidies	Debt interest	Government investment and other items	Total general government expenditure
1870	5.3	0.0	0.0	3.6	0.9	9.8
1900	10.1	0.3	0.0	1.8	2.3	14.5
1910	8.9	0.4	0.0	2.0	1.5	12.8
1920	9.0	2.5	2.1	6.0	1.8	21.4
1930	10.8	4.9	0.5	8.2	3.3	27.7
1938	15.5	4.9	0.8	5.6	3.9	30.7
1950	19.7	5.6	4.0	4.7	3.9	37.9
1960	19.0	6.2	2.1	4.4	4.6	36.3
1970	21.4	8.8	2.0	4.5	8.4	45.1
1980	25.4	11.6	2.4	5.3	3.7	48.4
1990	23.3	11.9	1.0	4.1	4.4	44.7
2000	23.7	12.9	0.5	3.1	1.9	42.1
Wartime peaks						
1917	39.3	0.9	0.5	4.4	1.4	46.5
1944	57.7	5.0	2.7	4.5	0.3	70.2
Recent years						
2001	24.2	13.1	0.5	3.1	1.7	42.6
2002	25.4	12.9	0.6	2.6	2.1	43.6
2003	26.2	12.9	0.7	2.2	2.6	44.6
2004	26.9	12.9	0.6	2.2	2.7	45.3
2005	27.4	12.8	0.7	2.4	2.8	46.1
2006	27.5	12.6	0.8	2.3	3.1	46.3
2007	26.8	12.6	0.7	2.5	3.2	45.8
2008	27.5	13.0	0.7	2.5	4.0	47.7
2009	29.5	14.9	0.8	2.2	5.4	52.8
2010	29.6	15.3	0.9	3.4	4.4	53.6
OBR forecasts						
2010/11	29.7	15.1	0.7	3.4	4.2	53.1
2011/12	29.1	15.1	0.8	3.6	3.6	52.2
2012/13	27.9	14.8	0.8	3.6	3.2	50.3
2013/14	26.7	14.1	0.7	3.8	3.0	48.3
2014/15	25.3	13.6	0.7	4.0	3.0	46.6
2015/16	24.3	13.3	0.8	4.0	2.7	45.1

Sources: As described in Smith (2009) and Office for Budget Responsibility, *Economic and Fiscal Outlook*, March 2011, Table 2.25, 'General government transactions by economic category'

Figure 2   Ratio of UK general government expenditure to UK GDP at factor cost 1870–2010, with implied Office for Budget Responsibility forecasts to 2015

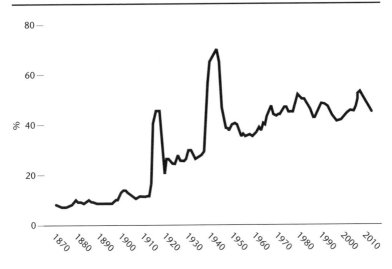

using calendar-year data and also to put the latest forecasts from the Office for Budget Responsibility (OBR) on the same consistent basis for fiscal years up to 2015/16 (see Smith, 2009, for a fuller account). This exercise has been carried out in Table 7 and in Figure 2, which presents the ratio of government spending to factor-cost GDP using annual data back to 1870. Figure 2 suggests that even if the coalition achieves its spending targets they will have achieved little more than the consolidation of the spending burden on the same high plateau that has prevailed since the early 1970s. A similar conclusion can be drawn from Figure 3, which shows the ratio of non-oil taxes to GDP back to 1900. Figure 3 suggests that it is almost impossible to get the non-oil tax burden significantly above 40 per cent of non-oil national output for any length of time. The coalition's apparent policy of jamming the tax burden against its maximum possible ceiling – rather than going for a lower tax ratio

Figure 3   **Ratio of UK non-oil taxes to non-oil GDP at factor cost 1900–2010, with implied Office for Budget Responsibility forecasts to 2015**

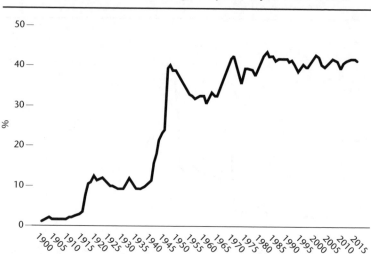

to optimise economic welfare as proposed throughout this monograph – suggests that the UK government's fiscal ambition has been limited to consolidating the position reached by the last Labour government at around the time Gordon Brown became prime minister.

Regional differences in government spending

The national spending ratio conceals huge differences between the main UK regions. Table 8 shows how these spending ratios have altered since 2005/06. A fuller account of the calculations involved is given in Chapter 5 of Smith (2006). The basic-price measure of GDP used for the main calculations is the basis on which regional activity is calculated, but anyone who prefers the factor-cost measure only has to multiply the 2009/10 basic-price ratios by 1.0138. The market-price GDP ratios used in Tables 2 and 3, which appear in the penultimate column of Table 8, show that the 36.9 percentage point difference between the least and most socialised regions within the UK is greater than the 30.8 percentage points range observed within the OECD as a whole. This is consistent with the point made earlier about the heterogeneity within the broad categories into which government activity is conventionally broken down.

Table 8 **General government expenditure in 2009/10 by country and region on a residence basis**

	Scaled public spending 2009/10 (£m)	Estimated GDP at basic prices 2009/10 (£m)	Ratio to GDP at basic prices in 2009/10 (%)	Ratio to GDP at basic prices in 2005/06 (%)	Change in basic-price ratio 2005/06 to 2009/10 (%)	Ratio to GDP at market prices in 2009/10 (%)	Proportion employed in public sector in 2010 Q2 (%)
North-East	29,942	41,214	72.7	62.8	9.9	65.2	24.6
North-West	78,193	121,572	64.3	54.8	9.5	57.7	21.9
Yorks & Humber	54,566	88,947	61.4	51.8	9.6	55.1	22.0
East Midlands	43,280	78,840	54.9	46.2	8.7	49.3	18.2
West Midlands	57,224	93,087	61.5	51.1	10.4	55.2	20.5
East	54,162	120,263	45.0	37.3	7.7	40.4	16.4
London	96,977	246,315	39.4	35.2	4.2	35.3	20.9
South-East	77,512	193,793	40.0	33.8	6.2	35.9	16.5
South-West	51,028	97,262	52.5	44.7	7.8	47.1	20.5
England	542,885	1,081,293	50.2	43.0	7.2	45.1	19.8
Scotland	63,412	104,699	60.6	56.1	4.5	54.4	24.8
Wales	35,767	45,449	78.7	67.6	11.1	70.6	26.1
Northern Ireland	23,211	28,848	80.5	70.4	10.1	72.2	29.1
UK	665,275	1,260,288	52.8	45.6	7.2	47.4	20.8

Sources: HM Treasury, *Public Expenditure Statistical Analysis 2011*, and Office for National Statistics data bank. Fuller details of the calculation methods can be found in Smith (2006).

The Office for Budget Responsibility

The OBR was established shortly after the May 2010 general election, with the intention of providing demonstrably independent forecasts for the UK economy and fiscal outlook. Apart from the OBR's chairman and one other member of the Budget Responsibility Committee, however, the OBR has been largely staffed by ex-Treasury officials and has been employing what was previously the HM Treasury (HMT) forecasting model. This suggests that the OBR might have to struggle hard to escape the intellectual legacy that it has inherited from HMT, despite its palpable institutional independence. This is worrying because there were serious flaws in the HMT methodology that it has inherited. One is that long-run economic output is set exogenously 'off-model'. This means that there are very few adverse supply-side feedbacks from raising taxes in the official forecasting framework. This explains why officialdom – and not just Labour Chancellors – had been persistently overoptimistic about the public finances during a decade in which the welfare- and tax-induced disincentives to work, invest and take risks had risen massively. It also means that the supply-side growth benefits stemming from low taxes, and the adverse second-round effects of high taxes on inflation and growth, are both largely ignored in the official framework. There is a real danger that the OBR has absorbed an unconscious institutional bias in favour of higher taxes because of the inept forecasting procedures it has inherited from HM Treasury.

An alternative independent projection for the public finances

The author has tried hard to remove such biases in his Beacon Economic Forecasting (BEF) model. The BEF model has been used to produce regular decade-ahead forecasts since 1984 and a detailed model manual is available in Smith (2011a).

The government sector of the BEF model divides government spending into current and capital spending and the associated subcategories. In the BEF model, some categories simply use the implied ratios to GDP contained in the 2011 Budget projections. There are other areas where economic relationships are used, such as debt interest payments which reflect the budget deficit and the interest paid on new government debt, and 'net social grants', which reflect claimant-count unemployment. The largest single expenditure item, however, is the government's current consumption of goods and services, which accounts for almost exactly one half of total spending. Here the volume is set using the figures given in the OBR projections up to 2016 Q1 (after which a flat level is assumed). In the BEF projections, however, the cost of government consumption is set independently of the OBR figures using a statistical relationship with the double-core retail price index (RPI) and a time trend. This equation has the long-run properties that government costs rise by 1.3 per cent per annum more than the double-core RPI inflation rate. As a result of this the BEF projections for the cash value of general government current expenditure end up £36.2 billion (9.9 per cent) higher than the OBR forecast by 2015/16. The adverse 'relative-price' effect (RPE) in the cost of current government expenditure also helps to explain Mr Osborne's attempt to freeze public sector earnings, which account for just over 52 per cent of public consumption. There was a long history during the 1960s and 1970s, however, of attempts to improve the public finances by imposing incomes policy controls on government wages. These attempts were successful for a year or two but tended to be followed by a burst of 'catch-up' growth later on. Fortunately, this may be less of a risk this time round because total public sector reward packages are starting at an unusually high level compared with those in the private sector. The RPE also means that real GDP has to grow by 0.3 per cent a year simply to stop the cash share of government spending in money GDP from rising when the volume ratio is constant.

General government fixed investment is projected using a similar approach, and also employs the OBR volume forecasts up to 2016 Q1, although core producer output prices are employed to predict the government investment price deflator instead of the underlying RPI. General government employment, which amounted to 5,672,000 people in 2010 Q4, is estimated by a statistical relationship with the properties that employment grows in line with the volume of general government current expenditure, but with a negative time trend of 1.2 per cent each year. This allows the employment consequences of spending cuts to be simulated in the BEF model, an issue that had proved controversial in the early 'Interim-OBR' forecasts. Finally, there are tax receipts from the North Sea, which are projected as a lagged share of the sterling value of North Sea oil and gas production, and non-oil taxes, which are officially projected to account for 93.7 per cent of all receipts in 2011/12.

For modelling purposes, the ratio of non-oil taxes to non-oil GDP is 'explained' statistically using a weighted average of the various UK tax rates, the ratio of government spending to GDP and a time trend. This equation has the property that tax receipts fall as the share of government spending (defined to exclude debt interest) in national output increases. The implication is that only the non-socialised part of the economy generates tax revenues. HM Treasury has consistently overestimated tax receipts when the government spending burden has risen because officialdom assumes a given ratio of taxes to the total 'tax base' rather than to its private sector component. This error works the opposite way round when the private sector is growing rapidly.

Increased taxes have adverse effects on a wide range of private sector activities in the BEF model, including household consumption, private investment, net trade, employment and the exchange rate. At a more detailed level, different taxes have different effects, with a VAT increase being more inflationary than a rise in income tax, for example.

Central forecast for the public accounts

All macroeconomic forecasts are prone to error and the errors tend to open out like a trumpet mouth the farther ahead one looks. Pre-announced tax changes have been incorporated in the BEF projections. Otherwise, the model has largely been allowed to run free throughout the forecast horizon to 2021 or fiscal 2021/22.

The central projection shows real GDP growing by an average of 1.5 per cent in 2011, 3.1 per cent in 2012 and 2.6 per cent in 2013 before eventually slowing to a trend rate of some 1.7 per cent by 2021. The average growth rate over the period from 2010 to 2021 is 2.3 per cent. This falls to 1.6 per cent, however, if 2007 is taken as the base, because UK GDP fell by 0.1 per cent in 2008 and 4.9 per cent in 2009. Such sluggish growth implies that the UK has become 'Euro-sclerotic' now that the public spending burden has reached levels previously observed only in heavily socialised francophone and Scandinavian societies. The presence of a large negative output gap in the OECD area – and the prospect of some recovery in the external value of sterling – means that inflation is not expected to be a major problem in the longer term, despite the substantial overshoot being observed at the time of writing. The annual rise in the target Consumer Price Index (CPI) is expected to average 2.5 per cent between 2011 and 2021, compared with the 4.1 per cent recorded in the first quarter of 2011. Claimant unemployment is expected to start easing back from 2012 onwards as the recovery in the private sector gathers momentum, ending up at some 837,000 by 2021. This is despite the projected loss of some 1,166,000 government jobs and 850,000 manufacturing positions during this period. It reflects the 3,290,000 new jobs expected to be created in the 'other private' sector (i.e. mainly services) between 2010 and 2021.

This projected background could prove too optimistic, however, if:

- There are renewed shocks to the world economy.
- Financial regulators cause an implosion of money and credit through ill-considered interventions.
- Taxes are raised even further.

The BEF projections suggest that Public Sector Net Borrowing (PSNB) could be wiped out by 2017/18, with increasing surpluses emerging subsequently, if the coalition possesses the stamina to implement such unprecedented spending discipline over such a long period.

One reason the public finances improve is the existence of important negative feedbacks between public borrowing and taxes and private sector activity. These feedbacks mean that fiscal parsimony generates a virtuous upward momentum in private activity and the tax base. This phenomenon could be observed during Mr Brown's flirtation with 'Prudence' between 1997 and 2000 and under Conservative administrations in the 1950s and 1980s. In contrast, Mr Major's high-spending policies in the early 1990s and the fiscal recklessness of 2000 to 2010 culminated in peak-to-trough contractions in the volume of private domestic expenditure (PDE) of 10 and 16 per cent respectively, although real PDE had recovered by 5.6 per cent from its 2009 Q4 trough by the first quarter of 2011.

While the BEF forecasts show a substantial long-run improvement in the fiscal position by 2021, they also indicate that the cash PSNB will be some £150 billion in 2011/12, compared with the £139.4 billion outcome for 2010/11, before it starts to fall back from 2012/13 onwards. There are several reasons for this, but one important one is the relatively small size of the tax-generating private sector of the economy. The PSNB is expected to fall from 9.7 per cent of the officially preferred market-price measure of UK GDP in 2011/12 (OBR forecast 8.3 per cent) to 8.6 per cent in 2012/13 (OBR 6.5 per cent), 6.7 per cent in 2013/14 (OBR 4.3 per cent), 4.6 per cent in 2014/15 (OBR 2.7 per cent) and 2.7 per cent in 2015/16 (OBR 1.9 per cent), when the OBR forecasts expire. The BEF projections show that the PSNB continues to fall in 2016/17, prior to moving into surplus from 2017/18 onwards. The improvement gathers momentum later in the forecast period because the share of the non-socialised economy in national output is 10.6 percentage points higher in 2020/21 than in 2010/11. This engenders a 6.3 percentage point rise in the ratio of non-oil taxes to GDP. These figures are generally more pessimistic than the OBR figures because more realistic assumptions have been made about government spending and the supply side of the economy. If the government is successful in reducing spending according to its cash targets – which may require a bigger reduction in volumes than the government itself anticipates – the OBR forecast could be fulfilled.

Alternative scenarios

This prospect assumes, however, that the financial markets will be prepared to finance the borrowing necessary over the next few years and gives rise to the question of whether the improvement in the public finances can be brought forward by a different strategy from that which Mr Osborne is attempting. To investigate this issue, a series of alternative scenarios were run on the BEF model. These incorporated a range of policies, including a 'big-cuts' scenario and a 'counter-factual' model run in which VAT was held at 17.5 per cent in January 2011, rather than being raised to 20 per cent. These simulations revealed *inter alia* that the January 2011 VAT hike did enough wider damage to exacerbate the budget deficit by some 0.1 to 0.2 percentage points of GDP, while adding 256,000 to claimant unemployment in 2021 and reducing the volume of GDP by 1.2 per cent.[2] More generally, the 'big-cuts' scenario somewhat arbitrarily assumed that the volume figures for general government current expenditure set out by the OBR were permanently reduced by 5.75 per cent from 2011 Q2 onwards. This is equivalent to a cash reduction of £20.75 billion in the cost of government consumption in fiscal 2011/12. The presence of government spending in GDP meant that real GDP rose by 0.6 percentage points less in 2011 than in the base run and was still 0.5 per cent lower in 2021. There was no discernible adverse affect on real private domestic expenditure (PDE), however, even in the short run, and this ended up 1.5 per cent higher by 2021. The consequent rise in private sector employment largely compensated for the extra loss of government jobs. Claimant unemployment was a relatively modest

---

2   The VAT hikes from 8 to 15 per cent in 1979, and from 15 to 17.5 per cent in the early 1990s, also appear to have exacerbated the then ongoing recessions. It would be interesting to know whether the equivalent simulations were run on the HMT/OBR model before the June 2010 Budget decision to raise VAT and, if not, why not.

93,000 higher than in the base run by 2021 as a result. The 'big-cuts' scenario also improved the PSNB/GDP ratio by just over 1 per cent in 2011/12 and almost 1.5 per cent in 2012/13, and brought forward the emergence of a small fiscal surplus to 2016/17.

The 'best buy' among the various options simulated, however, was to combine the large front-end-loaded spending cut with a run in which both the rates of VAT and NICs were held at their 2010 levels. This aggressive fiscal consolidation through the spending side maximised the virtuous circle arising from the feedbacks in the model and meant that additional private sector jobs more than compensated for the loss of government employment, with the result that the claimant count was 301,000 lower by 2021 than in the base run. By 2021, also, real GDP was 1.3 per cent higher than in the base run, the volume of PDE increased by 3.1 per cent and PSNB was improved by 1.4 per cent of GDP. There is room for concern that, instead of following this route, the coalition has embarked upon the 'worst-case' scenario by implementing Labour's pre-election tax increases, and raising VAT, while ring-fencing too large a share of public expenditure and thus combining 'small cuts' with damaging tax increases.

The main purpose of the model, however, is to demonstrate that a truly independent approach to modelling which incorporates the supply side of the economy leads to quite different projections. The OBR is not providing the Treasury with this sort of genuinely independent analysis.

Conclusions

One of the most disappointing aspects of the May 2010 election was that all three major parties treated high government spending as having no adverse consequences for the wider economy. This meant that the electorate had to choose between three, almost identical, fiscal 'Ponzi' schemes and that the coalition has no moral platform from which to justify the much-needed spending retrenchment.

The retrenchment was needed for several reasons, not least of which is that one effect of Labour's pre-2010 spending binge may have been to slow the growth of UK productive potential to a Euro-sclerotic 1.5 per cent or so each year. The need now is to rebalance the economy by nurturing the private sector. Otherwise the UK's ability to generate wealth, tax receipts and genuine employment opportunities is likely to become vanishingly small.

Indeed, the spending burden in Britain is so high that the economy is probably on the wrong side of the aggregate Laffer curve, particularly where taxes such as VAT are concerned (Smith, 2011b). Attempts to tax a way out of the current fiscal crisis are likely to lead to an exacerbated budget deficit as private activity falls away and joblessness rises. The coalition seems to be blissfully unaware of this. There should have been no tax increases in the fiscal consolidation plans. Simulations using the BEF forecasting model confirm that the hike in VAT to 20 per cent was pointlessly damaging, leading to higher unemployment, reduced national output and a *larger* budget deficit than would have been the case otherwise. This does not mean that alternative tax increases would not have been at least as harmful, particularly the Labour opposition's proposal that employer's NICs should have been raised instead. Direct surcharges on employment costs represent the most damaging tax of all and are an impost where the adverse Laffer-curve effects appear to be indisputable.

Simulations carried out on the BEF model strongly suggest that the 'best-buy' policy package would have been to cut spending more aggressively and not to raise taxes in the way that the coalition has done. This would have maximised the virtuous-circle 'crowding-in' effects of the policy stance. The institutional separation of the OBR from the Treasury, however, makes it difficult for the Chancellor to evaluate alternative tax and spending options using a properly specified macroeconomic model. There are major flaws in the forecasting methodology inherited by the OBR from HM Treasury. These flaws give rise to an undue bias in favour of higher taxes rather than expenditure cuts.

There have been several interesting studies of historic fiscal consolidations published since the literature was reviewed in Smith (2006). The subsequent studies by Lilico et al. (2009) and Reading et al. (2010) can both be recommended. What is surprising, however, is that more attention has not been paid to the successful rolling back of the state under Winston Churchill's post-war administration in the 1950s.[3] This government took a heavily socialised economy in which people were eating whale meat and in which bread had been rationed for the first time three years after the end of World War II and left a situation where 'most of our people have never had it so good'.

It is clear from the memoirs of R. A. Butler, who was Chancellor of the Exchequer throughout much of this period (he subsequently became Lord Butler), that he understood the importance of low taxes and deregulation as a means of triggering a virtuous circle of enhanced growth. Butler was aware also of the damage done by unpredictable taxes on capital. Indeed, there seem to have been remarkably few of the ideas of the 1980s US supply-side school that had not been anticipated by Butler in the 1950s, probably because both had their intellectual roots in pre-Keynesian microeconomic analysis. The remarkable thing, however, was how much was achieved with so little political fuss compared with the intense opposition that faced Lady Thatcher's reforms.

There are lessons here for the present government. From the government's rhetoric, the first lesson seems to have been grasped – even if little action has been taken. That is that supply-side reform is vital to the general health of the economy, especially during a fiscal retrenchment. The second lesson – to which only lip-service has been paid at best – is that the supply-side aspects of public finance are crucial. This includes

3   Churchill took office in late October 1951, following the election defeat of the post-war Labour government, and retired as prime minister in April 1955, after which he was followed by Sir Anthony Eden until January 1957. R. A. Butler was Chancellor of the Exchequer between October 1951 and December 1955. The share of general government spending in factor-cost GDP was 41.1 per cent in 1951 and 36.4 per cent in 1955, which was close to a post-war low and in line with Tanzi and Schuknecht's one-third optimum rule after allowing for definitional differences. As Chancellor, Butler reactivated monetary policy, eliminated rationing, and toyed with the idea of a floating exchange rate, but was overruled.

considering the supply-side aspects of public spending and taxation in general and also the specific supply-side effects of particular taxes and welfare policies.

References

Butler, R. A. (1971), *The Art of the Possible: the Memoirs of Lord Butler*, London: Hamish Hamilton.

HM Treasury (2011), *Budget 2011; March 2011*, HM Treasury/House of Commons, HC 836, www.hm-treasury.gov.uk.

IMF/ Independent Evaluation Office (2011), *IMF Performance in the Run-Up to the Financial and Economic Crisis: IMF Surveillance in 2004–07*, Independent Evaluation Office of the International Monetary Fund, 10 January 2011, www.Imf-ieo.org/eval/complete/pdf/01102011/crisis.

Lightfoot, W. (2010), *Sorry, We Have No Money: Britain's Economic Problem*, London: Searching Finance.

Lilico, A., E. Holmes and H. Sameen (2009), *Controlling Spending and Government Deficits: Lessons from History*, London: Policy Exchange, www.policyexchange.org.uk.

Office for Budget Responsibility (2011-I), *Forecasting the Public Finances*, Briefing Paper no. 1, January, www.budgetresponsibility. independent.gov.uk.

Office for Budget Responsibility (2011-II), *Economic and Fiscal Outlook; March 2011*, Cm 8036, www.budgetresponsibility.independent.gov. uk.

Reading, B., R. Roberts and G. Opie (2010), *Sharpening the Axe*, London: Lombard Street Research, www.lombardstreetresearch.com.

Smith, D. B. (2006), *Living with Leviathan: Public Spending, Taxes and Economic Performance*, London: Institute of Economic Affairs.

Smith, D. B. (2009), 'How Should Britain's Government Spending and Tax Burdens be Measured? A Historic Perspective on the 2009 Budget Forecasts', *Economic Affairs*, 29(4): 37–47.

Smith, D. B. (2011a), *Beacon Economic Forecasting (BEF) Quarterly Macroeconomic Model of the UK and International Economies, February 2011 Edition*, Beacon Economic Forecasting, xxxbeaconxxx@ btinternet.com.

Smith, D. B. (2011b), *Restructuring the UK Tax System: Some Dynamic Considerations*, IEA Discussion Paper no. 35, March, London: Institute of Economic Affairs.

Tanzi, V. and L. Schuknecht (2000), *Public Spending in the 20th Century: A Global Perspective*, Cambridge: Cambridge University Press.

Tanzi, V. and L. Schuknecht (2005), *Reforming Public Expenditure: Great Gain, Little Pain*, London: Politeia.

3 THE RECKONING UP
Philip Booth

The total government spending cuts proposed in the later parts of this monograph are listed in Table 9. Some qualifying points are worth making:

- In some areas, such as health, reforms are proposed that will lead to more pre-funding of healthcare and therefore to reduced government spending year on year.
- In further areas such as education, training and childcare the author has taken a relatively pragmatic approach and there would be opportunities for further radical reform in future years.
- In other areas, most notably privatisation, the revenues (listed here as 'reductions in spending') will be temporary. The road privatisation plans, however, will continue for at least a decade and a conservative approach has been taken to estimating all spending reductions, including privatisation proceeds. The total headline government spending cuts of £215 billion would, on balance, seem to be the minimum that is achievable and sustainable.
- There are some areas of government spending that are not included in Office for National Statistics or Treasury figures. These include elements of public sector pensions spending and some climate change measures. We have not examined all such 'off-balance-sheet' items but have identified cuts in those items of £27 billion.
- The main items of government spending not shown in government accounts relate to the accrual of future liabilities. We have proposed that this accrual of future liabilities (for example, public sector pensions) is reduced and this will also lead to long-term downward

Table 9 **Proposed spending cuts by 2015**

Area of expenditure	Proposed cut (£bn)
Health	44
Education, training and childcare	15.5
Pensions and the elderly	15.5
Defence	17
Foreign aid	12
Income transfers	31
Transport (including first year of road privatisation programme)	30
Privatisation	40[a]
Energy and climate change measures	10
Total 'headline' spending cuts	**215**
Reduction in spending that the Office for National Statistics does not currently count as spending	
Public sector pensions	17
Energy and climate change measures	10
Total cuts in underlying government spending	**242**
Removal of tax expenditures[b]	
Changes to taxation of pensioners' incomes	3
Move to a flat-rate VAT	25
Total fiscal adjustment	**270**

a This figure has not been uprated to allow for possible increases in asset values before 2015.
b To be recycled into lower tax rates. This revenue gain is calculated before the other reforms to the tax system have been proposed. As such, some of the measures, such as removal of the age allowance, could become irrelevant because all tax allowances would be raised.

pressure – or a lessening of the upward pressure – on government spending.

- Authors have identified cuts in exemptions from general taxes which would, at current tax rates, yield a further £25 billion as well as giving rise to a more efficient tax system.
- It has been implicitly assumed that the cuts to elements of government spending not discussed in the monograph will follow the trajectory proposed by the government. Again, this takes a conservative approach.

It is also important to note that both the reduction in government spending and the simpler tax system that is proposed will stimulate economic growth. This should have the effect of reducing spending pressures in some areas. While assumptions have already been made about the impact of welfare changes on labour market participation, it has been assumed implicitly that there is no beneficial impact from reduced taxes on tax avoidance and evasion, welfare fraud, labour market participation, household formation or saving.

The programme proposed by the authors of this monograph has been devised for implementation in 2015 – therefore the focus has been on calendar years rather than fiscal years. A reasonable estimate of government spending in calendar year 2015 is £750 billion or 40 per cent of national income. The proposals in this monograph would therefore lead to a reduction in government spending to about 29 per cent of national income using the government's own measure – a little more if the factor-cost measure of national income is used.

The shape of a new tax system

This reduction in government spending will allow a substantial reduction in taxation and a reshaping of the tax system. In recent years, not only has the level of taxation increased but the tax system has become more complicated. Various allowances are given and then withdrawn. Indeed, even the personal allowance is now withdrawn from individuals earning over £100,000 a year, leading to a sudden rise in the marginal tax rate to 62 per cent followed by a fall to 42 per cent and a rise again to 52 per cent when the top rate of tax starts. The UK tax system is now completely incoherent. Furthermore, the level of income at which higher-rate tax is paid has been gradually falling relative to average earnings – only 2 million people paid higher-rate tax in 1997 whereas it is likely that over five million people will pay higher-rate tax by 2014.

It is not only the income tax system which has become complex and punitive. It could also be argued that the extent of mobility of capital is such that the burden of corporation tax at current rates falls on workers through reducing capital investment in the UK (see Arulampalam et al., 2009). More generally, it is certainly difficult to justify a rate of corporation tax above the basic rate of income tax, which leads to a situation whereby the provision of equity capital to corporations is penalised as compared with the provision of debt capital. The corporation tax system is also extremely complicated, thus contributing to the UK's complicated tax code, which is the longest in the world (see Chittenden et al., 2010). Furthermore, arbitrary taxes such as stamp duty impair labour mobility and raise travel-to-work costs and the capital gains tax system provides no allowance for illusory gains as a result of inflation and often leads to the double taxation of certain forms of investment returns.

It is not the purpose of this monograph to propose or justify a very specific tax system. We do suggest, however, illustrative changes to the tax system and the abolition of a number of taxes. A broad picture of how a reformed tax system might look is also sketched out. Any estimates given of the costs of tax changes are crude and ignore second-round, or dynamic, effects of tax cuts that will arise from increases in economic activity. The estimates also ignore the costs of collection that are imposed upon the private sector and ignore the administrative costs of collection by government – reductions in those costs of collection would be a further advantage of radical tax reform. All the figures below should therefore be seen as indicative.

Tax abolition and substantial reductions

With the proposed reforms to government spending, a number of taxes could be abolished. These are shown in Table 10. The taxes that have been proposed for abolition either yield relatively little revenue or are economically damaging or both.

A number of taxes should also be cut significantly. For example, given that road users would be paying for road use via direct charges, there is very little justification for fuel duty except if it is believed that

Table 10 **Tax death list**

Tax	Cost to exchequer of abolition 2015 (£bn)
Stamp duty land tax	12.5
Stamp duty on shares	3.9
Capital gains tax	2.0[a]
Inheritance tax	2.9
Bank levy	2.4[b]
Climate change levy	1.7
Vehicle excise duty (VED)	6.3[c]

a It has arbitrarily been assumed that half of the revenue from this tax would be clawed back as a result of identifying more effectively income that was disguised as capital gains and taxing this as and when it accrued. The amounts involved are trivial but such an approach is necessary to prevent avoidance.

b The government argues that the bank levy is to compensate society for losses borne by taxpayers in the event of bank failure. The government simultaneously argues that banking legislation will be reformed so that future costs of bank failure will not be borne by taxpayers. This is clearly inconsistent and it is therefore proposed that the levy is abolished.

c The abolition of vehicle excise duty would begin when the process for privatising roads starts and would be phased out as the road privatisation programme progresses. Fuel duty would also be phased out as road-user charging developed (see below).

it is appropriate to reflect the externalities of road use arising from carbon emissions through fuel duties.[1] A reduction in corporation tax to the basic rate of income tax would be highly desirable. Other priorities would be a major flattening of the UK income tax system, which currently has some of the highest marginal tax rates in the developed world.

A case can also be made for increasing some very specific taxes. There would no longer be special tax allowances for pensioners (though these might be made redundant by the increase in the personal allowance). It would also be appropriate to extend the VAT base, though rates of VAT would be much lower.

---

1   Congestion externalities should be reflected in the road user charges. Environmental externalities could justify a generalised carbon tax: the Stern Report suggested that a tax of 11 pence a litre would be appropriate for this purpose.

An alternative tax system

The principles that form the basis of a good tax system are discussed in detail in the Mirrlees Report (Mirrlees et al., 2011). One such important principle is that the tax system should be neutral in the way it treats different forms of economic activity. While a case for departure from neutrality can be made in some cases, our current tax system has provided various reliefs and additional taxes that go beyond any reasonable justification for departures from neutrality. There are probably two reasons for this. As tax rates have risen, governments have had to design taxes in more complex ways to avoid levying taxes in overt ways that the electorate understands. Secondly, as tax rates have risen, both the economic and the political arguments for a departure from neutrality become more intense. If there is a theoretical argument for a tax exemption for a particular activity (such as work-related childcare) the economic distortion from not giving the relief is greater when the income tax rate is 40 per cent than if income tax is 10 per cent, and the political pressure to grant the relief is also greater. In many senses, therefore, low taxes are a prerequisite for simple taxes.

The revenue that it is necessary for the government to raise in order to finance government spending, given the proposals in this monograph, is of the order of 29 per cent of national income. This sort of revenue could be raised with a relatively flat income tax system with reliefs for charitable giving and certain types of saving; a corporation tax[2] at the same rate as the basic rate of income tax; an expenditure tax (value added tax); and a national insurance system to fund those insurance-style benefits that are still provided by the state.[3] It would also be necessary to find an appropriate system of local taxation that ensured that local government could be more or less fiscally autonomous. National insurance contributions could remain proportionate to salary, even

---

2   An entirely different method of taxing corporations could be justified, but we do not follow up those arguments here: again, see Mirrlees et al. (2011).

3   Individuals would be able to contract out of the main benefit – pensions – and receive a rebate of contributions as outlined in Chapter 6.

though most of the benefits are flat-rate, but the system should certainly return to the relative simplicity that existed before 1997.

Overall, it would seem feasible that the level of spending suggested could be financed by the following taxes:

- A single flat-rate income tax of about 15 per cent on income above the tax threshold, which would be determined by household size. A single person's allowance could be around £12,000. Larger households would have much higher tax allowances so that a four-person household on median earnings would pay little income tax.
- Corporation tax of 15 per cent.
- National insurance rates of about 10 per cent split between employer and employee above a lower threshold than the income tax threshold so that all workers made some contribution. Contracting out of the most important national insurance benefits would be possible. The proportional character of national insurance rates would mean that there would be redistribution within the state pension system.
- A value added tax of about 10 per cent across a broad base of spending.

Others may make a case for a land value tax rather than taxes on consumption and work. It could also be argued that there should be a comprehensive income tax *or* a consumption tax, but not both. These debates are beyond the scope of this monograph but are discussed in standard texts, including the Mirrlees report.

There would be other decisions to take within this overall framework, but the trade-offs would be easy to understand given the much simpler nature of the proposed tax system. The particular issues that would need to be addressed would include:

- Whether excise duties on alcohol and tobacco were retained.
- How local taxation and service provision fitted within this

framework and whether a property tax was retained or replaced with a local sales or income tax. Higher levels of local taxation would imply lower levels of national taxation.

- Whether a generalised carbon tax was introduced. The simplicity of the tax system would be such that the choices between a carbon tax and reduced taxes on general consumption would be very straightforward to understand. Any carbon tax would lead directly to a reduction in the taxes proposed here.
- Whether there were tax allowances for charitable giving and long-term saving.

Despite the horrendous complexity of the UK tax system, it is remarkably flat with regard to marginal rates. Those at the bottom end of the income scale pay marginal rates of tax (after withdrawal of tax credits) that are not very different from those paid by those who earn the most. The ending of employees' national insurance contributions at approximately the same earnings point as higher rate tax starts also leads to a hidden element of 'flatness' within the UK tax system. A typical marginal tax rate for a '40 per cent' taxpayer is around 58 per cent (after allowing for indirect taxes and taxes paid by the employer). This figure is around 50 per cent for those below the higher-rate tax threshold. Of course, taxes can be reduced by pension contributions and in other ways, and the average rate is less than the marginal rate because of tax allowances. The marginal rate of tax suggested here would be around 20 per cent for poorer families (they would pay value added tax and employees' national insurance contributions and their employer would be liable to employers' national insurance contributions).[4] For households earning above the household tax allowance the marginal rate of tax would be about 34 per cent after taking into account all forms of taxation. The marginal rates of direct tax would be much lower. The administrative costs of this tax system would be very low and the incentives for

---

4 The interaction with the proposed negative income tax system has been ignored here.

avoidance would be much reduced. Taxes would be transparent and politicians would be easily held to account if they increased them. The remaining parts of this monograph show how we could reach such a low tax burden in practice.

References

Arulampalam, W., M. P. Devereux and G. Maffini (2009), 'The direct incidence of corporate income tax on wages', Oxford University Centre for Business Taxation Working Paper 09/17, www.sbs.ox.ac.uk/centres/tax/Documents/working_papers/WP0917. pdf.

Chittenden, F., H. Foster and B. Sloan (2010), *Taxation and Red Tape: The cost to British business of complying with the UK tax system*, Research Monograph 64, London: Institute of Economic Affairs.

Mirrlees, J., S. Adam, T. Besley, R. Blundell, S. Bond, R. Chote, M. Gammie, P. Johnson, G. Myles and J. Poterba (2011), *Tax by Design*, Oxford: Oxford University Press, forthcoming.

PART TWO: THE WELFARE STATE

4 HEALTHCARE – TRIMMING THE FAT OR FIT FOR THE FUTURE?

Sam Collins

Introduction

The National Health Service (NHS) takes up almost a sixth of the UK government's budget (HM Treasury, 2010a), costing £104 billion in 2010/11 (HM Treasury, 2010b). The public sector is responsible for 83 per cent of all health spending in Britain (OECD, 2010: Chart 3). During the years 2000–08, government spending on health increased by more than double the rate of GDP growth (ibid.: Chart 1). Indeed, despite the budget cuts affecting almost every other government department, health spending is projected to rise to £114 billion in 2014/15, a real-terms increase of 0.4 per cent (HM Treasury, 2010b).

The future is almost certain to see upward pressure on total health spending, as the population ages, more treatments become available and life expectancy improves. In the absence of a significant increase in outputs for each unit of inputs, the government will face some stark choices. It will have to allow spending in the National Health Service to continue to take up a larger and larger proportion of government spending; reduce the level of healthcare provided through the NHS; increase taxes; or find a way to reduce government spending on healthcare without reducing total spending on healthcare or healthcare outputs.

The coalition government's Health and Social Care Bill[1] is likely to reduce the costs of local bureaucracy and, according to McKinsey, will lower annual spending on health provision by between £13 billion and

---

1   At the time of writing the Bill has not cleared the House of Commons, so any assumptions made are regarding the unamended Bill.

£20 billion by 2014 (Department of Health, 2011). This is a good start, but this money will be recycled into the health service and will simply produce a restructured nationalised health system.

This chapter will assume that access to healthcare should remain universal. It makes no further assumptions about how that should be achieved. It will look at two options: changes to the NHS model to improve productivity and increase private sector involvement, and, secondly, a shift from the single-payer model to an alternative model.

The first model, which could be called the 'cuts' model, reduces government spending through improvements in productivity, the introduction of user fees and streamlining bureaucracy. The second model is the 'reform' model – moving from the existing NHS framework to a different approach – specifically to private health savings accounts.

There are a number of underlying non-economic reasons for deeper reform. The UK has poor healthcare outcomes compared with most other European and industrialised countries. Whether the test is the comparative five-year cancer survival figures (Eurocare, 2007; Spiers, 2008: 112); deaths from circulatory disease (Gubb, 2007: 18); stroke outcomes (Gray et al., 2006); or mortality amenable to healthcare (Taxpayers Alliance, 2008), the NHS performs badly against other European countries which have different and more consumer-driven healthcare models. It is also notable that our government-dominated system also weakens the incentives for people to take responsibility for healthy lifestyle choices, by shielding them from the costs of their decisions.

A government-dominated system can also be captured by producer interests. As public choice theory makes clear, actors within a publicly owned body can act in their own self-interest (Buchanan, 1984: 11). Of such groups, two of the most powerful are workers (such as nurses, doctors, managers and consultants) and politicians. Politicians will (rationally) seek re-election and the continued support of the public. Workers will (again, rationally) seek to maximise their budgets, pay and conditions. For each of these groups the advantages of collective action to try to maximise these benefits are great, while the barriers to them engaging in this kind of action are low. In comparison, end-users of healthcare (patients) are highly dispersed and heterogeneous, making successful collective action difficult to organise, maintain or advance (Meadowcroft, 2008: 434). Most NHS staff work in close proximity to a number of other, equally interested, people. This makes it easier to act collectively, and use this lobbying power to force concessions and benefits from the employer. The capturing of an organisation by producers often leads to increases in budgets and changes to management structures benefiting the producers of a product or service, rather than the end-users, consumers and (in this case) patients (Spiers, 2008: 138).[2] This same producer capture makes any reform in the health system extremely difficult.

The third problem with government-provided services is overt and covert rationing. There is a fixed budget allocated to the NHS and, in the absence of pricing, care is essentially rationed by queuing. Others will continue to maximise their use of the system whether or not any other individual does. This means that the self-interested, rational outcome for many individuals will be to maximise their use of healthcare. After all, if the individual bears no extra cost for choosing to use the health service more often, why would anyone not maximise their usage? This leads to what Hardin termed the 'tragedy of the commons' (Hardin, 1968: 1244). This has meant that demand for services has exceeded (and continues to exceed) supply. When this happens there must be rationing. Therefore, while healthcare may be free at the point of use, it certainly is not completely accessible. As with any completely publicly funded system, doctors in the NHS find themselves not only acting as physicians but also as allocators of scarce resources (Evans, 2008: 6). Given this system of rationing, the surprisingly high level of health inequalities that exists in the UK (in a system that is designed to provide equal healthcare to all – see Marmot et al., 2010) may be explained by the ability of those who are most articulate to obtain the best care.

---

2   For a fuller discussion of budget maximisation, see also Niskanen (1971).

The 'cuts' model

Principles of the 'cuts' model

The cost of universal healthcare has increased dramatically since the formation of the NHS, and it is difficult to argue that there is no scope for cuts to the health budget. Real-terms spending increased by almost 200 per cent from 1980 to 2010 (Appleby et al., 2009: 5). And spending will continue to grow in real terms until 2014/15. The rate of growth of spending accelerated in the first decade of the 21st century. Productivity in the NHS, however, declined by more than 10 per cent between 1995 and 2006 (ONS, 2011: 1). In addition, the rate of improvement in the health outcomes of the NHS (measured by 'life expectancy amenable to healthcare') fell substantially between 2001 and 2004 (Taxpayers Alliance, 2008: 16). This suggests a decline in the marginal utility of every extra pound invested in the NHS, perhaps resulting from a lack of capacity within the service to spend the extra money productively. We will therefore examine the scope for cutting NHS spending by finding productivity gains, cutting bureaucracy and introducing co-payments and user fees. There is a strong rationale for all three improvements to the current NHS structure.

User fees, or co-payments, are already a feature in most healthcare systems (Irvine and Gratzer, 2009: 9) and have been examined in a number of studies over the past quarter-century. Although one of the founding principles of the NHS was that medical care should be free at the point of delivery, the NHS has charged fees for certain services almost since its inception (Meadowcroft, 2008: 430; Evans, 2008: 6).[3] It is therefore odd that user fees have not been more widely considered by government as a possible solution to the growth in NHS spending. User fees add a significant level of price discretion for 'non-urgent' care and bring major reductions in drug costs (Goodman, 2004: 8), emergency room visits (Selby et al., 1996) and outpatient costs (Dixon, 2002: 413).

Cutting bureaucracy could lead to a relatively pain-free reduction in

---

3   Fees for dentures and spectacles were introduced in 1951 and fees for prescriptions in 1953.

spending and also have beneficial effects on the provision of healthcare, though the potential savings are hard to quantify. Reducing administration costs will lead to productivity gains by enabling greater output for a given unit of input.

A further area for reform is the monopoly power exercised by groups such as the General Medical Council over the certification of medical professionals. While the supply of doctors is controlled, preventing the market from finding equilibrium, the 'price' of seeing a doctor will remain artificially high.[4] To quote David Friedman (1991: 302): 'Both barbers and physicians are licensed; both professions have for decades used licensing to keep their numbers down and their salaries up ... Government regulation of physicians makes medical care more expensive; one result, presumably, is that we have less medical care and shorter lives.'

While it can be expected that an increase in the supply of doctors will reduce the price to those purchasing healthcare in the market (whether government or individuals) it is also difficult, if not impossible, to quantify the possible savings.

Cost reductions from the introduction of user fees

User fees are an under-explored option for improving the fiscal position of the NHS. A broad introduction of user fees has never been seriously debated, despite the fact that most health systems in other countries have user fees for some or all non-emergency treatment (see Irvine and Gratzer, 2009: 9).[5] The use of user fees in a centralised NHS-style model has not been widely trialled (although they are used in other fully publicly funded and operated systems). Nevertheless, studies indicate that major savings could be obtained from even small user fees placed

---

4   For a much more in-depth discussion of this topic, see Evans (2008: 3).
5   For example, New Zealand has user fees for GPs and prescriptions and Australia for GPs and specialists – and Sweden, Austria, France and others charge for GPs, specialists and outpatient hospital care

on non-urgent healthcare – such as GP visits and outpatient operations. The HIE study[6] estimated falls in total health costs of between 20 per cent and 45 per cent,[7] while Selby et al. (1996) estimated a 15 per cent reduction in emergency room use. In South Africa (which uses a health savings account system further discussed below) outpatient costs are 50 per cent lower and pharmaceutical costs 25 per cent lower than for those patients who are not charged user fees (Dixon, 2002: 413; Goodman, 2004: 8). Even significantly smaller savings than these (and there is no reason to assume that the results would not be closely replicated) would lead to large amounts saved, especially in pharmaceutical costs. It should be noted that savings in government budgets can come about for a number of reasons. If there is some element of user charging, this provides an income stream for health service providers independent of government subsidies; secondly, user charging can regulate demand and encourage private provision; thirdly, user fees will make consumers of healthcare more price conscious and will sharpen competitive forces and should especially reduce the level of wastage from pharmaceutical usage that currently exists within the NHS (Craig, 2010). The range of possible savings is wide, but we can estimate that low-level universal user fees could save the NHS between £10.4 billion and £25 billion – and possibly more.

Back office costs

While many claim that the 'low-hanging fruit' of spending cuts through 'efficiency savings' has already been plucked, there are still significant savings that can be made in the back office. One such saving is from the inefficient use of the NHS estate. Both internal (Healthcare for London,

---

6 A summary of the findings of the HIE study can be found in both Irvine and Gratzer (2009), and HIE (2006). The full findings can be found in Lohr et al. (1986), Keeler (1992) and Newhouse and the Insurance Experiment Group (1993).

7 The extremes of co-payment leading to the quoted falls in outpatient expenses were 25 and 95 per cent of expenses up to $1,000 (1984 US dollars).

2007) and external research (May and Price, 2006; Appleby et al., 2010) has discussed the underutilisation of the NHS estate. Research suggests that between £500 and £600 million a year could be saved if this estate were used to its full potential (May and Price, 2006; McKinsey, 2009). Further savings can be made from a reduction in the number of managers and a reorganisation of support services. Research by McKinsey (2009) has identified up to £2.5 billion in savings through procurement/supply chain efficiencies. The Department of Health (2010) has itself shown that significant savings can be made in this area, through the success of the NHS Shared Business Services initiative, which has been forecast to save £25 million a year over the next ten years (Appleby et al., 2010: 12).

The size and remuneration of NHS management are frequently cited as a problem in the media (Smith, 2010; Ramesh, 2010). While the media has overhyped the proportion of the NHS budget that is spent on management, significant savings are possible in this area. The number of managerial full-time equivalent staff in the NHS has increased substantially over the past decade[8] (NHSIC, 2010a). If one were to remove every single manager and senior manager from the NHS, the government would save £1.9 billion a year (NHSIC, 2010b). But a centrally run single-payer system cannot hope to operate without any kind of management structure. The more realistic goal of seeking a reduction in the number of managers and central managers to 1999 levels[9] would save £880 million a year (ibid.).

There is further scope for savings in procurement (National Audit Office and Audit Commission, 2010). The public sector is not exploiting the benefits of commissioning in large volumes and, according to Appleby et al. (2010), a more efficient national framework agreement could save up to £240 million a year. These back-room savings could

---

8   Rising from 23,378 managers and senior managers in 1999 to 42,509 in 2009, an average annual increase of 6.2 per cent, against a 3.6 per cent annual increase in general infrastructure support staff, and a 3 per cent annual increase in total NHS staff (NHSIC 2010a).

9   8,592 senior managers and 14,786 other managers.

SHARPER AXES, LOWER TAXES: BIG STEPS TO A SMALLER STATE

be expected to reduce the NHS total bill by approximately £3.8 billion a year – approximately 3.6 per cent of the NHS budget.

Front-line savings?

A very large reduction in NHS spending would inevitably involve cutting staff costs, which make up some 60 per cent of total NHS spending (NHS Choices, 2011). As spending on the NHS has increased in the last decade, productivity has declined by 10 per cent. It would seem that there is plenty of scope to reduce the amount of staff time spent on paperwork and unnecessary bureaucracy[10] and by increasing the productivity of medical practitioners who are performing under the median level of productivity. It has been estimated that between £3.1 billion and £4.9 billion could be saved through these kinds of productivity gains, which would involve a reduction in the number of nurses by around 10 per cent (McKinsey, 2009). There is also some scope for savings on the front line through replacing national pay bargaining in the NHS with regional or individual pay awards, which some calculations indicate could save more than £1 billion annually in England.[11]

Some notes of caution

While the savings potential may appear large, some reasons for caution must be noted. Many of the savings enumerated come from theoretical studies, from extrapolations, from estimates based on different countries (with different healthcare systems) or from a combination of these three approaches. Therefore, it cannot be assumed that these savings can be achieved across the NHS in a uniform way. Indeed, if the basic problem is that efficiency cannot be achieved in a state-run system because it

---

10   It has been estimated that up to 25 per cent of GPs' time and 12 per cent of acute nurses' time is spent doing administration (McKinsey, 2009).

11   Based on a reverse weighting for those areas where the cost of living index is below the national average.

lacks the economic structures that provide signals and incentives, efforts to reduce expenditure may not be possible without structural reform. There may also be short-term costs of achieving longer-term savings. Furthermore, if one aspect of the strategy outlined above is implemented without the other aspects, or if implementation of one type of reform is partial, the whole reform strategy might fail. For instance, the introduction of user fees in only certain areas of the service may lead to higher consumption of other (sometimes more expensive) types of healthcare – such as a person going to an emergency room to avoid GP fees.

Arguments against the 'cost-cutting' model

There are also five major problems with reforming the existing model. First, there is the unavoidably politicised nature of the government-provided healthcare model. This model has, across the world, been accompanied by major increases in public spending on healthcare, since the total level of resources allocated to healthcare is not the result of consumer choice. In democratic countries around the world we have seen political parties seek to outbid one another to increase government spending on healthcare.[12] It must therefore be considered doubtful whether any major spending reductions in the NHS would survive multiple elections.

Secondly, the model of health provision not only prevents individuals from determining how much they spend on healthcare, it also prevents the processes of competition and discovery that can lead to consumer needs being satisfied in the most efficient way. Inefficiency – both in the dynamic and static senses – is hard-wired into a state-run health service. As has been noted, the NHS has not even achieved the equality of outcomes that a state-run system is supposed to guarantee.

---

12   Two examples are the US Republican Party's support for increasing Medicare and Medicaid spending and the UK Conservative Party's pledge to ring-fence NHS spending during the 2010 general election campaign.

A single-payer government-funded health system is also highly susceptible to special pleading by stakeholder groups. Producer interests and other stakeholder groups have been highly successful in obtaining preferential treatment from the NHS and avoiding exposure to competition. The nature of democratic competition makes it difficult for government to manage these interests and maintain efficient resource allocation in the face of well-organised campaigns by special interest groups that can obtain a high media profile.

The fourth major problem relates to the ageing population. The percentage of people aged 65 and over increased from 13 per cent in 1971 to 16 per cent in 2003 and is projected to rise to 23 per cent in 2031. The number of people over 85 is likely to rise from 2.8 million to 4.5 million in the next fifteen years. Spending per head on people aged over 65 is three times that of those aged between 20 and 64 (Hagist and Kotlikoff, 2006). Spending per head then continues to increase with age. As such, the argument is frequently made that the coming demographic difficulties will inevitably lead to a healthcare financing crisis. In fact, this is not true. Ageing will lead to a funding crisis only if we maintain our current system of financing healthcare. The most important factor affecting healthcare costs is proximity to death. If the population ages owing to rising longevity, death will occur later on average and healthcare costs will therefore be incurred later. That does not automatically make healthcare costs per person higher. The key issue is the relationship between healthy life expectancy and total life expectancy. If people live, for example, ten years longer and have ten years more healthy life, then population ageing is not necessarily a problem for healthcare systems. The data suggest that the number of years of ill health seem to be a relatively stable proportion of the total lifespan – though the proportion is growing slowly. Owing to improving technology, we are also better able to adapt to ill health.

If healthcare is financed by people saving throughout their lives for the time when they need healthcare then the ageing population alone will not cause a problem with regard to healthcare funding. The financing problem arises if the healthcare of the elderly is financed by a shrinking working population through taxation. If taxpayers in general are paying for healthcare, an increase in the number of old people per taxpayer will lead to a huge increase in costs.[13] If we save to finance healthcare costs, however, the total cost does not fall but there is a pool of capital to meet those costs. As such, just as we can talk about unfunded pensions, we can talk about unfunded health liabilities. The model proposed below addresses this problem – merely seeking efficiency savings within the current model does not.

Finally, any attempt at improving efficiency within the service will be met with the problem of the Baumol effect. While some industries, such as retail and manufacturing, can use improvements in technology to increase productivity, other service industries cannot do so.[14] There is, it can be argued, a minimum amount of time it will take a doctor to diagnose a patient, a nurse to change a bandage, a drug to be administered, and so on. It may be the case, however, that technological advancements in healthcare have made the Baumol effect less important. For example, improvements in technology may well lead to better treatments for the same level of resources, treatments that can be administered at home, diagnosis through the Internet, and so on. In the face of the Baumol effect, however, it is surely wrong that we rely on a system of healthcare funding and provision that eradicates the forces of competition which can deliver technological innovation and productivity improvements at the quickest possible rate. To some extent at least, the Baumol effect in healthcare might be the result of its central provision undermining the rapid adoption of new treatments and approaches to care (see Bartholomew, 2004).

---

13 Studies by the King's Fund and the Institute for Fiscal Studies have estimated that demographic pressures will add more than £1.1 billion to the annual cost of the NHS (in 2010 prices) and will require annual growth in spending of 1.1 per cent in order to maintain quality of care (Appleby et al., 2009).

14 The famous example used was a string quartet – no matter what improvements there were in technology, it would still take just as long to play a piece of music, and there was no scope to cut a member from the quartet and play the piece with three musicians.

Radical reform

While the coalition government is trying to achieve greater efficiency within the current model, there are, as we have seen, important reasons why this will be insufficient. There is therefore a strong case for more radical reform. Most health systems based on compulsory or regulated insurance have begun to suffer from some of the problems observed in the NHS. Such models are particularly vulnerable to the problems of population ageing if the state finances healthcare for the better off. In this chapter the introduction of individual Health Savings Accounts (HSAs) is advocated. This would lead to a radical opening up of the market economy in healthcare, a reduction in healthcare costs and the retention of the universal access to treatment, assuming that the government finances health provision for the poor.

What is a Health Savings Account?

A Health Savings Account is a type of personal savings account used to finance healthcare. It is used in the USA,[15] South Africa (Goodman, 2004: 6), China (Dixon, 2002: 412) and Singapore (Irvine and Gratzer, 2009: 7). HSAs combine the two usual methods of financing healthcare. These are pre-payment and point-of-service payments (Dixon, 2002: 409).

In a pure HSA model there is a voluntary or compulsory contribution to an individualised account from which each person is responsible for their own healthcare costs. Most HSA systems, however, combine this with insurance provision for acute and emergency operations (usually through catastrophic health insurance). Non-emergency outpatient care and pharmaceutical use tend to be charged to the individual.

Indeed, this combination of insurance and saving is important. Insurance provides the opportunity to pool risk and reduce the costs

---

15   Although it has been claimed that the passage and introduction of Comprehensive Health Care Reform ('Obamacare') will make many of the existing state-based HSA systems non-compliant with federal law.

to the individuals. In principle, all health risks are insurable risks and the insurance model prevails in most developed countries. Under certain assumptions, we might expect to see all health risks covered by insurance. Even in private systems, however, insurance brings with it economic problems such as transactions costs, information asymmetries and so on, which are difficult to resolve and which lead to high costs. The benefits of insurance might therefore be outweighed by the costs in certain circumstances and direct payments by the patient might be preferable.

Different health risks need not be covered in the same way. Some risks lead to large costs but arise with a low frequency; other risks have more predictable costs over a person's lifespan. The point at which the costs of insurance outweigh the benefits will depend on an individual's preferences, their risk aversion and other factors (including the ability of health systems to find ways of managing the additional costs of insurance-based systems). Thus, within any HSA system, it is important that individuals are able to determine for themselves the extent to which they fund potential healthcare costs through saving in individualised accounts and the extent to which they will be covered by insurance. There is one condition, however. There would have to be sufficient mandatory insurance so that all individuals would be protected against high-cost emergencies.

While there are few examples of HSAs in practice, those countries which have introduced HSAs recently (South Africa and the USA – particularly Indiana) have witnessed major cost reductions since their introduction. Singapore introduced Health Savings Accounts in 1993 and spends a comparatively low level of GDP on healthcare – predominantly in the private sector.[16] The state of Indiana has witnessed a reduction in long-term healthcare cost forecasts of more than 10 per cent (Mercer, 2010); the system trialled in some cities in China led to

---

16 Singapore spends only 3.4 per cent of its GDP on healthcare – of which 35 per cent is spent by the government (WHO, 2010a), compared with 9 per cent spent by the United Kingdom – of which 83 per cent is spent by the government (WHO, 2010b).

an average 18 per cent decline in health costs (Dixon, 2002: 410) and research from South Africa indicates that individuals with HSAs spend around half as much on healthcare compared with those who have regular insurance (ibid.: 413; Matisonn, 2000). Prescription costs have fallen by more than a quarter (Goodman, 2004: 8).

Prima facie, HSAs can be expected to bring about greater efficiency both in the static and dynamic senses, while retaining the universality of healthcare. In many areas they are likely to do so to a greater extent even than private insurance-based models. The removal of the insurance intermediary gives incentives to the direct payer to reduce costs, take preventive health measures (including lifestyle choices) and not consume wastefully. Insurance provides a 'backstop' for high-cost health events.

How would a UK Health Savings Account system work?

One possible model is as follows. An individual would pay a given sum from pre-tax income, which we assume to be £1,000 per annum,[17] into an account controlled by the individual for healthcare expenses. From this account a yearly fee would be paid for private catastrophic health insurance.[18] A minimum level of such insurance would be compulsory, but individuals could choose higher levels if they wished. The remainder of the account could be used for care not paid for through insurance, for deductibles, for non-urgent care, or would be saved for future years. The monies in the HSA would be the property of the individual, and would become the property of the relatives of any deceased person. It is possible that they could be used for other purposes in later life (see below).

There are various important practical details that would have to be

---

17 This is a reasonable sum, considering that (based on updated health spend figures using the proportions of Hagist and Kotlikoff (2006) and the original figures of Willetts (2010)) we can estimate healthcare consumption is approximately £800 per annum during working age, £1,600 p.a. between 65 and 74, £2,000 p.a. between 75 and 80 and £4,900 p.a. for those over 80.

18 We assume there will be significant choice in health plans offering lesser or greater levels of insurance using greater proportions of this £1,000 for insurance premiums.

determined on implementation of this policy in the UK. The most important detail for those who are in full-time work is the amount of money they are required to pay into the Health Savings Account. But we must also decide how to treat those groups that may not be able to make the contribution themselves. This would include the unemployed, those earning low salaries and the dependants of those who are employed. Payments in respect of the low-paid could be made directly by government. Alternatively, government could adjust the negative income tax system proposed in Chapter 9 to ensure that welfare payments were sufficient for the low-paid to make contributions for themselves and their dependants. Based on current economic inactivity figures (ONS, 2011), the cost of completely subsidising those not currently in work within the proposed system would be approximately £12.5 billion per annum,[19] while using a sliding scale of government subsidies for those earning less than £10,000 per year adds approximately another £1.7 billion.[20] The government financing all children would cost another £14.5 billion.[21]

It should be noted that there are many potential solutions to the problems of financing care for those who cannot afford it themselves – especially given the very substantial reduction in taxes that would be possible if all the proposals in this monograph were implemented. For example, instead of the state financing contributions to healthcare costs for children, this could be financed by their parents and the tax system adjusted appropriately to reduce taxes on families with children.

A further group that needs to be considered is the elderly, many of whom would be in no position to build up the level of health savings required to pay for their increasing health bills. Future generations of

---

19   It is hoped and expected that changes to the general welfare system will result in a significant fall in this number over the medium to long term.

20   Figures calculated from income distributions from HMRC (2010).

21   All these figures are approximations which make conservative assumptions about the behaviour and actions of those involved. For example, the costs of financing young people assume that no one within the age range of 0–19 will hold any job which pays tax. The figures are derived from Statistics UK (2010). In coming to a figure for the total level of savings, they have been indexed to 2015.

elderly people will be able to finance HSAs during their working life and reductions in the tax burden should ensure that they can continue to pay money into their accounts while also, of course, drawing money out of their accounts when they need care. One of the purposes of HSAs is to spread costs of health provision more uniformly across the lifespan and, as such, there should be no need (unlike in an annual-premium insurance model) to increase contributions as people become older.

With regard to the current generation of elderly, the best option is probably to accept that those nearing retirement age (say age 50) will have their healthcare paid for by the government until their death, and those beneath that age will be expected to begin saving through an HSA. Those below state pension age would still be required to contribute to HSAs but no insurance element would be required, and when funds were exhausted the state would finance care. The government would still be responsible for health expenditure for a large population cohort for one generation. This policy would mean the British government had an unfunded mandate for the next 40 years of approximately £780 billion,[22] with a maximum approximate yearly cost of £29 billion in 2014 declining to £12 billion in 2040 and further from there.

A further – relatively small – group for which the government might have to provide some finance is that consisting of the chronically ill who develop chronic conditions before middle age. Such individuals could be covered by the insurance element of the HSA. Alternatively, the government may make additional direct payments into HSAs for the chronically ill in the same way it would provide direct payments for those with long-term care needs, while leaving the individual free to spend the money in the best way possible.

---

22 These results come from a model put together showing the England and Wales age structure (Statistics UK, 2010) and using the estimates of average yearly healthcare costs discussed above. Obviously this model is not perfect – the cost of healthcare is more often than not related to proximity to death, rather than age itself, so an ageing population could lead to a longer and more expensive liability for the government. On the other hand, no account has been taken of the saving that would be undertaken in HSAs by those between age 50 and state pension age.

As a person grows older and is in need of personal care, it would seem reasonable to allow individuals to use the proceeds of the HSA to finance long-term care. Individuals could add to the fund out of pre-tax income in order to provide a greater sum to meet long-term care needs. This would also facilitate a less disjointed approach to meeting medical and personal care needs, in contrast to the current approach of attempting to split these two elements.

Overall, the total that the government would be expected to pay under a Health Savings Account system would be approximately £58 billion per year.[23] This is a conservative estimate. It is based on the most expensive year for existing expenditure mandates for older people, the number of unemployed at the height of a recession and the assumption that the state would pay contributions for all children. It also assumes no efficiency savings arising from this reform – such savings would be reflected in better-quality care. On the other hand, the figures on which this estimate of government subsidies is based were calculated about a decade before the proposed implementation in 2014. To make some allowance for that, we have increased the amount that government may need to pay by a further 20 per cent to £70 billion. Nevertheless, it would lead to spending being reduced by £44 billion.

While it is not the place of this chapter to discuss tax cuts, some distributional issues should be noted. It is likely that individuals will want to spend more on health as they become better off – especially on the 'hotel services' that come with healthcare. To some degree at least, however, within any country, one would expect desired health spending to be relatively income inelastic. As such, it is proposed that at least some of the savings are used to reduce taxes that bear relatively heavily on the less well off.

---

23   This figure is made up of the four different groups who would need to be subsidised by the government – £1.6 billion for those earning under £10,000, £11.5 billion for the economically inactive, £13 billion for those under eighteen, and £29 billion for those in the current over-50 cohort.

Conclusion

The long-term sustainability of a universal healthcare system is likely to be one of the great political problems of the next 40 years. As the 'baby boomers' retire and start to incur higher health costs, the fiscal position of the NHS is only likely to worsen. Little can be done about this, but policymakers can ensure that the health system is put on a sound footing for the long-term future. The aim should not simply be to reduce government spending but to develop health policy in such a way that personal choice, efficiency and dynamism are at the heart of health provision. The current system has not achieved the ideal of equality and has rarely been copied by other countries. Certainly the NHS does not achieve the same quality of outcomes as healthcare providers in other developed countries.

Even so, compulsory insurance-based models also have their shortcomings. Many of them do not deal well with the problems of demographic decline. We have therefore proposed a radical reform that will be more effective than insurance models and more financially sustainable in the long run.

One option is to keep the current single-payer model and to make efficiency and productivity gains, leading to a leaner and more effective NHS. This is likely to lead, however, to major political conflict, and will not solve the underlying long-term problems of state-financed and state-provided healthcare. Approximately £34.7 billion could be saved by this mechanism, though how long those savings would prevail before inefficiencies developed again is a matter for conjecture. Assuming the same proportion of the health budget, this would translate to savings of £37.6 billion in 2015.

The alternative option is to develop a radically new health policy based on Health Savings Accounts. This would lead to better health outcomes and restore consumer sovereignty, innovation and competition – which were, before the creation of the NHS, widely admired aspects of UK health provision (see Bartholomew, 2004). The accounts could also be used to better integrate the provision of long-term care, social care and healthcare, and would provide better incentives for preventative care. Insurance against particular health risks would be compulsory and further voluntary insurance would, of course, be allowed. There would also be a safety net for specific groups. This model could be expected to save between 35 and 50 per cent of the health budget. In 2014/15, this would translate into savings of a minimum of £44 billion, even if the state continued to finance care for the current generation of old people, children and those on low incomes. This estimate makes no allowance for improvements in preventative care or for efficiency savings and makes conservative assumptions about the groups for which the state would continue to finance – though not provide – healthcare. In many respects, this proposal achieves what many reformers set out to achieve when the NHS was set up: we would have healthcare finance for all without undermining what was best about the pre-war systems of health provision. Such a system would be particularly appropriate as we face the challenges of an ageing population.

References

Appleby, J., R. Crawford and C. Emmerson (2009), *How Cold Will It Be? Prospects for NHS funding 2011–2017*, London: King's Fund.

Appleby, J., C. Ham, C. Imison and M. Jennings (2010), *Improving NHS Productivity*, London: King's Fund.

Bartholomew, J. (2004), *The Welfare State We're In*, London: Politico's.

Baumol, W. and W. G. Bowen (1965), 'On the performing arts: the anatomy of their economic problems', *American Economic Review*, 55(1/2): 495–502.

Buchanan, J. (1984), 'Politics without romance: a sketch of positive public choice theory and its normative implications', in J. Buchanan and R. Tollison (eds), *The Theory of Public Choice*, vol. 2, Ann Arbor: University of Michigan Press.

Craig, G. (2010), 'Commissioning under NHS budget cuts', *Chemist and Druggist*, 10 March.

Department of Health (2010), 'NHS Shared Business Services: quality and productivity', www.library.nhs.uk/qipp/ViewResource. aspx?resID=330700&tabID=289.

Department of Health (2011), *Health and Social Care Bill 2011: Coordinating Document for the Impact Assessments and Equality Impact Assessments*, London: Department of Health, www.dh.gov. uk/prod_consum_dh/groups/dh_digitalassets/documents/ digitalasset/dh_123635.pdf, accessed 5 March 2011.

Dixon, A. (2002), 'Are medical savings accounts a viable option for funding health care?', *Croatian Medical Journal*, 43(4): 408–16.

Eurocare (2007), F. Berrino et al., 'Survival for eight major cancers and all cancers combined for European adults diagnosed in 1995–99: results of the EUROCARE-4 study', *Lancet Oncology*, 8(9): 773–83.

Evans, H. (2008), 'NHS as state failure: lessons from the reality of nationalised health care', *Economic Affairs*, 28(4): 5–9.

Friedman, D. (1991), 'Should medicine be a commodity? An economist's perspective', in T. Bole and W. B. Bondeson (eds), *Rights to Health Care*, Norwell, MA: Kluwer Academic Publishers, pp. 259–307.

Goodman, J. (2004), *Statement on Health Savings Account before the US Senate Special Committee on Aging*, 19 May, www.ncpa.org/pdfs/ tst20040519.pdf.

Goodman, J. (2010), 'Testimony before Senate Finance Committee Subcommittee on Health Care', www.ncpa.org/speech/ statement-on-health-savings-accounts.

Gray, L., N. Sprigg, P. Bath, P. Sorensen, E. Lindenstrom, G. Boysen, P. de Deyn, P. Friis, D. Leys, R. Marttila, J. Olsson, D. O'Neill and A. Turpie (2006), 'Significant variation in mortality and functional outcome after acute ischaemic stroke between western countries: data from the tinzaparin in acute ischaemic stroke trial (TAIST)', *Journal of Neurology, Neurosurgery and Psychiatry*, 77(3): 327–33.

Gubb, J. (2007), *Just How Well Are We?*, London: Civitas.

Hagist, C. and L. Kotlikoff (2006), *Health Care Spending: What Will the Future Look Like?*, Boston, MA: National Centre for Policy Analysis.

Hardin, G. (1968), 'The tragedy of the commons', *Science*, 162(3859): 1243–8.

Healthcare for London (2007), NHS London, *Healthcare for London: A framework for action*, www.healthcareforlondon.nhs.uk/assets/ Publications/A-Framework-for-Action/aFrameworkForAction.pdf, accessed on 15 December 2010.

HIE (2006), Brooke et al., *The Health Insurance Experiment: A Classic RAND Study Speaks to the Current Health Care Reform Debate*, Rand Corporation, http://www.rand.org/pubs/research_briefs/RB9174. html, accessed on 15 March 2011.

HM Treasury (2010a), 'Public expenditure statistical analyses 2010', www.hm-treasury.gov.uk/pespub_pesa10.htm.

HM Treasury (2010b), 'Statement by the Chancellor of the Exechequer to the House of Commons on the Comprehensive Spending Review', www.hm-treasury.gov.uk/spend_sr2010_speech.htm.

HMRC (Her Majesty's Revenue and Customs) (2010), 'Number of taxpayers in each income bracket', www.hmrc.gov.uk/stats/ income_distribution/3–5table-jan2010.pdf.

Irvine, C. and D. Gratzer (2009), *Medicare and User Fees: Unsafe at any Price?*, Halifax, Nova Scotia: Atlantic Institute for Market Studies.

Keeler, E. (1992), 'Effects of cost sharing on use of medical services and health – medical practice management', *Journal of Medical Practice Management*, 8: 317–21.

Lohr, K., R. Brook, C. Kamberg, G. Goldberg, A. Leibowitz, J. Keesey, D. Reboussin and J. Newhouse (1986), *Use of Medical Care in the RAND Health Insurance Experiment: Diagnosis- and Service-Specific Analyses in a Randomized Controlled Trial*, Santa Monica, CA: RAND Corporation.

Marmot, M., J. Allen, P. Goldblatt, T. Boyce, D. McNeish, M. Grady and I. Geddes (2010), *Fair Society, Healthy Lives: The Marmot Review*, London: The Marmot Review.

Matisonn, S. (2010), *Medical Savings Accounts in South Africa*, Dallas, TX: National Center for Policy Analysis, www.ncpa.org/pdfs/st234. pdf.

May, D. and I. Price (2006), 'A revised approach to performance management for healthcare estates', *Health Services Management Research*, 22(4): 151–7.

McKinsey (2009), *Achieving World Class Productivity in the NHS 2009/10 – 2013/14: Detailing the Size of the Opportunity*, London: Department of Health/McKinsey & Co., www.nhshistory.net/mckinsey%20 report.pdf.

Meadowcroft, J. (2006) 'In the NHS, more can mean less', *Economic Affairs*, 26(3): 82.

Meadowcroft, J. (2008), 'Patients, politics and power: government failure and the politicization of U.K. Health Care', *Journal of Medicine and Philosophy*, 33(5): 427–44.

Mercer (2010), *Analysis of Health Insurance Benefits for Public Employees*, Chicago, IL: Mercer, www.in.gov/legislative/senate_republicans/ files/Indiana_School_Corp_Opportunity_20100706-FINAL.PDF.

National Audit Office and Audit Commission (2010), *A Review of Collaborative Procurement across the Public Sector*, London: National Audit Office and Audit Commission, www.nao.org.uk/ publications/0910/collaborative_procurement.aspx, accessed 16 December 2010.

Newhouse, J. and the Insurance Experiment Group (1993), *Free for All? Lessons from the RAND Health Experiment*, Cambridge, MA: Harvard University Press.

NHS Choices (2011) 'About the NHS', www.nhs.uk/NHSEngland/ thenhs/about/Pages/overview.aspx.

NHS History (2010), 'NHS core principles', www.nhs.uk/NHSEngland/ thenhs/about/Pages/nhscoreprinciples.aspx.

NHSIC (2010a), 'National Health Service Information Centre staff overview', www.ic.nhs.uk/webfiles/publications/workforce/ nhsstaff9909/NHS_Staff_1999_2009_Master_Table.xls.

NHSIC (2010b), 'National Health Service Information Centre staff
earnings', www.ic.nhs.uk/webfiles/publications/workforce/staff_
earnings/NHS_Staff_Earnings_January_March_2010_Tables.xls.

Niskanen, J. (1971), *Bureaucracy and Representative Government*, Chicago,
IL: Aldine-Atherton.

ONS (Office for National Statistics) (2011), 'Labour market statistics',
www.statistics.gov.uk/pdfdir/lmsuko411.pdf.

OECD (2010), 'Growing health spending puts pressure
on government budgets, according to OECD Health
Data 2010', http://www.oecd.org/document/11/0,374
6,en_21571361_44315115_45549771_1_1_1_1,00.html, accessed 15
March 2011.

Ramesh, R. (2010), 'NHS management increasing five times faster than
number of nurses', *Guardian*, 25 March.

Selby, J., B. Fireman and B. Swain (1996), 'Effect of a copayment
on use of the emergency department in a health maintenance
organization', *New England Journal of Medicine*, 334(10): 635–42.

Smith, R. (2010), 'Rise in NHS managers outstrips doctors and nurses',
Daily Telegraph, 26 March.

Singaporean MOH (2010), 'Ministry of Health – healthcare financing',
www.moh.gov.sg/mohcorp/hcfinancing.aspx?id=104.

Spiers, J. (2008), *Who Decides Who Decides?*, Oxford: Radcliffe
Publishing.

Statistics UK (2010), 'Age structure of England and Wales', www.
statistics.gov.uk/populationestimates/flash_pyramid/
EW-pyramid/pyramid6_30.html.

Taxpayers Alliance (2008), 'Wasting lives: a statistical analysis of
NHS performance in a European context since 1981', http://www.
taxpayersalliance.com/wasting_lives.pdf, accessed 15 March 2011.

WHO (World Health Organization) (2010a), 'United Kingdom health
accounts', www.who.int/nha/country/gbr/en/.

WHO (World Health Organization) (2010b), 'Singapore health
accounts', www.who.int/nha/country/sgp/en/.

Willetts, D. (2010), *The Pinch: How the Baby Boomers took their children's future – and why they should give it back,* London: Atlantic Books.

5 EDUCATION, TRAINING AND CHILDCARE
J. R. Shackleton

This chapter makes proposals for short-term cuts in spending on education, training and childcare, but the main focus is on the longer-term question of government involvement in these areas of our economy. Why do we do what we do? What could be gained and lost if we did things differently?

Education, which now accounts for 13 per cent of all government expenditure, is an example of a wider phenomenon where spending initially occurs to meet a perceived 'market failure'. It then expands, partly as a result of demographic factors, but more importantly as a result of 'mission creep'. The original rationale for spending becomes overlaid with other considerations, many resulting from pressure from special interests which the initial intervention has itself created. Those on behalf of whom the original intervention was undertaken become marginalised while government-funded experts and insiders determine the agenda, and ordinary folk are almost infantilised as a consequence. As a result they become increasingly dependent on state funding despite its limited responsiveness to their concerns. And once something becomes the state's responsibility it requires a real effort of political imagination and will to reduce or abandon such responsibilities. There are always shroud-wavers pointing out the dire consequences of removing a benefit or service without which people lived quite happily till a few years back.

This chapter returns to the general principles which should inform debate about public spending cuts in general and applies them to education and the related areas of training and childcare. I look at the rationale for government intervention and how far this can justify government

spending; I look at areas where substantial new programmes were introduced under the last government and ask whether they have succeeded
or indeed can succeed; and I compare the UK with other countries which
do things differently.

State schooling

Let us begin with schools. In his classic text *Education and the State*
(West, 1965) the late E. G. West reviewed the early history of state intervention in Britain's classrooms. This began with the commendable
principle of protection of minors: it was felt that some parents would be
unwilling or unable to provide education themselves or through school
enrolment and this would deprive children of effective choice later in
life. This principle could be used to justify some compulsory schooling,
though Professor West shows that even without such compulsion the
vast majority of parents arranged some education for their children and
that literacy rates were high in early modern England. The nineteenth-
century advocates of compulsion did not envisage universal free education. They recognised that the vast majority of parents could afford some
schooling, and that their spending power ensured that school would be
responsive to their wishes. Parish subsidies, it was argued, should go
only to the poorest.

Later, however, other arguments were used. Subsidies to some
favoured schools led to others being driven out of the market, and the
resulting apparent 'shortage' of private or voluntary provision in turn
led to the 1870 Forster Act creating new Board (state) schools. Around
the same time arguments were heard about the 'neighbourhood' or
'external' benefits of education in discouraging crime and disorder, and
later on as a means of stimulating economic growth in a world where
Britain's lead in industrialisation was being undermined by countries
such as Germany and France: these countries had strongly developed
state education systems, and a causal link was inferred.

The argument that education stimulates growth is one which has never gone away since. But not everybody believes that this view holds up. Alison Wolf's *Does Education Matter?* looked in detail at the reasons put forward to support it. She argues that the social spillovers from education are limited, that huge amounts of government money have been wasted on pursuing illusory links between education and economic performance, and that economic history shows no consistent linkage between rapid growth and government investment in schooling: 'There is no clear indication at all that the UK, or any other developed country, is spending below some critical level, or that pumping more money into education will guarantee even half a per cent a year's extra growth,' she concludes (Wolf, 2002: 53).

The other modern rationale for state involvement in education is that it can reduce inequality and raise social mobility. This was a prime motive behind New Labour's expansion of funding over the last decade, and led to such developments as the 'pupil premium' for schools, which is being introduced by the coalition government. The details of the premium are limited at the moment. It involves the payment to schools directly of extra funding (initially £430 per free-school-meals pupil), but whether it must be spent directly on these pupils, or will just go into general school funds, remains to be seen.[1]

What extra educational spending on the scale contemplated (£625 million in the first year, rising eventually to £2.5 billion) can do to bring disaffected and disengaged pupils to engage in learning is difficult to see. The idea seems to be that it will encourage high-performing schools to take on more 'difficult' pupils, but will this happen? The initially modest premium, which in many schools may simply replace funding cuts elsewhere, is unlikely to do much to encourage good schools to take on additional poorer students. Even if it did, what will the result

---

1   Poverty 'czar' Frank Field has argued that it should not go to schools at all, but directly to parents to spend on suitably uplifting activities such as cultural visits and out-of-school courses. This sounds like a good idea, though Mr Field might go farther and argue that this principle should also apply to core educational funding – essentially a voucher system (see later).

be? The assumption seems to be that disadvantaged children will gain from mixing with the more academically oriented middle class. But it could equally well be that a large influx of disruptive children could undermine the ethos of successful schools. In any case, fear of such an outcome may stimulate what David Cameron calls the 'sharp-elbowed middle classes' to find ever more ingenious ways to game the system – or encourage increasing numbers to opt out into the independent sector. A more likely result will be that schools already teaching large numbers of difficult students will get a bit more funding, but without a fundamental change of ethos and approach – will this really make much difference?

But suppose for the sake of argument that the premium works, in the sense that the average performance of children from poor backgrounds improves. What would the outcome be for social equality? In theory increasing the supply of educated people can reduce the 'rent' which educational qualifications carry in the labour market and thus reduce wage inequality. In practice people possessing similar qualifications can be very differently motivated, and the wage distribution is so dynamic, with ever-changing patterns of demand, the advent of new skills, emigration and immigration flows, that marginal changes in educational outcomes cannot have much overall impact on the income distribution.

Even if the overall income distribution changes little, can education nevertheless contribute to greater social mobility? The idea of education as a means by which individuals from humble origins can rise through society has a great deal of intrinsic appeal and resonance. But the evidence that education promotes wider social 'churn' is unclear. What is supposed to happen? In a society where the number of jobs at the top and bottom of the hierarchy remained the same over time, children of the poor could gain in status only if the children of the better off fell in status. In a society like ours, which is gradually growing richer and the numbers of higher earners are increasing, this principle is mitigated slightly. It is still the case, however, that greatly increased overall social mobility can happen only if significant numbers of children from well-off families do, in relative terms, markedly worse in life than their parents – something which those parents are anxious to prevent by all means possible. Thus we have continuous genteel class warfare around our 'good' state schools.

Belief that education (and, in particular, educational qualifications) is associated with faster economic growth and greater social mobility lay behind New Labour's continual experimentation and detailed involvement in the curriculum and educational practice. It has also led in the last few years to a big increase in spending. The total workforce in English[2] schools rose from 568,000 in 2000 to 811,000 in 2010 – largely the result, incidentally, of employing more teaching assistants and administrators rather than extra qualified teachers – despite pupil numbers having fallen. As a share of GDP, state-funded education now accounts for more expenditure than in countries such as the USA, Canada and the Netherlands.[3]

Yet despite our teachers being relatively well paid by international standards, and our schools increasingly well resourced, our educational achievements remain modest. The Progress in International Reading Literacy Study (PIRLS) saw the UK falling to fifteenth place out of 40 in 2006, down from third in 2001. We now rank below Russia, Bulgaria, Hungary and Latvia, as well as Italy, Germany, the Netherlands and Denmark. The OECD's Programme for International Student Assessment (PISA), which looks at fifteen-year-olds' achievements, placed the UK in 2006 at 14th out of 57 for science, 17th in reading and 28th in maths. These figures are an important counterpoint to the ever-rising pass rates and average grades in public examinations.

Improvements in these uninspiring results are unlikely to come simply from throwing more money at unreformed schools, while giving

---

2   Note that education in the four countries of the UK is separately administered and funded. This indicates some potential for longer-term savings. For instance, it appears that per-pupil funding is significantly higher in England than in Wales with no obvious gains in outcomes.

3   Adding in private spending would boost the figure still higher, as the perceived deficiencies of state schools lead a higher proportion of UK parents than in most other developed countries to pay for private schools.

parents no financial or other leverage and allowing highly organised teaching unions to determine working patterns.

Market liberals have long argued for the use of education vouchers,[4] for greater freedom of entry and exit in the education sector, and for a much greater crossover between the state and independent sectors. The government's 'free schools' initiative – which allows parents, independent schools and other non-profit groups to set up new, publicly funded schools – is an interesting initiative. It may encourage different educational philosophies and improved teaching methods, and promises to allow the new institutions to negotiate different types of teacher contracts. Some may feel, however, that it is too timid in excluding the profit motive: Sahlgren (2010) argues that the introduction of for-profit schools into the Swedish state education system has improved performance. In particular he claims that for-profit schools produce better outcomes for pupils than either standard state schools or non-profit independent publicly funded schools.[5]

An even more fundamental reform would be to move back towards a system where all parents (except the very poor) made a financial contribution to schooling, as they did in the nineteenth century. If taxes were reduced by an equivalent amount, the vast majority of parents would be no worse off over a lifetime. This need not involve parents funding the entire cost of the school system. Capital costs could be paid by the state, or each school could be given a nominal endowment, with 'top-up' fees being charged, rather like those in the university sector.

Parents expect to pay for pre-school childcare (but see next section) and extra piano lessons, and students increasingly expect to pay for higher education, but nobody advocates payment for mainstream

---

4   See Forster (2008) for some recent evidence from the USA on the benefits of voucher systems and school choice. Forster also makes the important point that such benefits are contingent on schools being able to compete on matters such as curriculum and selection. A degree of deregulation is needed as well as changes to the funding mechanism.

5   It also seems likely that a significant introduction of the profit motive into schools could in the medium term lead to capital investment being provided by the private sector rather than the public purse.

schooling. Yet without some form of price mechanism, parents face rationing devices which encourage them to move house unnecessarily or falsely profess a religious faith, or else take part in absurd lotteries such as those pioneered by Brighton and Hove Council.[6]

If we charged parents around one quarter of the average cost of education (allowing for exemptions for the poorest and possibly for multiple children) this should reduce public spending by around £8.5 billion by 2015 and cost parents about £1,000 per annum (though more for older children). This would have to be implemented alongside reforms to ensure that all funding was directed to schools through children. Introducing charging, however, would not improve the quality of education unless there was free entry into the schooling system from alternative providers who could receive the same funding as state schools. The cost to parents from this limited charging would be less than is often spent on pre-school nursery care and could probably be more than recouped by the extra opportunities to work that exist for most parents once children start school. Schools could, of course, be allowed to operate more efficiently and thus lower the charge made to parents, or they could spend the money on providing out-of-school activities, clubs, etc.

In addition to this we could rescind the pupil premium and also abandon the proposed increase in compulsory education. As Table 11 shows, we already subject British children to one of the longest periods of compulsory schooling in Europe.

Despite our long period of compulsory education, the coalition government seems to be pressing ahead with Labour's plan to increase the upper age limit of compulsory education or training to seventeen in 2013 and eighteen in 2015 even though both the Conservatives and the Liberal Democrats opposed this move in the last parliament.

---

6   Imagine a world where the government provided cars 'free' but rationed the better ones by means of a lottery. You might still be allowed to buy a car outside the scheme, but you would have to pay the tax cost of a car anyway. Nobody would seriously advocate this (I hope). But in the far more important area of children's education, this is exactly what we do.

Table 11 **Compulsory education in Europe 2009/10, selected countries**

Country	Start age for compulsory education	Leaving age for compulsory education	Duration of full-time compulsory education
Belgium	6	15	9
Denmark	6	16	10
Finland	7	16	9
France	6	16	10
Germany*	6	15/16	9/10
Italy	6	16	10
Netherlands	5	18	13
Spain	6	16	10
UK (except Northern Ireland)	5	16	11

*Differs between Länder

The public expenditure cost of the move was estimated by the Labour administration in 2007 to be a recurring £793 million in prices of that year. This was offset against a highly speculative benefit of £1.4 billion resulting from wage gains and greater employability for young people who stayed on in education or training and achieved higher qualifications. In reality the costs to the government (and also those to business) are likely to have been significantly underestimated and the benefits exaggerated (Wolf, 2007). A high proportion of those currently not in education or training in the sixteen-to-eighteen age group are going to be very difficult to motivate to acquire further (largely so-called 'vocational') qualifications as they have typically had a poor experience in compulsory schooling. They are going to end up mainly in further education colleges[7] as employers will be even more reluctant to employ young people under eighteen as the time they will be required to spend in education/training will make them expensive to employ relative to slightly older young people – while schools will continue to prefer higher-scoring students taking academic qualifications as these boost their league-table standing.

---

7   In a fuller discussion it would be useful to reflect on the way in which post-sixteen education is split between school sixth forms and FE.

Abandoning this commitment would save around £1 billion a year in current money, and would probably lead to slightly lower youth unemployment (thus lowering expenditure on benefits and increasing tax take) without any obvious victims, since anybody who genuinely wants to stay in education till eighteen can still do so.

We might go even farther in the longer term and consider whether we should start compulsory full-time schooling later, say at age six, like most other comparable countries. While this would be difficult to organise in the short run, a reshaping of the school year and an emphasis on the quality, rather than the quantity, of school years would be welcome.

Early schooling and childcare

But rather than raising the age of entry into state schooling, the last government began steps effectively to lower it. A range of initiatives was started which have amounted to a stealthy nationalisation of the pre-school years.

One element has been the guarantee of a limited number of hours of 'free early education' for three- and four-year-olds: this has now been extended for some groups to two-year-olds. It is difficult to cost this commitment as there are elements of cross-subsidy involved, but at a conservative estimate the cost must be of the order of £1.5–2 billion per year.

As with many areas of spending in education, it is difficult to see what exactly the rationale is for non-compulsory provision of this kind. Reports – for example, Hopkin et al. (2010) – suggest that the gains in terms of enhanced performance later in pupils' school careers are small. If the purpose of early-years education is to improve the *relative* performance of children from poorer backgrounds it probably achieves little, as the take-up among middle-class families is at least as high as that from poorer families.

In addition New Labour introduced the childcare element of working tax credits.[8] A system of childcare vouchers was also introduced. These are made available through employers, who either administer them directly or through an agent. Under the scheme employees can pay for up to 55 per cent of childcare costs and employers make some savings on national insurance contributions. The scheme has been costing the taxpayer around £250 million a year. Again, the purpose is not entirely clear. It is not a significantly redistributive measure. The take-up rate among all groups is rather similar, and 87 per cent of all childcare voucher users do not receive tax credits, suggesting that they are not among the poorest. Up to 17 per cent of the benefits went to higher-rate income tax payers in 2007/08, though the scheme is being reformed to stop this (Konings, 2010). A further element in the expansion of government into the pre-school years is a comprehensive system of regulation of childcare providers, which has brought them into an unprecedented state-determined curriculum for under-fives. This scheme has thirteen assessment scales, each of which has nine points against which children's development must be measured. Providers of childcare are subject to Ofsted inspection in the same way as schools for older children.

The requirement to implement this 'Early Years Foundation Stage', together with a set of demanding regulations about premises, food safety and so forth, has meant that many informal providers of childcare have simply left the market. The number of registered childminders fell from nearly 100,000 when Labour came into power in 1997 to 57,000 in 2010. This in turn has led more and more people to use formal childcare and to increased public expenditure either on state nursery and pre-school education or on subsidies to the private commercial sector.

The centrepiece of Labour's strategy, however, was Sure Start. This

---

8   As this is a welfare benefit, it is not discussed farther here except to point out that it has been costing well over £5 billion a year and was not particularly well targeted: thus it is now being trimmed back so that it will eventually be available only to those families with an annual income of less than £23,000. While much of the political rhetoric focused on the way in which child tax credits would encourage many parents back into work, both theoretical reasoning and empirical evidence suggests that the effect would be small and possibly even negative (Chzhen and Middleton, 2007).

scheme, which began in 1999, was inspired by the American Head Start scheme, which concentrated a range of services and support on children in disadvantaged areas. There is evidence from Head Start that early intervention of this kind can lead to improved performance at school.

This aim was copied in the Sure Start scheme, but over the last decade it changed its focus considerably as Labour's Strategy for Childcare evolved. By the end of Labour's period in power resources were spread nationwide in 3,500 Children's Centres, which provided drop-in centres, childcare and early education for the community as a whole. The focus on disadvantaged children was lost, with many middle-class parents taking advantage of Sure Start facilities, and evidence suggests that, so far at least, few inroads have been made into the disadvantage suffered by children from poor backgrounds.

Although some positive results have been reported in Wales, the evidence for England is more ambiguous. And the National Audit Office (2006, 2009) has suggested that the scheme has been relatively poor value for money. There is also some evidence that private sector childcare and nursery provision have been 'crowded out' by public expenditure.[9]

The doubts about the effectiveness of Sure Start are such that it is difficult to see that ending this scheme would produce any significant loss to the wider community in the medium term. It would save over £1 billion a year. Scrapping childcare vouchers completely would save another £200 million or so. More controversially, cutting back on Labour's plans to expand further the provision of nursery places within primary and infants' schools could also make further unspecified savings.

The coalition government seems to be moving in the opposite direction, however, towards further state involvement in childcare. It has retained Sure Start, albeit claiming that it will reorient it towards the disadvantaged. It has extended the entitlement to 'free' nursery

---

9   This is an echo of the nineteenth-century experience, touched on earlier, where state regulation and subsidies drove out private educational providers.

provision for all three-to-four-year-olds. Instead, policymakers should look for ways in which to encourage more private sector provision, by relaxing the excessively expanded regulatory framework of childcare.

Training

A succession of government reports going back over a hundred years – the most recent being the Leitch Report – has bemoaned the low skill level of the British workforce and argued for government regulation and public spending.

The pace has accelerated since the 1980s, and a dizzying parade of soon-abandoned organisational structures, vocational qualifications, training schemes and funding mechanisms has rarely produced anything resembling success. Much of the theoretical argument for the existence of market failure in this area depends on the belief that employers will not provide an economically optimal level of investment in training because they cannot capture the return on this investment. Workers are mobile and can take their newly acquired skills to other non-training employers who would get a 'free ride'.

The argument is unconvincing. For one thing, as Gary Becker (1964) pointed out nearly half a century ago, training (a special form of education) can take two forms – specific and general. Specific training – induction into a particular organisation's technology, practices and procedures, for example – is non-transferable and thus avoids the free-rider problem because the worker gains no advantage from taking this knowledge and skill to another employer. It will make financial sense for employers to provide it. General training, on the other hand, inculcates skills which are valuable to other employers and, because of the fear of poaching, is potentially under-provided.

In a free market, however, various devices can arise enabling employers profitably to provide such training. One is to define contractual rights in such a way that the training employer can prevent employees leaving without paying compensation themselves or having it paid by a new employer. Another is for the trainees or their families to pay up front for training. An alternative is for trainees to pay for training by working for very little until they are fully qualified, when their pay rises to reflect the fact that their skills are now valuable in the outside market.

Nowadays various legal judgements have made restrictions on employee mobility and enforced compensation difficult to rely on. The introduction of the national minimum wage has restricted the possibility of taking little or no pay during training. In any case, some forms of general training – becoming a doctor or an airline pilot, for example – are too expensive for trainees to fund without borrowing. And employees often lack the collateral to borrow large sums of money. Alison Wolf among others has recently argued (Wolf, 2009) that trainees should be treated like university students and have access to guaranteed loans for training. The coalition appears to have accepted this argument although details are not yet forthcoming.

Providing training out of public funds often leads to a deadweight loss – training being paid for which would have been financed privately. This was certainly true of Gordon Brown's 'Train to Gain' programme – to which £1.37 billion was allocated in Labour's March 2010 budget. The scheme offered employers taxpayer-funded training and accreditation in the workplace. The idea was to deliver government-approved qualifications in partnership with employers. Alison Wolf, however, a fierce critic of the scheme, has pointed out (ibid.; Wolf, 2011) that, in order to maximise the numbers of individuals obtaining positive results, resources have been concentrated on low-level qualifications. She claims many of the qualifications are unpopular and produce low or zero productivity and wage gains.

Train to Gain has been scrapped by the coalition. Instead, it seems to be putting its faith in expanding the numbers of apprentices by 75,000 a year to 200,000 by 2014/15 at an extra cost of £250 million. This ambition is endorsed by Professor Wolf in her recent report, although she points out the need to reform the funding of apprenticeships. At the moment some apprentices seem to be supported by government subsidies even where other young people on identical company programmes are not – suggesting that 'apprenticeship' is just a convenient label to attract state funding,[10] another example of deadweight loss. She argues that funding should be available only to compensate employers for the time apprentices spend 'off the job' in college or in bespoke apprentice training (Wolf, 2011: 123). Such off-the-job training is characteristic of apprenticeships in other European countries.

In light of this, we might wonder whether the extra £250 million in funding is really necessary, and whether we could not boost apprenticeship numbers by more effective use of existing funding and by facilitating the downward adjustment of wages for apprentices: Alison Wolf claims that UK apprentice pay is 'probably the highest in Europe' (ibid.: 122). Indeed, a specific minimum wage for apprentices has been brought in by the current government.

Higher education

Educational policy at all levels is excessively preoccupied by the pursuit of equality, which makes it very difficult to evaluate policy in economic terms. In higher education (HE) it is treated as axiomatic that more and more young people should be participating. Year after year we have achieved this (see Urwin et al., 2010) – but inevitably expansion has been uneven among different social groups, as it is in every country in the world. A desire to put this right has immensely complicated questions of funding, admissions standards, curriculum and pedagogy.

Government subsidy of higher education, and its provision by the state or para-state bodies, is common throughout the world. Although estimates differ, higher education probably cost the UK taxpayer over

---

10 Rather than a distinct economic status characterised by very low initial productivity and thus justifying only very low or even negative pay (the historical position where parents or others had to pay employers to take apprentices on). See Shackleton et al. (1995).

£15 billion per year in 2010/11.[11] In one sense UK universities and colleges are a success story. We attract the largest number of overseas students after the USA, British universities feature prominently in international league tables, and numbers of research publications and citations outstrip those of most of our competitors, but all is not as rosy as it seems.

University education in the UK still operates on a medieval calendar, with long breaks for Christian religious festivals and the need to get the harvest in: as a consequence students see staff for only around half the year, and buildings lie substantially idle for the rest of the time. An undergraduate degree takes three or four years to complete, and its quality is not directly tested or monitored. A disturbingly high proportion of graduates – saddled with substantial debt – either cannot get work or are underemployed in jobs which 30 years ago could have been done by people with A-levels.

Heavily unionised staff largely dictate their own work patterns, including considerable amounts of time on esoteric research.[12] Contact with students is minimised in the name of 'independent learning', while the teaching that takes place is often poor and its method of delivery has not changed to reflect a world where students are continually online in their personal lives.

Universities have not competed for domestic students over price or over the format (or, some would say, over the quality) of their delivery. Instead they try to manipulate the inadequate league tables organised by the quality press. If you have a reasonable grasp of the mechanics

---

11   Something of a guesstimate, as UK total government spending on higher education is opaque. Higher Education Funding Council for England (HEFCE) funding, at £7.4 billion in 2010/11, does not include Welsh, Scottish or Northern Ireland spending, nor the Research Councils (around £3 billion going to universities), nor the subsidy to the Student Loans system through inflation-only interest payments – and these are only the most obvious ways in which the state funds our HE system. Universities UK estimated the total public support at £14.3 billion in 2007/08.

12   A big issue on campus recently has been outrage against the view that research might partly be judged in the forthcoming Research Excellence Framework on its impact on the outside world, away from the cosy clubbiness of peer review.

involved, it is possible to engineer higher positions. Or simply lucky features of your location and student intake may bias the indicators used. Thus in the recent *Guardian* league tables the University of Chichester appears to be doing better than the University of Manchester, while University College Falmouth has a more impressive performance than the universities of Reading or Essex.

Across the sector an unhealthy dependence has grown up on cross-subsidy from high overseas student fees. Without these students, many more universities would be in serious financial straits.[13] Yet there are issues about the quality of students admitted, and about the quality of experience which they are offered. Many academic staff continue to regard the notion of students as consumers, with the rights which this notion entails, as heresy. Yet without them, the still fairly comfortable lives of academics could not be sustained.

The case for subsidising higher education rests on the claim that both social and private returns on higher education are substantial. But the basis for this claim, endlessly repeated by ministers, trade unions, vice-chancellors and some economists who ought to know better, is not unassailable. Many studies purporting to show high rates of return do not hold ability constant when comparing graduates and non-graduates. They fail to account for the phenomenon of 'credentialism', whereby qualifications are used as a screening device rather than a measure of enhanced productivity. They are inevitably backward-looking, based on the experience of previous cohorts of students, and thus a poor guide to future labour markets, which may face a glut of graduates. And they inevitably focus on returns to the average graduate, while many weaker students may face very low or even negative returns to their university education – and of course there is a considerable drop-out rate at many universities.

---

13 There are no restrictions on fees charged to overseas (in this context, non-EU) students, whereas domestic fees have been subject to a cap. Recent immigration rule changes, which may well deter significant numbers of overseas students, have increased the risks associated with this funding stream.

Higher education is a mixed economy everywhere, but the proportion of funding provided by the state varies considerably with little apparent effect on participation rates for countries of similar levels of average national income. The state pays for about 65 per cent of tertiary education costs in the UK; over 95 per cent in Finland; 85 per cent in Germany; and 84 per cent in France. On the other hand, it accounts for only 48 per cent in Australia; 53 per cent in Canada; 34 per cent in the USA; and 32 per cent in Japan.[14]

Reducing the share of HE funding provided by the state has long been recognised as an important priority, both for its effects on public finances and in giving universities and colleges greater autonomy. The Blair government made important steps forward with the introduction of a £1,000-per-year fee in 1998, followed in 2006 by 'top-up' fees starting at £3,000 and raised annually in line with inflation.[15] The higher fees were to be repaid on an income-contingent basis from interest-free (in real terms) student loans.[16] The last government continued to restrict the amount that universities could charge home and EU students, and therefore had to continue funding well over half the costs of higher education. This arrangement was only ever a temporary compromise, and the cost to the state of direct funding and the subsidy element of student loans rose sharply as the numbers entering higher education increased.

The Browne Report, commissioned under the last government but reporting in October 2010, argued for a lifting of the fee cap, cutting of direct government funding and charging a positive rate of interest[17]

14   OECD (2009) – 2006 is the most recent year for which figures are available.
15   Scotland, however, did not charge the top-up element of the fees.
16   If there is believed to be a 'market failure' requiring state intervention in higher education, it primarily lies in the capital market. It can be difficult and costly for young people without collateral to pay up front for the substantial cost of studying for a degree. This is the justification for the government ensuring that all qualified young people have access to student loans. This does not, however, imply that these loans should be interest free. Indeed, interest-free loans boost demand artificially, with adverse consequences for individuals and higher education institutions.
17   Browne argued for an interest rate of 2.2 per cent above the rate of inflation, but this is

on student loans. These loans would be repaid, starting at a higher threshold income level (£21,000 compared with £15,000 at present), over a longer period. As higher fees would initially cause a substantial increase in public spending to cover the consequentially higher student loans, Browne recommended that institutions should pay a levy to the government on any fees set above £6,000 per year, the levy to rise as fees rose.

The coalition has got itself into a muddle over its response to Browne. While accepting the principle of higher fees, the government baulked at the idea of having no upper limit. It feared that 'elite' universities, Oxbridge and the Russell Group of research-intensive institutions, would raise fees so high that talented students from less-advantaged backgrounds would be deterred from applying. Accordingly it set an upper limit of £9,000. Unfortunately this seems to have had a perverse effect, although one that might have been predicted.[18] A flood of universities have announced that they will be charging the maximum, as they fear that to charge less than this would be interpreted as a signal of poor quality by potential students. This has also thrown the government's financial calculations out: it had assumed that fees would be set at an average of £7,500, but if fees cluster higher than this it will raise the costs of providing loans in the short run, and increase the likelihood of graduates never repaying. It is already being speculated that half of all loans will have to be written off in part or in whole.

This tendency is exacerbated because universities will suffer no direct penalties if they recruit students who fail to complete or have poor prospects on graduation.[19] Neil Shephard (2010) has made an

---

arguably below the real cost of finance. The coalition has settled on an interest rate of inflation plus 3 per cent. Very considerable government subsidy is implied even at this rate of interest because of the large number of recipients of loans who will never fully repay.

18 The same thing happened when top-up fees were introduced: the £3,000 was supposed to be an upper limit, not a standard charge.

19 Under the old HEFCE funding system, poor retention or poor graduate prospects in principle attracted penalties, although these were usually not onerous. The availability of loans for students they took on was not affected. When HEFCE funding disappears for most degree programmes it is not clear what constraints institutions will face.

interesting proposal which would force universities to share the financial risks currently being borne by students and (through the Student Loans Company) the taxpayer. The argument is that this would make universities much more assiduous in trying to ensure that their graduates were 'employer-ready'.[20]

One promising avenue to control government spending is to encourage new entry from private providers who have a lower cost base because of technological innovation, cheaper estate and employment policies unconstrained by union agreements. Companies such as BPP, recently given degree-awarding powers, offer a high-quality student experience more cheaply than traditional HE institutions. Competition from these providers is likely to be significant for non-traditional students who are not looking for a quasi-Oxbridge research environment but expect good teaching and support. Another possible way of encouraging competition would be to allow UK students to access student loans to study abroad, something which some other countries do.

A more immediate and much less liberal approach to controlling the drift towards high fees is seen in the new powers which have been given to OFFA, the Office for Fair Access.

When top-up fees were introduced in English and Welsh higher education, MPs' concern for widening participation led to the introduction of a bursary obligation on HE providers. Each university or college charging higher fees had to sign an 'access agreement' with OFFA, setting out its plans to use part (usually 20–25 per cent) of the extra fee income to encourage participation in HE from students from low-income backgrounds.

In fact MPs' fears were unfounded: over the last five years participation has continued to rise, but access agreements seem to have had little effect. Institutions spent around £350 million a year, much of which was spent on bursaries or scholarships. Last year a report by OFFA showed these to be ineffective, as few potential students were influenced by their

---

20 If, however, it led institutions to steer clear of weaker applicants this might lead them into conflict with OFFA (see below).

availability or even knew of their existence before applying (Office for Fair Access, 2010).

Now OFFA has been given a new remit and more powers. It has recently published 35 closely written pages of guidance to HE providers. If they want to charge more than £6,000 – as they all do, for it is less than most institutions currently get per student from HEFCE funding and existing fees – they will now have to submit much more detailed annual access plans, complete with targets, milestones and monitoring requirements.

Bursaries are now downplayed, although some universities are to be required to produce matched funding for the new National Scholarship programme (on which the government is going to spend £150 million per year), about which little is yet known and which could again largely be a waste of money. The focus of institutions' plans is to shift to 'outreach', which is not explained and is left up to universities to define.[21]

These plans will probably commit universities to spending around £700 million next year: it depends on what fees are charged. If OFFA thinks a university is not spending enough, it can refuse to agree to the plan, in which case (in theory at least) the university will not be able to charge more than £6,000 per student.

While saying it has no powers to determine universities' admissions criteria, OFFA has also made it obvious that it wants to see 'contextual information' being used to influence who is admitted. This means that admissions offers to potential students should be based on relative rather than absolute criteria: lower grades for those coming from schools with poorer average results.

This new dispensation is far more intrusive than before. Universities

---

21   It is likely to embrace similar ideas to the 'Aim Higher' scheme, funded until last year by HEFCE to the tune of £70 million a year – involving partnerships between universities, schools and colleges. Such approaches have not been particularly effective. They work best in areas where an HE provider has a clearly defined recruitment area: elite universities which recruit nationally and internationally have no such obvious partners.

and colleges are going to be spending very large amounts of money on nebulous objectives, a social engineering project which experience suggests is unlikely to succeed.

Elite universities already want to attract as broad a social mix as possible, but without really significant improvements in state schools they face an uphill struggle. The danger with the strengthened OFFA is that it will chip away at the reputation and the will of our leading universities until academic standards are seriously eroded in order to accommodate students whose academic abilities and commitment are inadequate.

It seems perverse to allow higher education institutions the freedom to raise fees and then dictate how a sizeable chunk of the extra funding is to be used. If the OFFA obligation and the National Scholarship programme were scrapped, US experience suggests that universities would still seek to widen their intake and offer appropriate scholarships. Without government interference they might be better placed to attract private donations – from individuals and businesses – to support such schemes. Such donations are currently 'crowded out' by government funding.

Allowing universities the freedom to spend their extra incomes as they see fit would justify further cuts in the direct government funding. Additional government funding will be provided mainly for the STEM subjects (broadly, Science, Technology, Engineering and Maths). Successive governments have taken the view that not enough students are pursuing these subjects, which are thought to be particularly important for economic growth. This is disputed by most economists who have looked at this issue. Sir Howard Davies, ex-director of the London School of Economics, was right to say, in July 2010, that the focus on STEM is 'economically irrational'.

Already around one in three students follows a STEM-related degree. Entry standards on many courses classified as STEM are low, however, and graduates from most of these subjects suffer a significantly higher level of unemployment than the average for other graduates. Moreover, among those in work, more than a third are in non-STEM occupations such as accountancy or finance.[22]

It is difficult to see that there would be serious consequences to the economy from a sizeable cut in STEM funding. If, say, £1 billion a year was cut from the HEFCE budget in this area, it would still leave substantial support for STEM. It would not lead to an exactly equivalent cut in public spending as tuition fees might rise and, to the extent that students were still willing to sign up, there would be higher student loan subsidy costs to cover.

Some reduction in HEFCE's direct research funding ('QR') of universities, currently costing about £1.5 billion a year and largely protected from cuts, could also make sense – in particular the absurdly elaborate (and expensive) Research Excellence Framework planned for 2014 could be scrapped.[23] More generally, we could fund research only through the Research Councils and reduce HEFCE research funding costs by around £1 billion. This would leave some of HEFCE's remaining research budget as well as any administration budget to be channelled through the research councils. The universities themselves would also save administrative costs through the abolition of the REF.

Conclusions

An environment where public spending cuts are being widely discussed

---

22 Accountancy, incidentally, has had the lowest level of core HEFCE funding in the past, and has suffered restrictions on numbers which have led to a considerable overspill into the private sector for undergraduate degrees or professional training.

23 Its predecessor, the Research Assessment Exercise, was a useful idea when first instituted in 1986 as it forced universities to be explicit in what they were doing with money notionally allocated to them to support non-specific research projects. We have now had six rounds of this exercise and diminishing returns have set in. The bulk of funding goes to a limited range of institutions and will do so whatever rules are applied, but this does not prevent huge amounts of time and resource being devoted by institutions in the hope of securing a slightly larger share of the pot. The rewards are largely in the eyes of researchers' peers, as much research continues to have little public benefit and is totally ignored (if even known of) by most undergraduate applicants to degree programmes.

is not an occasion for gloom, but an opportunity to rethink structures and assumptions which have gone unchallenged for decades. This chapter has suggested ways in which state involvement in education and related areas might usefully be rethought, but it has merely scratched the surface.

Even so, there are significant savings which the government could make without major hardship to the public – in many cases because they relate to only recently established, or planned future, activities. To summarise: in *schools*, scrapping the pupil premium would save £625 million this year, rising to £2.5 billion a year in 2014/15, while abandoning the raising of the age of compulsory education/training could save around £1 billion a year in 2014/15; a charge for education could save £8.5 billion while potentially increasing the quality of education significantly; in *childcare and pre-schooling*, ending most of Sure Start and scrapping childcare vouchers could save £1.2 billion a year from now on; in *training* extra savings of £250 million a year could be made by 2014/15 by cutting back on planned increases in funding for apprenticeships; while in *higher education* STEM funding could be cut back by £1 billion and QR funding for research by £1 billion. This would reduce the education budget by around £15.5 billion.

In the longer term, the suggestions here indicate a wider role for the private sector, which, while we expect it to provide our food, clothing, most of our housing, heating, energy, travel, communication and most of the ways in which we enjoy ourselves, we remain curiously reluctant to trust in the classroom, the seminar or the nursery.

References

Becker, G. S. (1964), *Human Capital: A Theoretical and Empirical Analysis*, New York: Columbia University Press.

Chzhen, Y. and S. Middleton (2007), *The Impact of Tax Credits on Mothers' Employment*, York: Joseph Rowntree Foundation.

Forster, G. (2008), 'Vouchers and school choice: the evidence', *Economic Affairs*, 28(2): 42–7.

Hopkin, R., L. Stokes and D. Wilkinson (2010), 'Quality, outcomes and costs in early years education', National Institute of Economic and Social Research Working Paper, June.

Konings, J. (2010), *Childcare Vouchers: Who Benefits?*, London: Social Market Foundation.

National Audit Office (2006), *Sure Start Children's Centres. Report by the Comptroller and Auditor General NAO*, London: Stationery Office.

National Audit Office (2009), *Sure Start Children's Centres Memorandum for the Children, Schools and Families Committee*, December.

OECD (2009), *Education at a Glance*, Paris: Organisation for Economic Co-operation and Development.

Office for Fair Access (2010), *Have Bursaries Influenced Choices between Universities?*, Bristol: OFFA.

Sahlgren, G. S. (2010), *Schooling for Money: Swedish Education Reform and the Role of the Profit Motive*, IEA Discussion Paper no. 33, London: Institute of Economic Affairs.

Shackleton, J. R. (1992), *Training Too Much? A sceptical look at the economics of skill provision*, Hobart Paper 118, London: Institute of Economic Affairs.

Shackleton, J. R. with L. Clarke, T. Lange and S. Walsh (1995), *Training for Employment in Western Europe and the United States*, Aldershot: Edward Elgar.

Shephard, N. (2010), 'Deferred fees for universities', *Economic Affairs*, 30(2): 40–44.

Urwin, P., M. Gould and L. Page (2010), 'Are there changes in the characteristics of UK Higher Education around the time of the 2006 reforms? Analysis of Higher Education Statistics Agency data, 2002/3 to 2007/8', Department for Business, Innovation and Skills Research Paper.

West, E. G. (1965), *Education and the State*, London: Institute of Economic Affairs.

Wolf, A. (2002), *Does Education Matter? Myths about Education and Economic Growth*, London: Penguin.

Wolf, A. (2007), *Diminished Returns: How Raising the Leaving Age to 18 Will Harm Young People and the Economy*, London: Policy Exchange.

Wolf, A. (2009), *An Adult Approach to Further Education*, London: Institute of Economic Affairs.

Wolf, A. (2011), *Review of Vocational Education: The Wolf Report*, London: TSO.

6 COMPREHENSIVE PENSION REFORM
Philip Booth and Corin Taylor

The purpose of this chapter is to examine non-means-tested government payments to older people: means-tested benefits are examined in the chapter by Kristian Niemietz. This chapter includes an examination of the pension system but also other non-means-tested benefits provided to older people. There has been an enormous growth in government financial provision in old age in the last thirteen years. Furthermore, increases above inflation in the basic state pension are planned in the near future. It is also the case that pensioners have received particularly favourable treatment in the tax system. They have a higher personal allowance than younger people and even have a marriage allowance.

This chapter does not merely propose cutting back on government transfer payments to the elderly; it also proposes making the remaining transfers more economically coherent. We address the problems that pensioners receive income from approximately eight different sources (assuming only one private pension) and face about twelve different marginal tax and benefit withdrawal rates over the income spectrum (see Booth and Cooper, 2005). We also propose significant cuts in public sector pension provision and long-term reforms of the state pension and tax system for older people.

It is notable that the elderly have been identified for special treatment by the government in the 2010 Comprehensive Spending Review. They have been more or less exempt from spending cuts, despite the creation of many anomalous benefits for pensioners in recent years. Furthermore, the government proposes to increase pensions in line with general wage increases and also guarantee that increases in pensions will not be below 2.5 per cent or the rate of inflation. At a time of apparent public spending stringency, this shows a remarkable degree of laxity, probably driven by the ageing of the electorate. The problems of reducing benefits to older people when electorates are ageing are discussed in the chapter by Booth in Booth et al. (eds) (2008). In this monograph, of course, we ignore the politically possible and propose a comprehensive programme of reform which, taken as a whole, will lead to dramatic reductions in taxation and improvements in economic welfare.

Abolition of non-cash benefits to pensioners

We begin by proposing the abolition of three non-cash benefits that are provided to pensioners. This is the extent of the immediate direct reduction in income to older people from the state that we propose, though there will be other indirect changes to pensioners' income levels. These proposals for direct reductions in pensioners' income have been chosen because the relevant benefits give rise to economic distortions, involve significant costs of administration (which have not been included in the estimated savings) and/or involve significant time costs by individual claimants.

Abolition of free bus travel

It is extremely difficult to produce a rationale for providing free bus travel for pensioners.[1] As a means of transferring income to older people, it suffers from the following problems:

- It benefits only those pensioners who are fit enough to travel unaided.
- It benefits only those pensioners who live near reliable bus services.
- It benefits mainly those pensioners who choose to travel by bus rather than by car or cycle.

---

1   In fact, at the moment, the free travel is for over-sixties. The age will change with state pension age equalisation.

- It distorts economic decisions: pensioners who, facing all the costs and benefits of their decisions, would choose to travel by taxi, car, foot, by cycle or not to travel will be artificially encouraged to travel by bus as a result of the existence of free bus travel.
- It changes the dynamics of the bus market as it makes the providers of these subsidies to the elderly (local authorities, financed by the government) the customers of the bus companies rather than travellers themselves. As elderly people are a significant part of the market, this is not unimportant.
- It prevents bus companies from finding their own packages of price discrimination to help fill buses at less busy times.
- It reduces the incentives for dynamic innovation in taxibus and minibus services that can potentially compete with buses but provide a more personalised service.
- The taxes used to finance the benefit themselves cause economic distortions.

It is suggested by some economists that providing free bus travel at off-peak times, with the costs being reimbursed to bus companies in the form of a subsidy, helps the industry cover average costs at a time of day when marginal costs are zero. As such, it is further argued that subsidisation in this way leads to a more efficient economic outcome. This ignores not just the arguments listed above but also the fact that bus companies themselves produce a range of innovative products that are designed to ensure that average costs are covered at times when marginal costs are low. Coach, rail and airline companies also handle this problem effectively.

It is difficult to obtain a precise estimate for the saving from the abolition of free bus travel because of the changing rules for the benefit. Probably, however, its abolition would save approximately £1.3 billion per annum by 2015/16.

Abolition of free TV licences[2]

In many senses the rationale for not providing free television licences is the same as the rationale for not providing free bus passes. Though it does distort how people spend their income to some extent, the demand for a television licence is, however, likely to be highly price inelastic. As such, the economic distortions are not considerable. This may change with the increase in demand for and supply of Internet, subscription and pay-per-view television.

Free television licences do, however, discriminate against those who do not wish to have their own television because they are poorly sighted or because they do not wish to watch television – they are receiving a benefit in kind which they do not value. The benefit also, rather bizarrely, is of value to young families who have a relative aged over 75 living with them.

There are also public choice arguments against providing free television licences. The television licence was generally regarded as a 'user charge' until recently. It was a rather strangely constructed user charge because owners of televisions had to pay for a licence even if they did not watch the channels the fee was designed to finance. The move towards free television licences, however, gives the licence fee, to an even greater extent, the features of a tax. The government requires a levy in the form of a television licence fee from households it deems *should* pay, as well as making a contribution to the BBC itself on behalf of other householders who benefit from free licences. This strengthens the direct links between the government and the BBC.

The abolition of free television licences would save approximately £725 million per year by 2015/16.

Abolition of winter fuel allowance

The winter fuel allowance is marketed by the government as a contribution towards the cost of fuel. In fact, it is a tax-free cash payment made to

---

2   We ignore, here, whether it is desirable to have what is effectively a state broadcasting service financed by a tax on televisions.

all households in which there is an individual aged over 60.[3] It is generally paid at the rate of £200. The rate is increased to £300 if the household contains somebody aged 80 or over.

It is very difficult to make any coherent argument in favour of this allowance. It is not related to fuel costs or how cold a particular winter happens to be (there is a separate payment made when weather is exceptionally cold): 'winter fuel allowance' is a misnomer. The benefit is also an anomaly because the payment falls outside the standard tax and benefits system. The payment has to be claimed (with a special form) and is administered separately. There is simply no reason for this additional source of income to be provided to pensioners.

The abolition of the so-called winter fuel allowance would save £2.1 billion per annum by 2015/16.

It is noteworthy that none of these benefits was cut in the coalition's recent spending review. Indeed, other forms of state finance for goods and services that have a stronger economic rationale (such as government provision for students[4]) were cut while benefits to pensioners remained untouched – indeed, provision for pensioners was actually expanded (see below). As has been noted, there is strong electoral pressure to retain benefits for the elderly.

Abolition of married couples' allowance for old people

It is not the intention of this chapter, in general, to propose tax increases. All the measures proposed will lead to significant government spending reductions and thus facilitate tax reductions. But it is desired to make the tax system – as well as the provision of benefits – significantly more economically efficient. Lower taxes should also lead to simpler taxes, but achieving this involves the removal of certain tax exemptions.

---

3   This will rise in line with female state pension age.

4   That is not to say that the authors support government finance for students but there is arguably a stronger rationale for such finance than there is, for example, for free television licences to households with a member aged 75 or over.

It is very difficult to justify the existence of a married couples' tax allowance for older people. For younger people, the proposal for a transferable tax allowance has been justified by the bias in the benefits system against couples with children. The married couples' allowance is not, however, a transferable allowance to facilitate the using of unused tax allowances on a household basis, and few pensioner couples have dependent children.

The rules for the married couples' allowance are bizarre in the extreme and have evolved from a series of decisions to limit the allowance and then to abolish it for younger people from April 2000. Older people were exempt from that latter decision for purely political reasons.

The rules for receiving the allowance are as follows:

- One person in a couple must be 75 or over.
- The amount of the allowance is £7,295.
- The rate at which the allowance can be claimed is 10 per cent; it therefore reduces the marginal rate of tax for one person within a married couple by 10 per cent over that band of income.
- If income is above £24,000 then the allowance is withdrawn at the rate of £1 for every £2 of income after the additional age-related personal allowance has been withdrawn until a minimum married couples' allowance of £2,800 is left.

Confused? It is not surprising. The net result of withdrawal is that pensioners have a marginal tax rate of 5 per cent in addition to the standard rate of income tax on a band of income of about £8,000 starting at about £29,000. This is in addition to a marginal tax rate of 10 per cent above the standard rate of income tax on a band of income of about £5,200 over approximately £24,000 because of the withdrawal of the age-related personal allowance (see below). The tax system should not be this complex and this tax relief has no economic rationale.

Abolition of the age allowance

In addition to the married couples' allowance, pensioners receive an age-related personal allowance. This reduces the marginal rate of tax to zero on a tranche of income of £2,615 above the standard personal allowance of £7,475 (in 2011/12). The age-related allowance is then withdrawn when income reaches £24,000 at a rate of £1 for every additional £2 of income. At the current basic rate of income tax this raises the marginal tax rate to 30 per cent on a tranche of income of approximately £5,200 above £24,000. There is a small additional allowance for those over 75. Table 12 shows the marginal tax rates at specimen income points for an individual under age 65, an individual over age 75 and somebody who is married over age 75.

Table 12 **Pensioners' marginal tax rates**

Income level	Individual under age 65	Individual over age 75	Married person over age 75
£5,000	0%	0%	0%
£7,500	20%	0%	0%
£10,000	20%	20%	10%
£17,500	20%	20%	20%
£25,000	20%	30%	30%
£30,000	20%	20%	25%
£39,000	20%	20%	20%
£50,000	40%	40%	40%

It is very difficult to see a rationale for the age allowance and for the varying marginal tax rates to which this system leads. It increases incomes to pensioners in very particular circumstances. Married pensioners who have a high income and whose partners have a low income might well not benefit from the age allowance, whereas a married pensioner who was over 75 whose income was split evenly between the couple could obtain about £20,000 of tax-free income in addition to a tranche of income of over £7,000 on which tax of 10 per cent was charged. The withdrawal of the two allowances is fiendishly complex. The whole system seems to be designed to reward effective tax planning.

We therefore propose to abolish the age-related personal allowance. This, together with the abolition of the married couples' allowance, would save £3.14 billion.[5] There would be significant administrative savings both for government and individuals and significant savings in tax planning costs. This saving could be reduced in 2011/12 when the personal allowance for all individuals is increased, but other factors before 2015/16 would lead to an increase in the cost of these two allowances. We have therefore assumed that the saving from their abolition would be £3 billion per year.

Two groups on modest incomes would lose out from these proposals, and we might consider how to reduce taxes in a simple, transparent and economically coherent way using some of the savings from cuts to other areas of government expenditure in the other proposals in this monograph. The first group would be pensioner couples whose income was unevenly split so that one member of the couple did not make full use of their personal allowance. This group will become smaller as pension provision among women increases. The second group would be single pensioners on small incomes who will pay a maximum amount of additional tax of £520 a year. If it is wished to reduce taxes for the first group, then it should be done through a simple transferable tax allowance between members of a couple. The second group will gain from the general increase in the personal allowance that is already proposed and being implemented with effect from April 2011. Given the other proposals in this monograph, it should be possible to raise the basic personal allowance very significantly above the age allowance in any case.

The above two proposals would lead to nearly all pensioners paying a marginal rate of tax at either 0 or 20 per cent on all their income. No tax returns would be necessary and the tax that would be due could be worked out by inserting three numbers into a pocket calculator.

---

5   http://www.hmrc.gov.uk/stats/tax_expenditures/table1–5.pdf.

Not linking UK state pensions to earnings from 2011

The UK government has recently announced that the state pension will be linked to increases in earnings from 2011. Furthermore, the government will guarantee that the state pension will rise at the higher of the increase in the retail price index, national average earnings growth or 2.5 per cent. It is difficult to justify this decision and it exposes the government to considerable risk if there were to be a period of sustained deflation, negative real earnings growth or high real earnings growth. Pensioners' real incomes will depend arbitrarily on the relationship between earnings growth, prices growth and 2.5 per cent – as will the real cost of pensions to government. At a time when the population is ageing, a decision to raise the real level of pensions within a pay-as-you-go pension system financed by taxes of the working generation is imprudent.

In the long term, as discussed below, the government should develop a pensions system that maximises the scope for private pension provision. Meanwhile, the government should not expand the real level of spending within the current system. We propose that the basic state pension and all means-tested benefits through the pension credit system be frozen in real terms.[6] Given the increase in means-tested benefit levels in recent years, as well as above-inflation rises to the basic state pension, this is an entirely reasonable approach. Indeed, it could be argued that real pensions should be reduced if real earnings fall in the current climate.

It is likely that real wage growth will be subdued over the next few years but, assuming wage growth of 2.5 per cent per annum above inflation (which is about 0.5 per cent per annum less than the government's GDP growth forecast), not increasing pensions in line with earnings will save about £5.6 billion per year by 2015/16. Additionally, increasing the minimum income guarantee for pensioners in line with the rise in prices rather than the rise in earnings is likely to save about £0.8 billion per annum.

---

6   Though further proposals for pension credit are given in the chapter by Niemietz.

Raising state pension age to 66 in 2015

The government has already legislated for the state pension age to rise from 65 to 68. The rise to 68 will not take place until 2046. There is a strong case for a considerable rise in the state pension age very soon. In 1952, life expectancy for a male at age 65 was 11.7 years. By 2010, it was 21 years (see DWP, 2010). Indeed, even the rise in state pension age to 68 will not reduce the average number of years for which the state pension is received because, by 2046, life expectancy at age 65 is likely to have increased by at least a further five years.

The age at which people retire should be a matter of free choice. We propose below methods by which greater choice in this matter will be facilitated in the long term. As an interim measure, however, we propose a rise in the state pension age of half a year in 2014 and a further half-year in 2015 for both men and women (for the latter this would be half a year each year above already planned increases). The savings from this would depend on the extent to which additional older people could be absorbed into the labour market and the relationship between pension payments and means-tested benefits. A conservative estimate of the savings would be about £5 billion.

Reduction in public sector pension contributions

There has been much discussion in recent years about the level of pension provision given to public sector workers (see, for example, Record, 2006). This discussion culminated in the publication of a report by the Public Sector Pension Commission (Pension Commission, 2010) and action by the government to set up its own commission.[7]

There is no particular need for the government to resolve this issue by designing new pension schemes for every group of public sector workers. Two reforms are important, however. First, the full costs of

---

7   This commission is known as the 'Independent Public Service Pensions Commission', though unlike the 'Public Sector Pensions Commission' it is not independent as its only member was a prospective public sector pensioner.

all pension promises should be revealed and charged to public sector employers and employees as new pension accrues: the public sector should face the same discipline as the private sector. Secondly, public sector employees and employers should be free to negotiate pension arrangements: these arrangements may well be different in different areas of the public sector. Whatever pension arrangements they design, the full cost should be charged to employers and employees.

Currently, the cost of public sector provision is about 40 per cent of the public sector salary bill – though it varies widely between different parts of the public sector (see ibid.). Because of the way in which the government accounts for public sector pensions, however, only about half that figure appears in headline public spending numbers. We propose that all public sector budgets are adjusted so that they contain an allowance for current salaries (after allowing for cuts proposed elsewhere in the monograph) plus an allowance of 20 per cent of salary for pension provision. It would then be a matter for public sector employers (schools, hospitals or health authorities, the Defence Department and so on) to agree pension arrangements with their employees. If pension arrangements cost more than 20 per cent of salaries, cuts would have to be made elsewhere; if pension arrangements cost less, there would be scope for salary increases.[8]

This change to public sector pension arrangements would not change headline spending at all. The reason for this is that about half of public sector pension costs are currently hidden from government accounts. This policy change will, however, reduce underlying public spending on public sector pensions by £17 billion to £18 billion a year.

A case could be made for going farther. Pay increases in the public sector have outstripped those in the private sector in recent years. The

---

8   This 20 per cent figure represents an average: it could be higher in some departments and lower in others. The authors believe, however, that, even in areas such as police and defence, pension arrangements should be such that they do not treat early retirement generously. There is no reason why workers in those services cannot continue working, even if in less strenuous occupations.

Institute for Fiscal Studies estimates that the difference between private sector and public sector pay, after allowing for differences in skills and so on, is relatively small – about 5 per cent. However, employer pension provision in the private sector costs, on average, considerably less than 10 per cent of salary.[9] The difference between the 40 per cent of salary that pension benefits are currently worth in the public sector and the 10 per cent of salary that represents a generous estimate of the average private sector employer contribution towards pensions is a reasonable estimate of the extent of the generosity of public sector pay packages relative to private sector packages – excluding the small amount by which headline rates of pay are higher in the public sector. We do not propose that this issue of superiority in public sector pay is addressed further in this chapter – proposals in other chapters will have implications for public sector pay and will lead to a radical decentralisation of pay setting.

Comprehensive pension reform
The problems with government pensions

The purpose of this monograph is not simply to suggest short-term budget savings. We are also proposing long-term policies to radically improve the functioning of the economy. In the field of pensions, comprehensive reform is desirable.

Most Western countries have very high levels of explicit government debt. Though this is not unprecedented, previous situations where high levels of explicit debt existed were at times when government spending and taxation were at much lower levels than today – for example, after the Napoleonic wars. In addition, the explicit debt is only the tip of an iceberg. For perhaps the first time in economic history, developed countries use the taxes of the working generation to provide income and healthcare for the retired for a long proportion of their total lifespan. As has been noted above, life expectation at age 65 has doubled in just 60 years. Currently, an

---

9   See http://www.statistics.gov.uk/cci/nugget.asp?id=1278.

individual who retires at age 60 can expect to be in retirement for a period equal to perhaps two-thirds of the length of his working life.

Where pensions are provided by the state, this leads to an implicit debt: that is, it leads to an unfunded obligation on the younger generation to provide income and healthcare to the older generation. The explicit and implicit debt combined has been estimated to be around 550 per cent of national income (see Hagist et al., 2009).

In the past, people provided for needs in old age through their extended families (older members being supported by younger members), through saving or through insurance (see Bartholomew, 2004, for more discussion). The portion of an individual's life for which provision of this type was made, of course, was much shorter than the period for which we expect to be in retirement today.

There are very good reasons to make a clean break from the post-war pension settlement. The most important is the burdens that pay-as-you-go pension systems place on future generations when the population is declining. When savings, insurance and family provision are the methods of providing for old age, there are automatic processes of adjustment to changing economic conditions. For example, when longevity improves and the working population shrinks, annuity prices increase and there will be upward pressure on wages. These effects increase the incentives for individuals to work longer and to defer retirement. The desirable outcome for the individual is also desirable for society as a whole.

The problem with the approach of using tax-financed pensions and healthcare – whereby taxes are levied on the young and those to whom promises are made make no funded provision themselves – is that the risks are inherently systemic and not self-correcting – indeed, they are self-reinforcing. When the working generation pays taxes to provide the pensions and healthcare of the older generation, the key variable that determines the burden is the number of children the older generation had when it was the working generation. There were no incentives whatsoever, however, for today's retired generation to have sufficient children when they were the working generation in order to provide the means to pay for their pensions and healthcare. Furthermore, as the population ages, reform of state pension systems becomes more difficult because of the weight of older people among the electorate. The median age of an active voter in the UK is already over 50. In many continental European countries the median age of active voters is rising rapidly to the high fifties (see the chapter by Booth in Booth et al. 2008). It is interesting that, in the recent Comprehensive Spending Review, there was very little downward adjustment made to the benefits of older people and state pensions are due to increase in real terms – possibly quite rapidly. No other group has been treated this way except the users of the health service, who are also disproportionately older. A further problem is that, as the working generation shrinks relative to the retired generation, the taxes necessary to finance pay-as-you-go pensions increase also. This can reduce the incentive to work and save, which then has a second-round effect on both tax revenues and the savings individuals themselves make for old age.

Of course, it should be stressed that savings, insurance and family provision are not risk-free methods of transferring income across time and for making long-term income provision in old age, as the last few years have shown us. Those risks can be managed, however, and, as has been noted, savers can respond to price signals as they approach retirement when real wages and annuity prices change. It is also often contended that, when people use private forms of pension provision, their retirement incomes can be inadequate. Here we should bear in mind two points. The first is that, if government provision of income, goods and services were less, people's net incomes would be greater, from which saving could take place. Secondly, the only way in which government pension schemes have provided large pensions without huge contributions throughout working life is by the government throwing the burden on to generations as yet unborn.[10] It is, indeed,

---

10   As has been noted above, Record (2006) and Pensions Commission (2010) show that contributions of 40 per cent of salary would be necessary to provide an income in retirement

expensive to save throughout a 35-year working life to provide a pension for 25 years – brushing the cost under the carpet does not make it cheaper.

Proposed reform

The current UK state pension schemes are extremely complicated and their existence and interaction with the social security system substantially reduce – or even eliminate – incentives for most people to save.[11] We propose a very simple system which would provide a small but adequate pension from which people would be able to contract out and make their own private provision. Individuals would be able to finance whatever retirement period they wished to supplement a small state pension that would be received from age 70 with that age being adjusted upwards as life expectancy increased. The system would be designed so that rights would be accrued within this system in such a way that they could not be increased arbitrarily by future governments.

In line with the general practice of pension reform, we propose leaving accrued rights in existing systems unchanged. With regard to future state pension accrual, we propose a new approach, but one that is based on the contributory principle. The principles of a new, sustainable, state pension system are enunciated below. The details can, of course, be changed without changing the underlying logic and sustainable nature of the system.

We suggest that, for each year of work in which an individual earns income above the lower earnings limit in the national insurance system,[12] he would accrue a right to a pension equal to 1/45th of a full state pension. The new model could be implemented immediately,

---

equal to that received by most public sector workers. To the extent that the contributions that are made are smaller and not invested, future generations are bearing the burdens through implicit debt that is accumulating.

11 See Field in Deacon (2002) – the situation has not improved since this time.

12 This is currently just over £5,000 per annum and is designed to be at a level that makes the notion of a contributory system relevant.

though it would be many years before the old model was completely phased out – transition arrangements would be needed for those who had accrued pension under both the new and existing state pension schemes.[13] The full state pension would be set at a level of around £140. This level is close to the current pension credit minimum income guarantee and somewhat below the level of the current combined Basic State Pension and Second State Pension. The pension would be financed by national insurance contributions levied, as now, separately from the income tax system.

Other features of this pension regime would be as follows:

- The accrued pension would be indexed to median wages before retirement, as would the basic level of pension which determined how much pension was accrued each year.
- Once in payment the pension would be linked to increases in the retail price index.
- All individuals could contract out of the system on simple and actuarially neutral terms so that they would receive a rebate of national insurance contributions to invest in a private pension scheme. Full privatisation of pension provision would therefore be possible on a voluntary basis.
- Some accrual of pension would be given for those who were not paying national insurance contributions in certain circumstances, as is the case now.
- State pension age would be adjusted every five years so that life expectation at pension age would remain the same as life expectation at age 70 today.
- The number of years that it would be necessary to work to receive a full pension would rise in line with the state pension age.
- Once a full pension was accrued, no further state pension could be

---

13 It might be possible to phase out the old systems quickly if transition arrangements allowed rights in older systems to be transformed into rights in the new system of equal actuarial value.

accrued, but no further national insurance contributions in respect of the state pension would be payable.

- After a phasing-in period, no special level of means-tested benefits would be given to older people: those who had not contributed to the system would not be treated any differently above state pension age than they are below state pension age.

Such a system would bring significant economic advantages over the current state pensions system. These advantages would include the following:

- Two complex – indeed incomprehensible – schemes with completely separate rules would be replaced by one simple scheme.
- The currently incoherent national insurance system would be radically simplified.
- The proposed scheme would considerably limit the extent of pay-as-you-go pension provision and fix the level of that provision in advance.
- Individuals could opt out of the scheme if they so wished, thus facilitating full privatisation of pensions on a voluntary basis and a further reduction in state pay-as-you-go pension liabilities.
- Costs for national insurance payers would be reduced significantly, but it would be possible, at limited cost, for an individual to save to pay for extra benefits either to facilitate longer retirement or to facilitate a higher retirement pension. This additional saving could be through either formal pension schemes or more flexible savings products.

There would be significant long-term savings arising from the increase in the state pension age and a reduction in the total extent of the state pension scheme. Contracting out would lead to further long-term savings.

In many ways, this would take us back to Beveridge's original intention for the social insurance system. Beveridge (1942: para. 9) suggested: 'The state organising security should not stifle incentive, opportunity, responsibility; in establishing a national minimum, it should leave room and encouragement for voluntary action by each individual to provide more than that minimum for himself and his family.'

We go farther, however, and allow that 'national minimum' to be provided by private means. This proposal would extend one of the most successful aspects of UK pension policy – that of contracting out. In recent years, contracting out has been undermined as a result of the government reducing national insurance contribution rebates below fair actuarial value; the government is now in the process of removing the ability of most workers to contract out.[14]

Conclusion

Recent UK governments have managed to create one of the most inco-herent systems of old-age support imaginable. There are two special tax allowances for the old – both of which are withdrawn once income reaches a certain level. Older people are also entitled to a range of different means-tested and non-means-tested benefits, as well as to benefits in kind. Few of these benefits have any coherent economic justification. In addition, the government has created an extraordin-arily complex state pension system which few people understand. Over several years, the government has also been undermining private

---

14   There would be a practical problem with contracting out that could be resolved in various ways. Currently, percentage-rate national insurance contributions are paid for a flat-rate pension. This leads to significant redistribution within the scheme. Either national insur-ance contributions would have to return to being flat-rate (together with reductions in other taxes paid by the less well off in order to compensate) or the rebates would have to be larger than the national insurance contributions actually paid for those workers who are less well paid. Neither approach creates any particular practical difficulties and the best approach would depend on the shape of the tax system after taking into account all the tax reductions that would be possible across government given the proposals in this book.

provision and making it more difficult for individuals to contract out of the state pension system.

We propose that many of the benefits currently given to old people are abolished, that older people do not get special treatment in the tax system, and that we have a long-term sustainable settlement for the state pension system which allows people to make alternative private provision if they wish to do so. Other short-term adjustments are proposed to the state pension system such as raising the state pension age. The total savings from these proposals are approximately £15.5 billion. In addition, tax revenues of an additional £3.0 billion would arise from removing special allowances for older people. Furthermore, underlying public spending would be cut by another £17 billion, though this would not affect headline public spending because of the way in which public sector pension costs are currently incorporated in government accounts. More important than the short-term savings would be significant benefits from a more coherent tax and benefits system and from long-term reforms to the state pension system.

It should be noted that there are other proposals in other chapters that also affect government spending on older people. The proposals for health savings accounts will ensure that healthcare for the elderly can be pre-funded and will also lead to the pre-funding of much long-term care. Also, the system of means-tested benefits for the elderly is dealt with in another chapter. The cuts suggested here, though radical in terms of the current political debate, generally only remove benefits that have been granted in the last fifteen years. The proposed reform of the state pension system would, however, have radical implications for spending in the long term.

References

Bartholomew, J. (2004), *The Welfare State We're In,* London: Politico's.
Beveridge, W. (1942), *Social Insurance and Allied Services,* London: His Majesty's Stationery Office.

Booth, P. M. and D. R. Cooper (2005), *The Way Out of the Pensions Quagmire*, Research Monograph 60, London: Institute of Economic Affairs.

Booth, P. M., O. Juurikkala and N. Silver (eds) (2008), *Pension Provision: Government Failure around the World*, Readings 63, London: Institute of Economic Affairs.

Deacon, A. (ed.) (2002), *Debating Pensions: Self-interest, citizenship and the common good*, London: Civitas.

DWP (2010), *When Should the State Pension Age Increase to 66? A call for evidence*, London: Department for Work and Pensions.

Hagist, C., S. Moog, B. Raffelhuschen and J. Vatter (2009), *Public Debt and Demography: An international comparison using generation accounting*, Germany: CESifo, DICE Report.

Pensions Commission (2010), *Reforming Public Sector Pensions – solutions to a growing problem*, London: Institute of Directors.

Record, N. (2006), *Sir Humphrey's Legacy*, Hobart Paper 156, London: Institute of Economic Affairs.

PART THREE: THE WARFARE STATE

7 THE FAT RED LINE: TIME TO CUT BRITISH DEFENCE SPENDING
Paul Robinson

Introduction

For reasons which are not entirely clear, politicians and analysts on the free market end of the spectrum, even while insisting that governments do less, are usually reluctant to accept cuts in defence spending.[1] Yet in the sphere of defence, doing less and spending less can often produce better results than doing more and spending more. Students of international relations learn about the security dilemma in almost their first class: a state's efforts to improve its own security may be misinterpreted by others as aggressive, causing them to spend more on their defences, thus making the first state actually less secure than it was to begin with (see, for instance, Glaser, 1990). Similarly, in the last few years we have seen how attempts to increase Britain's security by waging war overseas in Iraq and Afghanistan have probably made it less secure, radicalising certain elements of the British population and so increasing the likelihood of terrorist attack. The counterproductive nature of our policies does not excuse such terrorism, but it should make us consider alternative policies which will have a more desirable effect.

The recent Strategic Defence and Security Review (SDSR) brought predictable howls of protest from those who felt that the proposed cuts would endanger Britain's security. In fact, the SDSR represented a lost opportunity to reduce expenditure much more dramatically. A rational analysis of Britain's defence needs reveals that much of the country's current military capability is not only unnecessary but also dangerous.

1 There are a few exceptions in the USA, most notably Congressman Ron Paul, as well as conservative writers such as Andrew Bacevich and Christopher Preble. See Preble (2009).

The best way to serve the national interest would be to cut this capability. As this chapter shows, cuts of as much as 50 per cent of the current budget are not only possible, but desirable, and should be a priority of any British government in the future.

Rational defence planning

In an ideally rational world, defence policymaking would follow a five-step process in accordance with the model shown in Figure 4.

If on reaching Step 5 the planner discovers that there is insufficient money available to enact the chosen strategy, he must return to Step 2 and carry out a risk assessment. Perfect security is impossible. Decision-makers should determine which of the threats they will ignore, based on the likelihood of their occurrence and the damage that will result if they do occur. They can then redraw the strategy to bring it into line with financial constraints.

Of course, defence policy rarely, if ever, actually follows this process. Inertia plays an important role. It takes years to create new military capabilities, and so change strategies. In practice, therefore, Steps 3 and 4 are often reversed, with existing capabilities shaping strategy rather than strategy shaping capabilities. Furthermore, many factors, such as party politics, bureaucratic politics and the influence of interest groups, intervene to prevent the process from following the desirable course. Nevertheless, this model provides the most logical framework available for determining policy.

The model is an example of what is termed 'threat-based planning'. As such it poses problems for defence planners in the post-Cold War world, because the collapse of the Soviet Union removed the greatest threat to Western security, and military force is not a particularly good strategy for dealing with those threats that still exist. Planners using this model are likely to conclude that there is little of a serious nature in Step 2, and that there is little contribution military power can make in Step 3, thus meaning that few capabilities are needed, and little needs to be spent.

Not wishing to draw this conclusion, supporters of high military

Figure 4   **Defence planning process**

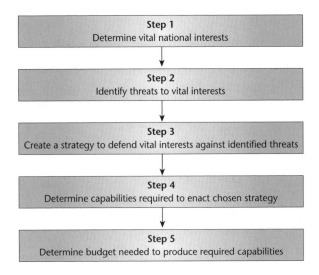

Source: Adapted from *Fundamentals of Force Planning*, vol. 1, Naval War College Press, Newport, RI, 1990, pp. 107 and 150.

spending respond either by exaggerating the threats (by claiming, for instance, that Islamist terrorism poses an existential threat to British security), or by simply jettisoning threat-based planning entirely and appealing to morality. This was the reaction of the Blair government, which envisaged the armed forces as a 'force for good', whose explicit role was to change the world for the better, rather than to defend the UK.[2] Although the coalition government has abandoned the specific language of 'force for good', references to 'global responsibilities' remain popular among supporters of high levels of defence spending, the idea being that Britain has a moral obligation to carry its share of

---

2   I have criticised this policy elsewhere: Robinson (2008).

the burden of making the world safe for all. Unfortunately, in the past decade this policy has failed even on its own terms, as it certainly has not changed the world for the better, while at the same time it has probably made the UK less secure at the cost of many billions of pounds of taxpayers' money. Furthermore, research indicates that activities such as preventing the spread of HIV/AIDS, reducing the incidence of malnutrition and malaria and liberalising trade do far more to improve the world, at a far lower cost, than any form of military or security activity (for instance, Lomborg, 2009). The bombing campaign against Libya is a case in point: its cost (several hundred million pounds at the time of writing) is high, but its security benefits are unclear, and its humanitarian impact is decidedly ambiguous. In short, moral arguments do not provide a good justification for defence spending.

Perhaps aware of this, the current government instead promotes the idea of uncertainty. This is encapsulated in the title of the SDSR issued in October 2010, *Securing Britain in an Age of Uncertainty* (HM Government, 2010a). This approach admits that the current security environment is benign, but declares that the future is uncertain (see, for instance, HM Government, 2010b: 3–4), thus requiring us to maintain strong and flexible defences just in case.

There is some logic to this point of view. The future *is* uncertain. We can never predict with total accuracy. Also, as noted, it takes time to create defence capabilities. If the situation changes rapidly, one may not be able to create defence capabilities fast enough to react. That said, the SDSR admits that 'we face no major state threat at present and no existential threat to our security, freedom, or prosperity' (HM Government, 2010a: 15). Nor can we envisage such a threat reappearing in the near future. By historical standards this is a degree of certainty of staggering importance. Furthermore, we know that the world has become more stable and less violent than at any other time since World War II, with fewer wars, fewer coups, fewer revolutions, and less terrorism.[3] The

3   For details of the good news about the international security environment see *The Human Security Brief 2007*, online at http://www.hsrgroup.org/human-security-reports/2007/

argument that we live in a particularly uncertain era is weak. In any case, uncertainty provides no basis for rational planning. If one does not know what the future holds, one set of capabilities is every bit as rational as any other set. There is no way of determining whether to build this or that, or spend this amount or that amount. Defence planning becomes entirely arbitrary. And creating military capabilities 'just in case' is not cost-free. It is also potentially dangerous because, when these capabilities are sitting around not being used, governments are tempted to use them in inappropriate circumstances, leading the country into unnecessary and costly conflicts. A certain amount of hedging of bets is necessary, but this is not best done by creating large regular forces to cover all possible eventualities. If the fear is that it will be difficult to re-create capabilities in the future, the solution instead is to retain a small core of competence in most areas, but hand this over to the reserve forces, who can then act as the cadre for future expansion should the security situation dramatically change.

Given these arguments, the threat-based planning model shown above retains its validity. It is, therefore, the model which the rest of the chapter follows below.

Vital national interests

International relations scholars sometimes define interests as being divided into 'vital' and 'secondary' ones. The former consist of interests the defence of which is essential to the continued existence of the state; the latter are ones which it is desirable, but not essential, to defend.[4] Politicians and security analysts have an unfortunate tendency to conflate the two, but a proper defence planning process needs to keep

overview.aspx; *The Human Security Report 2009: The Shrinking Costs of War*, online at http://www.hsrgroup.org/human-security-reports/2009/overview.aspx; and Center for International Development and Conflict Management, *Peace and Conflict 2010: Executive Summary*, online at http://www.cidcm.umd.edu/pc/executive_summary/exec_sum_2010.pdf.

4   For a discussion of these issues, see Sonderman (1997).

them separate and use a narrow definition of what truly constitutes a vital interest.

Any state's most vital interest is self-preservation. Beyond that, the state has an obligation to protect the life and property of its citizens, whose basic security constitutes another vital interest. This is self-evident, but still needs some further explanation. As noted, total security is impossible. It would be absurd to consider it a vital national interest that all citizens be absolutely safe from danger at all times anywhere in the world. The vital interest is actually a more modest one: that there be a reasonable level of security, sufficient to ensure that the normal processes of social and economic life may continue without excessive trouble. The state does not have to ensure total peace and stability everywhere to secure this interest.

Maintenance of citizens' preferred way of life constitutes another vital interest. This includes both continued economic prosperity and the protection of civil liberties. Again, this needs qualification. Not every economic interest is a vital one. Defence planners often cite the fact that Britain is a trading nation to justify defence spending, saying that Britain must secure its trade routes. There is some truth to this, but perhaps less than one might imagine. The top destination for Britain's exports is the USA; eight of the remaining nine states in the top ten are members of the European Union; the other top ten destination is China.[5] Some two-thirds of all the maritime trade entering and exiting British ports, measured by weight, goes to, or comes from, Europe.[6] Were Britain's trade with Europe to collapse, the consequences for British society would be catastrophic. If Britain's trade with much of the rest of the world were

---

5   HM Revenue & Customs, *Top 25 Trading Partners Monthly*, online at https://www.uktradeinfo.com/index.cfm?task=topPartners, statistics for September 2010.

6   According to figures provided by the Royal Navy, in 2005, 255 million tonnes of traffic arrived in British ports, of which 168 million tonnes came from Europe; 160 million tonnes left British ports, of which 112.8 million tonnes went to Europe. European trade therefore accounted for 67 per cent of the total: Royal Navy, 'The importance of maritime trade', online at http://www.royalnavy.mod.uk/linkedfiles/upload/pdf/the_importance_of_maritime_trade.pdf.

to collapse, the consequences, while undesirable, would not be so dire. In short, the trade with the former constitutes a vital interest, but the trade with the latter does not. Similarly, keeping the short sea routes to Europe open is a vital interest, but keeping sea routes open everywhere, however desirable, is not.

Another interest often considered to be of great importance in defence debates is national honour, often referred to as 'influence', 'credibility' or 'prestige'. Politicians want Britain to 'punch above its weight', a fact made clear by the first sentence of the foreword to the SDSR, in which David Cameron and Nick Clegg announced that 'Our country has always had global responsibilities and global ambitions ... we should have no less ambition for our country in the decades to come' (HM Government, 2010a: 3). Defence, it seems, is not really about defence, but about 'ambition' and pride. Many defence projects, the desire to retain nuclear weapons being the prime example, can be understood only in this context.

It is natural for people to wish to feel proud of themselves and their country. The question, though, is whether national honour is a vital interest. The argument in favour tends to be that countries which are perceived to be strong are safer; a reputation for weakness invites attack. Unfortunately for this argument, almost every academic analysis of the topic has concluded that this is not the case: 'credibility' does not deter attack (see, for instance, Press, 2005). Wars for honour make very little sense, and it is actually very hard to make a decent case that national honour constitutes a vital interest.

Threats to vital interests

Undoubtedly some threats to these vital interests do exist, but by historical standards they are on a remarkably small scale. For another state to be inclined and have the ability to attack the UK directly, the international system would have had to have undergone a collapse of such enormous dimensions that there would probably be very little we could do about it anyway. Planning has to stay within the realms of what is reasonably credible. Such a scenario falls outside those realms. For the foreseeable future, major state and existential threats will continue to be absent. This is a conclusion with very significant ramifications, since it immediately removes the justification for a very substantial portion of the defence establishment.

Nevertheless, some threats to the lives, prosperity and way of life of British citizens remain. Perhaps the most prominent of these is terrorism. Undoubtedly this will continue to be a problem for many years, but it is necessary to keep a sense of proportion. During the 30 years of the troubles in Northern Ireland, approximately three thousand people lost their lives. By contrast, in the nearly ten years since 11 September 2001, outside Northern Ireland, only 52 people have been killed by terrorists in the UK, all on one day in July 2005. If one excludes Iraq and Afghanistan from the figures, international terrorism has declined in both volume and lethality in the past 20 years.[7] According to Europol, there were 515 terrorist attacks in Europe in 2008; of these just one attack was deemed to be an act of Islamist terrorism (Europol, 2009: 11). In the UK, even now, Irish terrorism remains far more significant, with 129 shooting and bombing incidents in 2009, although these resulted in only two deaths.[8]

Threats to life are few. Threats to prosperity are more numerous, but more diffuse. The National Security Strategy identifies natural disasters, organised crime, the poor state of the country's finances and cybercrime as among the most important (HM Government, 2010b: 14, 27). To this one might add the danger of international instability, including state failure and connected phenomena such as piracy. Again, though, one must not be too alarmed by this list. Natural disasters in the UK do not take on the dimensions they do in many other countries, and our

---

7   *The Human Security Brief 2007*, pp. 8–21.
8   Police Service of Northern Ireland, *Annual Report of the Chief Constable 2009–2010*, Figure 5.3, online at http://www.psni.police.uk/chief_constables_annual_report_2009_-2010. pdf.

primary trading partners are not unstable. There is no notable threat to the trade routes to Europe on which the economy relies. Instability in parts of the world such as Africa, while undesirable, does not pose a threat to the UK's vital interests. Cybercrime, by contrast, is a rising and serious problem which deserves major consideration, but there is no reason why this should be a military responsibility.

Creating a strategy to meet identified threats

The lack of existential threats to the UK means that large armed forces to defend the country from direct attack are not necessary; nor are armed forces designed to invade others to pre-empt such an attack. Heavy military forces designed to fight other states do not, therefore, serve a useful purpose and should be largely eliminated. This includes equipment such as main battle tanks, heavy artillery, fighter aircraft, submarines and the larger surface vessels.

In terms of threats to life, this leaves only the threat from terrorism. Domestically, it would be wise to retain a reasonable infantry force with supporting services to provide aid to the civil power should the situation in Northern Ireland deteriorate, which is not impossible, and also to provide assistance in the event of a major terrorist attack on the mainland. Beyond that, though, military force has little role to play. A sensible strategy for fighting terrorism would concentrate on politics, intelligence and policing activities.

Also domestically, it is useful to have some military forces to provide aid to the civil power in the case of natural disaster, and also to provide services such as Search and Rescue, although the latter could easily be contracted out to the private sector. In any case, the number of troops needed is small.

As far as dealing with uncertainty is concerned, the optimal strategy, as mentioned above, is to retain a core capability in the reserves. As the regular force is cut, an expansion of the reserve force would make sense.

In general, power projection capabilities do not serve Britain's interests. The recent mania for overseas intervention has cost much blood and treasure and brought little observable benefit. One can make a case for naval operations such as minesweeping (such as those that took place to secure the Persian Gulf during the Iran–Iraq war), counter-piracy and counter-narcotics on the high seas, but most of the solutions to these problems lie on land rather than at sea, and the areas in which such operations would take place are generally not areas in which the UK has a vital interest. These activities do not justify retaining a large fleet.

Finally, the strategy of using military power to enhance Britain's prestige should be abandoned. Not only is there no evidence that it works, but prestige is not a vital interest, and there are many other, cheaper, ways of achieving the goal. A successful economy and a flourishing national culture will do far more for national prestige than any number of weapons.

Capabilities

With these considerations in mind, one can now draw some conclusions as to what capabilities may be cut.

In the first place, the nuclear deterrent should be eliminated. Other important states, such as Japan, Germany and Italy, manage perfectly well without one, and there is no obvious enemy to deter. The desire to renew Trident appears to be founded entirely on grounds of national honour, which, as we have seen, do not constitute a good basis for national strategy.

The elimination of the nuclear deterrent will enable the UK to also eliminate the seven Astute-class submarines called for in the SDSR. The only reasonable justification for these is defence of the nuclear deterrent; without it they are no longer needed.

As we have seen, Britain's vital trading interests are far more local than supporters of a large navy assume. There is, therefore, no great requirement for such a navy to protect trade routes, most of which are in any case not under serious threat. Most of the Royal Navy is thus no longer needed. The most notable examples are the two proposed aircraft carriers. The SDSR admits that these are not required in the short term, but provides no good reason why they will be needed in the long term (HM Government, 2010a: 5). They make sense only in the context of the sort of interventionist strategy which is here rejected. The UK government claims that the ill-advised terms of the contract mean that it is cheaper to build them than to cancel them, but this ignores associated costs such as the aircraft which must be bought to go on the carriers, long-term maintenance and personnel, not to mention the dangers which arise from having unused military capabilities sitting idle, tempting politicians to use them. The aircraft carriers should be scrapped.

This, in turn, enables one to eliminate the Royal Navy's new Type 45 destroyers. These are a bizarre choice of vessel, since their primary role is air defence, yet, as we have seen, there is no state enemy capable of attacking the UK and its fleet, nor is one likely to appear. With the elimination of Trident, the Astute submarines, the carriers and the destroyers, the Royal Navy could be reduced to a fleet of small ships, of far more relevance to the country's actual needs. Even here, though, there appears to be some slack. For instance, the SDSR envisages a fleet of fourteen mine counter-measures vessels, which it says will be used for a variety of roles 'such as hydrography or offshore patrol' as well as providing a 'significant level of security and protection of the UK's nuclear deterrent'. With the elimination of the latter, this requirement would disappear (ibid.: 21).

The strategy proposed above calls for the elimination of most of the heavier elements of the army associated with traditional conventional state warfare, such as main battle tanks and heavy artillery, and for the retention only of a small core of such forces in the reserve. This should enable the elimination of both 1 (UK) Armoured and 3 (UK) Mechanised divisions, as the Royal Armoured Corps is reduced to one reserve battalion of main battle tanks, the Royal Artillery loses its multi-barrelled rocket launchers and reduces its heavy artillery (AS90) to one reserve battalion, and the Army Air Corps loses most of its attack helicopters.

These reductions would in turn allow major reductions in support elements. This would include, perhaps, as many as seven out of eleven Royal Engineer field regiments, five out of seven Royal Electrical and Mechanical Engineer battalions, and similar proportions of signals, intelligence and logistics elements, as well as headquarters staff and their support services. The infantry would suffer less, but even here some cuts would make sense, perhaps reducing the force to about twenty-five battalions.

In the Royal Air Force (RAF), fighter aircraft would be cut en masse. Present plans call for the RAF to keep three types of fast jets – the Typhoon, the Tornado and the Joint Strike Fighter (JSF). The elimination of the aircraft carriers will provide an opportunity to cut the JSF completely. The Tornado, being the oldest of the three, should also go. This leaves only the Typhoon. At present the RAF has four squadrons of Typhoons, with a total of 55 aircraft. This is surely sufficient, given the lack of air threat and the growing obsolescence of fast jets in an air environment increasingly dominated by Unmanned Aerial Vehicles (UAVs). The proposed second tranche of Typhoons should therefore be cancelled. The RAF could retain its UAV capability, plus enough of its helicopter and transport aircraft to support the remaining elements of the army. Since this analysis no longer foresees the UK carrying out large-scale expeditionary operations overseas, however, the requirement for long-range in-flight refuelling of aircraft would disappear. This would allow for the cancellation of the Future Strategic Tanker Aircraft.

Inevitably, reforms on this scale would encounter serious opposition. The elimination of cherished regiments always produces resistance, while local economies which rely heavily on defence industries could experience major job losses. Sentimental attachments, however, are not sufficient justification for the expenditure of large sums of taxpayers' money. And while undoubtedly some areas of the country will suffer economic losses, the idea that military spending boosts the economy as a whole – 'military Keynesianism', in other words – lacks foundation. Economic suffering will be highly localised, largely temporary, and the economy as a whole should benefit.

The defence budget

The defence budget for the financial year 2008/09 was £38.6 billion, added to which an additional £4 billion was spent on the wars in Iraq and Afghanistan. The most notable items of expenditure were personnel (£11.7 billion), depreciations and impairments (£6.9 billion), construction of new equipment (£6.7 billion), maintenance of equipment (£4.3 billion) and research and development (£2.4 billion). Other significant expenditures include property management (£1.5 billion), PFI service charges (£1.5 billion) and war pensions (£1 billion).[9]

The single largest item is personnel. The proposals above would lead to very large savings. The cuts to the equipment of the Royal Navy would allow major reductions in personnel. These would include the crews of the vessels that are no longer required (about 100 per submarine, 180 per destroyer and 600 per aircraft carrier), plus the much larger 'tail' of support elements and training establishments. Overall, this would amount to a reduction of about 20,000 sailors out of a current force of 35,000. The Army would lose about 40,000 soldiers out of a current force of 102,000, and the RAF would face cuts of between 15,000 and 20,000 out of a current force of 38,000.

In total, this would permit the government to reduce the size of the armed forces from the current level of 175,000 to 90,000, a cut of almost 50 per cent. Assuming that the number of civilian personnel can be lowered in direct proportion to military personnel, this would allow the Ministry of Defence (MoD) to reduce its personnel budget by just under 50 per cent, or about £5.5 billion at 2009 prices.

A smaller military will wear out less equipment and other assets, will consume less stock, and will require less property, less management, fewer consultants, less fuel, less communications and IT support, and so on. Depreciations and impairments will be lower. Calculating the exact savings from these changes is difficult, especially as the gains will be gradual as the cuts are phased in. There are some benefits of

9   *UK Defence Statistics 2009*, online at http://www.dasa.mod.uk/modintranet/UKDS/ UKDS2009/pdf/UKDS2009.pdf.

scale, in that larger organisations need proportionally less real estate and management. Some items, such as the PFI service charges and war pensions, will have to be paid in full regardless. These disadvantages could, however, be offset to some degree with funds generated through one-time sales of defence equipment, property and estates. One would hope that after the dust has settled, the savings in all these items would be roughly proportionate to the reductions in personnel, that is to say something in the region of £6 billion at 2009 prices.

Savings on equipment are harder to calculate. Equipment support can be expected to be reduced in proportion to the overall size of the force, which given a 50 per cent reduction would mean a little over £2 billion a year. The move to a military with less high-technology weaponry designed to fight other states would permit even more significant cuts in research and development, perhaps in the region of £1.5 billion pounds per year. The rest of the equipment budget is for new equipment, and it is here that the real complications arise. The MoD is in effect in debt for many billions of pounds for equipment for which it has postponed paying. Furthermore, many of the proposed cuts are to projects that are already partly completed (e.g. the destroyers and submarines) or are based on contracts with punitive cancellation terms. This means that short-term economies will be less than one might hope.

Nevertheless, one can identify some savings during the next ten years. These include up to £10 billion for the JSF, another £10 billion for the Future Strategic Tanker Aircraft, £4 billion for Typhoon tranche two, and £3–4 billion for the Astute submarines. Together these amount to some £30 billion over ten years, or £3 billion a year. Thereafter, the cancellation of the Trident replacement will save £10–20 billion just in the initial purchase, and anything up to £80 billion over the project's lifetime, meaning that lower equipment costs can be sustained in the longer term. Also, once the proposed restructuring has taken place, the equipment requirements of the military will be much smaller than today, while bringing an end to the war in Afghanistan will reduce wear and tear and destruction of weapons and vehicles. Therefore, while bearing in mind that this figure is somewhat approximate, one should be able to expect initial savings of about £3 billion a year on the equipment budget, rising further in the future.

Overall, this means that after a period of restructuring the defence budget could be reduced from the current level of about £38 billion to about £21 billion at 2009 prices, a saving of £17 billion a year,[10] or 45 per cent. This compares strikingly with the 8 per cent cut proposed by the British government. Yet even the remaining £21 billion defence budget (in 2009 prices) would make British defence spending the ninth-largest in the world, and through NATO the UK would be allied to countries that collectively account for two-thirds of the world's defence expenditure[11] (and which would still account for over half of the global total even if they all followed Britain's example and cut spending by 45 per cent). In these circumstances, it is impossible to say that Britain would not be well defended and could not protect her vital interests. No country would suddenly invade the United Kingdom; terrorism would not suddenly increase; the economy would not collapse. At the same time, many lives would be saved as futile military interventions came to an end. In fact, by doing less and spending less, Britain would probably be more secure, while the British state could repair its public finances and put money back into the pockets of taxpayers. The case for cutting defence spending is overwhelming.

References

Europol (2009), *TE-SAT 2009: EU Terrorism Situation and Trend Report*, The Hague: Europol.

Glaser, C. L. (1990), 'The security dilemma revisited', *World Politics*, 50(1).

---

10   Given the cuts that are already taking place to the defence budget, this would lead to cuts of approximately the same magnitude in 2015.

11   For comparisons of defence spending around the world, see *The Military Balance 2010*, 110(1), 2010, pp. 462–8.

HM Government (2010a), *Securing Britain in an Age of Uncertainty*, London: The Stationery Office.

HM Government (2010b), *A Strong Britain in an Age of Uncertainty: The National Security Strategy*, London: The Stationery Office.

Lomborg, B. (ed.) (2009), *Global Crises, Global Solutions*, Cambridge: Cambridge University Press.

Preble, C. A. (2009), *The Power Problem: How American Military Dominance Makes Us Less Safe, Less Prosperous, and Less Free*, Ithaca, NY: Cornell University Press.

Press, D. (2005), *Calculating Credibility: How Leaders Assess Military Threats*, Ithaca, NY: Cornell University Press.

Robinson, P. (2008), 'Why it is time to stop being a "force for good"', *Defence and Security Analysis*, 24(4): 381–91.

Sonderman, F. A. (1997), 'The concept of national interest', *Orbis*, 21(1), Spring.

PART FOUR: THE TRANSFER STATE

8 HOW TO IMPROVE THE LOT OF THE POOREST BY CUTTING GOVERNMENT 'AID'

Julian Morris

In 2009, the UK government spent £7.4 billion on 'official development assistance' (ODA), representing 1.1 per cent of total government expenditure[1] and 0.52 per cent of Gross National Income (GNI).[2] ODA spending has increased substantially in recent years: 2009 alone saw an increase of more than £1 billion over 2008. The coalition government has stated that it is committed to increasing 'aid' spending to 0.7 per cent of GDP from 2013[3] and has made provisions for that increase in the recent Comprehensive Spending Review.

This chapter seeks to answer three questions: (1) whether the recent and proposed increases in ODA are justified; (2) whether ODA might be spent in such a way that it does more good and less harm; (3) which existing areas of UK ODA spending should be cut and which kept (or even added to).

Should ODA be increased?

After World War II, Europe's economies were severely wounded. Agricultural production had collapsed and malnutrition, even starvation, was widespread. To eliminate the famine and assist in the recovery, the US government provided aid of various kinds. The most significant of these, made under the auspices of the Marshall Plan, was a series of large low-interest loans to European entrepreneurs (governments acted as

---

1   http://www.ukpublicspending.co.uk/, accessed 1 October 2010.
2   http://www.dfid.gov.uk/Documents/publications1/ODA2009_statistical_release.pdf.
3   http://www.number10.gov.uk/news/latest-news/2010/09/deputy-pm-pledges-to-increase-uk-overseas-aid-spending-55267, accessed 1 October 2010.

intermediaries but were not directly involved in spending the money). In the space of four years the US government provided loans to the tune of $13 billion. This massive injection of capital contributed to a period of unprecedented economic growth; industrial production is estimated to have increased at an average rate of an almost unbelievable 35 per cent per year from 1948 to 1952 (Hubbard and Duggan, 2008; Grogin, 2001: 118)!

The apparent success of the Marshall Plan led to a widespread view that the problem of 'underdevelopment' in other parts of the world could be solved by injections of capital. It led to the invention of the 'investment gap' theory, which posited that countries were poor because they had low savings rates, so there was a lack of capital for investment. To solve the problem of a lack of local capital, it was proposed that capital be injected from abroad.

On the basis of this investment gap theory, the US government and, subsequently, various other governments and multilateral institutions, such as the World Bank and the IMF, made loans to the governments of poor countries. Unlike those made under the Marshall Plan, these loans were not primarily intended for entrepreneurs. Indeed, under the rules establishing the World Bank and the IMF, loans cannot be made directly to entrepreneurs.

For over sixty years, the governments of richer countries have sent taxpayers' money to the governments of poorer countries. Yet it is not at all clear that the more than $2 trillion thereby spent has actually done much to improve the lot of the poor.[4]

Figure 5 shows the relationship between per capita overseas development assistance and changes in per capita GDP (all figures taken from the World Bank's World Development Indicators (WDIs)) from 1975 to 2000. As can be seen, there is no statistically significant relationship.

---

4    $2 trillion is approximately ten times the annual Gross Domestic Product of Nigeria, Africa's most populous country; it is about three times the annual GDP of South Africa, the continent's largest economy; and it is about the same as the annual GDP of sub-Saharan Africa as a whole.

Figure 5   **ODA and economic growth, 1975–2000**

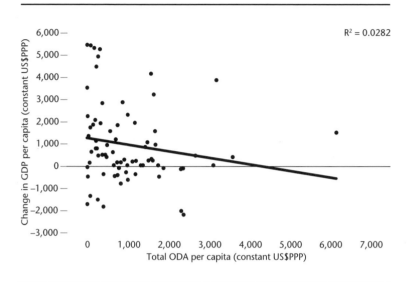

Of course, my simple analysis misses many subtleties – especially the problem of endogeneity (i.e. that countries which received more aid are the poorest). Fortunately, economists have sought to address those defects by developing much more complex econometric studies. Among the most detailed is that of Rajan and Subramanian (2008), who conclude: 'we find little robust evidence of a positive (or negative) relationship between aid inflows into a country and its economic growth'. In other words, even taking into account the fact that more aid tends to go to poorer countries, aid still has no (net) effect on growth.

Figure 6 shows the relationship between ODA and life expectancy over the period 1960–2000 (again, data is from the World Bank's WDIs; data on life expectancy was available for a longer period than per capita GDP for the range of countries under inquiry). Again, there is no statistically significant relationship.

Clearly, up until 2000 at least, aid had failed – on average – to improve the lot of the poor. Our taxes had been wasted. Why? There

Figure 6   ODA and life expectancy at birth, 1960–2000

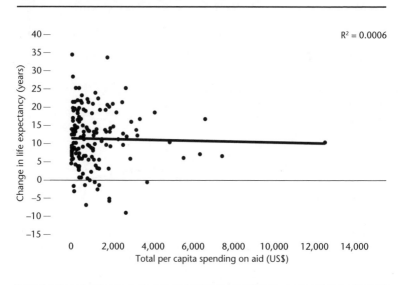

are many possible explanations, some more plausible than others. One commonly cited reason is that aid has been used to further foreign policy objectives rather than development. That is true, but it was also partly true of the Marshall Plan money, which was given preferentially to those countries that aligned themselves with the USA. And in any case, aid that was given ostensibly for development purposes does not appear to have been more successful in actually promoting development than aid given in furtherance of foreign policy objectives. Both have failed equally badly.

Another reason is that aid has been centrally planned by governments – and central planning doesn't work (Easterly, 2006). Development takes place as a result of millions of individuals transacting in markets. These transactions result in the creation of important information, including the establishment of prices for goods and services. Such market prices act as signals to entrepreneurs, who seek opportunities to profit, innovating new products and new production processes. The result is better, cheaper products. In economic jargon, the production possibility frontier is pushed outward. Wealth and average incomes rise.

Central planners do not have access to the decentralised information that is available to individual entrepreneurs operating in markets, so they set prices incorrectly and make mistakes about which goods and services to produce using what factors of production. There is little or no incentive within such systems to identify and develop new products or production processes. There are typically huge inefficiencies and horrendous levels of waste, not to mention environmental damage. Growth occurs very slowly, if at all.[5]

The curse of aid

Perhaps the most important reason for its failure, however, is that aid, like natural resources (Sala-i-Martin and Subramanian, 2003), becomes a 'curse', undermining rather than promoting economic development. There are numerous possible explanations for this phenomenon, including:

1. 'Dutch disease': this is the phenomenon whereby inflows from aid or receipts from the sale of natural resources distort the local economy by increasing the value of the local currency, making locally produced goods less competitive. The paradoxical effect is that low-income jobs are particularly adversely affected, undermining the prospects of the very people who arguably most need help.
2. Moral hazard: the prospect of future bailouts from international donors undermines incentives to utilise aid in ways that lead to economic growth. (This leads to what is known as the 'Samaritan's dilemma', since donors may feel obliged to help even though they know that their assistance is doing no good.)

---

5   See, for example, the various essays in Morris (2001).

3. Rent-seeking: individuals and groups seek to obtain their slice of the aid pie. Aid becomes a means of promoting patronage and feathering the nests of the incumbent political elite. Moreover, by enabling politicians to fund activities without recourse to taxpayers, it undermines democratic constraints on bad behaviour and disincentivises political and institutional reform (Moss et al., 2006).

Recent scholarly work has focused especially on this last factor.[6] The most comprehensive and persuasive of these analyses is that of Simeon Djankov, Jose Montalvo and Marta Reynal-Querol (Djankov et al., 2008). Using panel data (a combination of cross-sectional and time series data), Djankov et al. found that countries with higher levels of aid as a percentage of GDP tended to be significantly less 'democratic' – i.e. have institutions that were significantly less responsive to the concerns of their citizens and with fewer means of limiting autocratic power – than countries with lower levels of aid. And they tended to grow less quickly. Importantly, Djankov et al. found that higher levels of aid tended to be *followed* by poorer governance, suggesting a causal link.

The new paternalism

While the potential for such an institutional aid curse is widely accepted, the fervent belief that we must give to those apparently in need seems to blind many to the intractable nature of the problem.

In the past decade, billions of dollars have been given to the governments of poor countries on the premise that those governments have done the right thing. There was a twin premise to such giving: first, some evidence suggested aid was effective when given to governments with good institutions (Burnside and Dollar, 2000); secondly, good behaviour should be rewarded.

In a sense, this is a new take on an old modus operandi. Aid has

---

6   For an overview, see, for example, Brautigam and Knack (2004).

often been given in a conditional manner – such as support of the donor country's foreign policy or trade policy. Recipient governments have often been expected or required to spend some proportion of the aid they received on companies based in donor countries. In the 1980s, the World Bank and the IMF attempted to make aid conditional on macroeconomic improvements in recipient countries. Sometimes these 'structural adjustment programmes' had benefits, but often they were counterproductive; for example, balanced budget requirements were met by raising taxes and tariffs, instead of streamlining bloated bureaucracies. More often, they were simply ignored and, because the donor agency's interest lay in increasing (not decreasing) the size of their loan books, there was effectively no penalty.

The main difference with the new paternalism is that it focuses more on the micro-foundations of development – the institutions that underpin economic growth, such as well-defined and readily enforceable property rights, easily and cheaply enforced contracts, the absence of egregious government intervention in markets, and so on. The most ambitious attempt to implement this new paternalism is the Millennium Challenge Accounts, a US government project under which aid is ostensibly given only to governments that meet a minimum level on a set of governance-related criteria.

While arguably more rational in its focus, there are two problems with the new paternalism. First, the evidence that aid works when it is given to good governments turns out to be rather flimsy. Indeed, while the aforementioned analysis, by Craig Burnside and David Dollar, appeared to show a positive effect of aid over the period 1970 to 1993, a subsequent analysis by Bill Easterly, Ross Levine and David Roodman, extending the time frame to 1997 and adding some omitted data, eliminated any positive effect – suggesting it was merely an artifact of the data set chosen by Burnside and Dollar (Easterly et al., 2004). Secondly, it turns out to be extraordinarily difficult to structure aid in a way that actually incentivises good governance rather than the opposite: Rajan and Subramanian found 'no evidence that aid works better in better policy or geographical environments, or that certain forms of aid work better than others' (Rajan and Subramanian, 2008: n. 11).

The experience of Uganda, formerly a poster boy for good governance, shows how damaging aid can be. When Museveni came to power in 1987, following the devastating genocidal reign of Idi Amin (who allegedly spent around $1.5 billion of US and UK aid money on weapons), Uganda was in dire economic straits. Museveni implemented numerous economic reforms, such as opening the country to trade, stabilising the money supply, and removing some of the egregious restrictions on entrepreneurial activity. The consequence was a marked improvement in the nation's economy.

In 1998 and 2000, Uganda was given debt relief through the World Bank's Highly Indebted Poor County (HIPC) initiative. Overall, around $2 billion of the country's $3.2 billion in debts was written off. The World Bank's justification was that Uganda had created a 'good policy environment', which had led to sustained economic growth. Though, as Andrew Mwenda points out, the Bank also had a secondary and seemingly inconsistent justification that the debt burden was unsustainable (Mwenda, 2006).

If the debt burden really was unsustainable, then one would expect Uganda to have used the write-off to reduce its level of indebtedness. Instead, it continued to borrow heavily, with average inflows of aid in the six years after 1998 being greater than the average inflows of aid in the six previous years. Moreover, as Mwenda points out, instead of leveraging its reward for good behaviour to support further reforms, the government

> indulged the political elite and the military. It bought a jet for the president at a cost of US$35 million. The government also launched military adventures in Sudan and Congo. Consequently, Ugandan military spending almost doubled from US$110 million in 2000 to US$200 million in 2005. ... The Ministry of Finance 'Public Expenditure Review' of 2002 showed that the costs of political patronage increased by 16 per cent per annum from 1998 on. (Ibid.: 5–6)

But this is not a new problem. In his brilliant *Equality, the Third World, and Economic Delusion* (1981), Lord Bauer noted numerous examples of aid being given to military dictatorships, including the government of Vietnam in the late 1970s when it was forcibly suppressing all private economic activity; Idi Amin, while he was systematically murdering the Ugandan people; and Mengistu, while he was murdering and starving the people of Ethiopia. More recently, Paul Collier has estimated that around 40 per cent of Africa's military spending 'is inadvertently financed by aid' (Collier, 2008: 103).

Can ODA be spent in ways that do more good than harm?

After their rather pessimistic assessment of the historical impact of aid, Rajan and Subramanian observe that 'Our findings, which relate to the past, do not imply that aid cannot be beneficial in the future. But they do suggest that for aid to be effective in the future, the aid apparatus will have to be rethought.' A high priority in this respect would be to ensure that aid is not a curse.

For Djankov et al., one way to reduce the curse of aid would be to reduce the proportion of GDP represented by aid. Since the aid curse is worse for countries where aid represents a higher percentage of GDP, a reduction in that percentage would be expected to reduce the problem. This depends, however, on the reduction being made in a credible way. If recipient governments believe that donors will increase aid again if their country is seen to be suffering, the effect would be minimal. Moreover, if less aid leads to better outcomes, then why not simply end aid altogether?

Unfortunately, the prospects for eliminating aid seem distant. The aid bureaucracy in rich countries and the sycophantic aid-dependent NGOs have spent considerable resources promoting their well-intentioned but sadly largely counterproductive enterprise. Politicians have committed themselves to further aid spending, with many pledging to increase the amount of aid they give – as though what matters is inputs rather than outcomes. (To be fair, many of the inputs are predicated on outcomes – such as achieving the Millennium Development Goals – but even accepting the desirability of these outcomes, they are most unlikely to result from the proposed inputs.)

In such an environment, alternative solutions should perhaps be considered. Tim Harford and Michael Klein suggest that aid should either be supplied through non-governmental actors, or be made contingent on outputs (Harford and Klein, 2005). Either way, aid should in principle be less open to abuse: if the aid does not go into government coffers, then officials cannot misuse it (though merely channelling aid through private companies does not necessarily prevent it from being extracted by government officials); meanwhile, if aid is disbursed only when specific performance criteria are met, then in principle it would be easier to control its use.

Given the pervasive nature of the aid curse, it would be irresponsible for governments in wealthy countries to continue to supply aid to governments in poor countries without attaching very specific conditions on its use. But such conditions are often ignored, or structured in such a way that the aid is simply used for purposes that would otherwise require the use of tax funds. Moreover, donor countries rarely restrict aid when conditions are breached. So the only realistic option is to reduce the amount of aid that is given directly to governments.

That leaves us with the first option: provide aid through the private sector. Requests for proposals for the supply of specific services could be very clearly defined and offered to the lowest bidder that meets a set of criteria.[7] This would at least ensure that specific objectives could be met in an efficient manner without undermining democratic accountability. It is at least possible that such spending could improve the lot of the poor – if the specific goals are appropriately defined.

The problem even with this kind of aid is that the goals are likely to focus on short-term deliverables that do not necessarily enhance

---

7   For some examples of this in practice, see Stevens (2008).

the long-term prospects for development. Unfortunately, spending by aid agencies tends to be biased towards the obsessions of lobbyists in rich countries. As a result, vast amounts are spent on education, AIDS treatment and environmental issues. Yet such spending is at best highly inefficient and at worst counterproductive (for example, various aid agencies have funded campaigns to promote 'organic' agriculture, even though the use of such methods typically results in lower yields, reduces farm income, and leads to more extensive farming, reducing the land available for wildlife).

We know that the institutional environment is of utmost importance in creating the conditions for growth.[8] (Broadly speaking, the ability to own and exchange property without arbitrary or excessive interference from government is the most important condition.[9]) Yet without reform to the local agenda-setting process, aid spending is unlikely to significantly improve the institutional environment. The training of judges, for example, is not an activity that has a large constituency in rich countries, so is not high on most government aid agendas, yet it might well be the best way to inculcate the rule of law, which we know is of fundamental importance.

The 0.7 per cent solution

The UK government currently faces an unprecedented budget crisis. If it fails to curb government spending, the national debt will spiral upwards, imposing an unbearable burden on future taxpayers, stifling growth and perhaps leading to a mass migration of talent to more welcoming shores. In spite of this predicament, the government has committed itself to increase spending on ODA.

---

8   There is a seemingly endless literature on this, but I recommend especially Rodrik et al. (2004).
9   http://www.voxeu.org/index.php?q=node/568.

Table 13 **Proposed UK ODA spending, 2010–14**

Year	2010	2011	2012	2013	2014	Total
Amount (£bn)	8.4	8.7	9.1	12.0	12.6	50.8
ODA/GNI (%)	0.56	0.56	0.56	0.70	0.70	

Source: HM Treasury (2010: 60)

As Table 13 shows, Britain's coalition government recently committed itself to spending 0.7 per cent of Gross National Income (GNI) on ODA by 2013. Its justification for this input target is that 0.7 per cent is a UN General Assembly resolution from 1970 (which committed 'each economically advanced country' to meet the 0.7 per cent commitment by the mid-1970s).

The notion that rich countries should spend 0.7 per cent of their GNI on aid to developing countries is predicated on the investment gap theory. The 0.7 per cent figure was a back-of-the-envelope calculation based on a presumption of the scale of the 'gap'. A recent analysis using the same methodology 'yields an aid goal of just 0.01 per cent of rich-country GDP for the poorest countries and negative aid flows to the developing world as a whole' (Clemens and Moss, 2005). In other words, the 0.7 per cent solution has no empirical basis and should be scrapped.

Moreover, the investment gap theory has itself been discredited by the finding that what actually matters is the institutional environment. If a country is politically stable, has sound money and well-defined, readily enforceable and transferable property rights, a government that is not overbearing and does not interfere in an arbitrary, capricious or corrupt manner and is subject to the rule of law, then entrepreneurs will both create capital and attract capital inflows that will drive innovation and development.

If the British government wants to ensure that aid does more good than harm, the first thing it should do is reverse its decision to increase aid spending.

Aid to cut and aid to keep

There may be a role for government to provide some limited assistance to people in poor countries during emergencies. Given the sporadic nature of such emergencies, we advocate establishing a fund that would receive an annual allocation but would pay out only during emergencies. The amount to be spent could be determined by matching private donations. Perhaps it would amount to a few hundred million pounds; a considerable amount but small compared with today's aid budget. In order to ensure that such monies are spent in a cost-effective and accountable way, disbursements should be made through an open and transparent process of competitive tender, preferably a minimum-criterion (hurdle-based) low-bid auction open to both for-profit and not-for-profit entrants.

But so-called 'development aid' should be scrapped and the budget used to cut taxes. So, in financial year 2014/15, that would mean cutting the aid budget by about £12 billion – or about £200 for every man, woman and child in Britain. Taxpayers can then choose whether or not to spend their money on projects that might or might not help people in poor countries. If we were individually responsible for allocating the money currently spent on aid we would take more care to ensure that it is spent wisely. We might choose to put some of it into funds such as Kiva,[10] which invest in entrepreneurs in poor countries. We might choose to donate to a charity such as Mercy Corps[11] or Network for a Free Society,[12] which support market solutions to economic development. Or we might simply buy things with it. China and India are not growing rich as a result of aid; if anything they are growing rich in spite of it – by selling goods and services to us, to each other and to everyone else on the planet.

10   www.kiva.org.
11   www.mercycorps.org.
12   www.freesocieties.org.

Conclusion

The substantial increase in ODA spending in the past decade – both by Britain and by some other countries – can be seen as a response to campaigns run by anti-poverty groups, public intellectuals and, of course, those noted development experts, rock stars. These campaigns claim that such spending is necessary to reduce poverty and improve livelihoods in other countries. The foregoing analysis shows that not only is this not true but that increased government spending on development aid is likely to be counterproductive. I hope that I am proved wrong.

References

Bauer, P. T. (1981), *Equality, the Third World, and Economic Delusion*, Cambridge, MA: Harvard University Press.

Brautigam, D. and S. Knack (2004), 'Foreign aid, institutions and governance in sub-Saharan Africa', *Economic Development and Cultural Change*, 52(2): 255–86.

Burnside, C. and D. Dollar (2000), 'Aid, policies, and growth', *American Economic Review*, 90(4): 847–68.

Clemens, M. A. and T. J. Moss (2005), *Ghost of 0.7%: Origins and Relevance of the International Aid Target*, Working Paper 68, Washington, DC: Center for Global Development, www.cgdev.org/content/publications/detail/3822, accessed 5 October 2010.

Collier, P. (2008), *The Bottom Billion*, Oxford: Oxford University Press.

Djankov, S., J. Montalvo and M. Reynal-Querol (2008), 'The curse of aid', *Journal of Economic Growth*, 13(3): 169–94.

Easterly, W. (2006), 'Planners vs. searchers in foreign aid', *Asian Development Review*, 23(2): 1–35.

Easterly, W., R. Levine and D. Roodman (2004), 'New data, new doubts: a comment on Burnside and Dollar's "Aid, policies, and growth"', *American Economic Review*, 94(3): 774–80.

Grogin, R. C. (2001), *Natural Enemies: The United States and the Soviet Union in the Cold War, 1917–1991*, New York: Lexington Books.

Harford, T. and M. Klein (2005), 'Aid and the resource curse: how can
    aid be designed to preserve institutions?', *Public Policy Journal*,
    April, Washington, DC: World Bank.
HM Treasury (2010), *Spending Review 2010*, London: The Stationery
    Office.
Hubbard, R. G. and W. Duggan (2008), 'The forgotten lessons of the
    Marshall Plan', *Strategy + Business*, Summer, www.strategy-business.
    com/press/article/08203?pg=all.
Morris, J. (ed.) (2001), *Sustainable Development: Promoting Progress or
    Perpetuating Poverty*, London: Profile Books.
Moss, T., G. Pettersson and N. van de Walle (2006), 'An aid-institutions
    paradox? A review essay on aid dependency and state building
    in sub-Saharan Africa', Working Paper 74, Washington, DC:
    Center for Global Development, http://www.cgdev.org/content/
    publications/detail/5646/.
Mwenda, A. (2006), 'Foreign aid and the weakening of democratic
    accountability in Uganda', Foreign Policy Briefing no. 88,
    Washington, DC: Cato Institute.
Rajan, R. G. and A. Subramanian (2005), 'What undermines aid's
    impact on growth?', IMF Working Paper 05/126, Washington, DC:
    International Monetary Fund.
Rajan, R. G. and A. Subramanian (2008), 'Aid and growth: what does
    the cross-country evidence really show?', *Review of Economics and
    Statistics*, 90(4): 643–65.
Rodrik, D., A. Subramanian and F. Trebbi (2004), 'Institutions rule: the
    primacy of institutions over geography and integration in economic
    development', *Journal of Economic Growth*, 9(2): 131–65.
Sala-i-Martin, X. and A. Subramanian (2003), 'Addressing the natural
    resource curse: an illustration from Nigeria', IMF Working Paper
    03/019, Washington, DC: International Monetary Fund.
Stevens, P. (2008), *Foreign Aid for Health: Moving beyond Government*,
    London: Campaign for Fighting Diseases, www.fightingdiseases.org.

9 TRANSFORMING WELFARE – INCENTIVES, LOCALISATION AND NON-DISCRIMINATION

Kristian Niemietz

Introduction

In 2006, the UK's net expenditure on social protection benefits amounted to 25 per cent of GDP (Eurostat, 2009a). This is not just a remarkable share by domestic historical standards. It also contradicts a common international classification, which counts the UK among the so-called 'basic security welfare states', as opposed to the – supposedly much more encompassing – Scandinavian and Continental welfare regimes (British Social Attitudes Survey, 2010). Yet as far as aggregate social spending is concerned, the UK now belongs to the European Economic Area's top group: see Table 14.

Table 14 **Net government spending on social transfer benefits (% of GDP), selected EEA countries**

% of GDP	
>25%	Austria, Belgium, France, Germany, Sweden, UK
20–25%	Denmark, Finland, Italy, Netherlands, Norway
15–20%	Iceland, Ireland, Luxembourg, Spain

Source: Eurostat (2009a)

It may, at first sight, seem counterintuitive that spending on social transfers is so much higher today than half a century ago given that real incomes of the bottom deciles have almost doubled since then (based on Institute for Fiscal Studies data, 2010a). But welfare has long ceased to be a 'safety net', in the sense of a last-resort provider of temporary assistance in exceptional situations. As will be shown below, government transfers have become a regular income source for people at just about every point of the income distribution. Indeed, it has become almost impossible *not* to be a transfer recipient at some stage in life.

So in welfare reform, there is no such thing as a 'disinterested party'. There is hardly a voting bloc which does not have its own cherished benefit, allowance, discount, premium or something else at stake. From a public choice perspective, the extent of coverage of a spending programme is a much better predictor of its popularity than its net distributional impact. There are largely two sets of reasons for this. The first set can be summarised under the heading of 'fiscal illusions'. It was first articulated by Puviani (1903, translation from 1960), and systematised by Buchanan (1999 [1967]). The structure of public expenditure and revenue creates systematic perceptional biases about costs and benefits. Public finances will typically be structured in such a way that benefits are highly visible to the recipient while costs are more dispersed and opaque. Fiscal illusions come in various shapes, and in empirical studies many of them have been found to be powerful explanations of real-world phenomena (for a review of the empirical literature, see Dollary and Worthington, 1996).

Some examples of fiscal illusions clearly apply to welfare states. Recipients will usually be very well aware of the cash transfers they receive, and of the publicly financed services they use. The financing side will be obscured through devices such as indirect taxes, which merge with product prices,[1] contributions which are nominally paid by the employer and debt financing.

Secondly, voting for the retention of a 'middle-class benefit' can be a sensible strategy for self-interested middle-class voters, even if they are fully aware that they are net payers of the benefit. Since there is no direct link between any particular benefit and any particular tax, there is no guarantee that the abolition of a middle-class benefit will lead to a

---

1   For example, an average household in Britain pays £474 per year on 'sin taxes' (taxes on alcohol, tobacco and gambling) and £829 on 'green taxes' (based on data from Office for National Statistics, 2010).

corresponding reduction in middle-class taxes. The benefit is certain; the tax reduction that could correspond with its abolition is not.

Horton and Gregory (2009), who have recently proposed a drastic expansion of the British welfare state, argue in the same vein, albeit using the term 'middle-class buy-in' instead of 'fiscal illusion'. They examine public support for expansions of different types of welfare spending empirically, and find that, with some exceptions, there is a direct relationship between coverage and popularity. Increasing spending on universal or near-universal programmes (e.g. child benefit) is always popular; increasing spending on tightly targeted benefits (e.g. social housing) is not. They thus propose to move away from targeting and extend the coverage of benefits in cash and kind to wide segments of society, because 'while narrowly targeted policies will fail to draw on the strength of middle-class political pressure to defend welfare, policies with wider coverage actively recruit the sharp elbows of the middle class' (ibid.: 85).

This article agrees with Horton and Gregory's analysis of the expansionary effect of middle-class buy-in. But it argues for the precise opposite: i.e. it argues for a reduction of the amount of fiscal illusion in the welfare system, in order to enable a pronounced and lasting contraction of the welfare state's remit. Given that welfare spending is 25 per cent of national income, one wonders where the growth in spending would stop if fiscal illusion were increased.

Income replacement versus work incentives

The most widely discussed trade-off in welfare policy is between the aims of providing income replacement in emergency situations, and of preserving incentives to re-enter the labour market. The two main income replacement tools – Income Support (IS) and Jobseeker's Allowance (JSA) – are not particularly generous by European standards. Nevertheless, for those outside the labour market, financial incentives to re-enter are generally moderate, and can be very weak for some groups.

This is best captured in the replacement rate: the ratio of benefit income without work to disposable income in a realistically attainable occupation. Replacement rates among the economically inactive vary considerably depending on individual characteristics, but the median rate is around 60 per cent. For about a third of the non-employed, they even rise to 70 per cent and higher (see Table 15).

Table 15 **Replacement ratios among the non-employed**

Range of the distribution of the replacement rate	Replacement ratio in that range
Upper half	>60%
Upper third	>70%
Upper tenth	>80%

Source: Adam and Browne (2010)

Across household types, the system's incentive structure is highly polarised. Replacement rates are highest for single parents and parents with a non-employed partner, while being much lower for individuals with a working partner (Adam and Browne, 2010: 16–21). Inasmuch as financial incentives influence labour market decisions, we would thus expect the system to foster a polarised employment structure with many double-earner and many zero-earner households: this is precisely what we do see.

The transition to Universal Credit, which will merge the main out-of-work and in-work benefits from 2014 onwards, will generally lower replacement rates. But the magnitude of the effect will be moderate because the Universal Credit is meant to broadly retain the real level of out-of-work benefits.

Constraining spending versus constraining adverse incentives

The targeting of benefits is used as an instrument to keep welfare spending under control and to have the biggest impact on poverty with a given budget. As we have noted, in the long run, targeting can reduce fiscal illusions that lead to permanent electoral pressure for welfare expansion. For a set of wealthy OECD countries, Korpi and Palme (1998) show that the degree of targeting is inversely related to the size of the welfare budget.

But stringent income targeting comes with a severe side effect. It requires a steep withdrawal of benefits as the recipient's income rises, so it effectively acts like a second income tax on transfer recipients who attempt to progress gradually in the labour market. This effect is often discussed in terms of working hours, but it also leads to disincentives to train, obtain promotion and so on. Levying higher implicit marginal tax rates selectively on *any* population subgroup would be likely to deter that group's progression in the labour market. But levying higher implicit marginal tax rates on the weakest groups in the labour market is almost a guarantee for creating destructive dynamic effects. Indeed, labour market models for the UK context show that the low-skilled and single parents are most susceptible to adverse incentives (Blundell et al., 1998; Meghir and Phillips, 2008).

The inverse relationship between the degree of income targeting and implicit marginal tax rates shows in the comparison of a strictly income-targeted benefit, such as Jobseeker's Allowance (JSA), with a non-targeted one, such as Disability Living Allowance (DLA). JSA is reduced by £1 for every £1 the recipient earns. This makes the circle of recipients much smaller than that of any other benefit: 87 per cent of total spending on JSA goes to people in the bottom three deciles of the income distribution. But it also creates an effective marginal tax rate (EMTR) of 100 per cent, at least over a short range of income. DLA, on the other hand, is not tapered at all and does not therefore elevate EMTRs. But spending on DLA is anything but focused (and is not meant to be): only a quarter of the DLA budget goes to people in the bottom three deciles.

Table 18 will show that huge amounts of welfare spending end up in the pockets of middle- and higher-income groups. But curiously, this does not prevent very high EMTRs. On the contrary: what is characteristic about the present set-up is the *coexistence* of poorly targeted transfer spending with high EMTRs on those in employment. The latter are distributed unevenly across the working population, but, in summary, EMTRs below 40 per cent barely occur at all while a significant minority faces EMTRs above 50 per cent or even above 70 per cent (see Table 16).

Table 16 **EMTRs among the employed**

Range of the distribution of EMTRs	EMTRs in that range
Upper nine-tenths	>40%
Upper fifth	>50%
Upper tenth	>70%

Again, the distribution of EMTRs is highly polarised across household types. For single parents, as well as parents with a non-working partner, rates in excess of 70 per cent are the norm (Adam and Browne, 2010: 21–3). These high rates usually arise through the interaction of income tax, national insurance contributions and the withdrawal of benefits. So again, inasmuch as incentive variables influence employment outcomes, we would expect the system to foster a polarised pattern of labour market progression, with the latter groups being slowed down most.

The introduction of the Universal Credit will not fundamentally change this situation. There will be a sizeable fall in EMTRs for those who currently face the withdrawal of multiple benefits (combined with a tax liability), but this is a relatively small group. In the more common situation of the withdrawal of a single benefit (combined with a tax liability), EMTRs are more likely to remain constant or rise slightly (see Table 17). The taper rates are reduced substantially only for people who currently pay income tax and national insurance and receive working tax credit and housing benefit.

Table 17 **How EMTRs will change after 2014**

Present system Tax/benefit	EMTR	New system (after 2014) Tax/benefit	EMTR
Income tax (IT) + national insurance contribution (NIC) + Working Tax Credit and/or Child Tax Credit (WTC/CTC) taper	73%	Universal Credit taper	65%
		IT + NIC + Universal Credit taper	76%
IT + NIC + Housing Benefit (HB) taper	76%	IT + NIC + Universal Credit taper	76%
IT + NIC + WTC/CTC taper + HB taper	91%	IT + NIC + Universal Credit taper	76%

Contribution versus 'need'

Another common way to classify welfare regimes, or individual programmes within them, is by their way of assigning whether a recipient qualifies for payments. This can be on the basis of a previous contribution record, or on the basis of 'need'. Transfer systems serve two purposes: redistribution and risk provisioning. In need-based welfare systems, the former motive dominates, while the latter dominates in contribution-based systems. In other words, need-based systems are dominated by interpersonal redistribution (i.e. from Jones to Smith), while contributory systems are dominated by 'intrapersonal' redistribution (i.e. from the young/healthy/employed Jones of today to the old/sick/unemployed Jones of tomorrow). The ratio of intrapersonal to interpersonal redistribution in transfer spending is roughly 3:1 in Sweden and Denmark and 1:1 in Australia and Ireland (Sørensen and Bovenberg, 2007: 6–9).

The general advantage of contributory or 'Bismarckian' welfare states is that they provide a direct link between how much people pay into the common pool and how much they are entitled to take out of it. Therefore, social insurance contributions do not provide the same disincentives as taxes. However, Bismarckian welfare programmes are not intended to complement but to fully substitute for private provision.

They therefore tend to be much larger than need-based systems, and more aggressive in crowding out private savings and private insurance. On this measure, the UK's welfare state combines negative features from both regimes – the disincentive effects of needs-based welfare regimes, and the crowding-out effects of Bismarckian ones. In terms of the ratio of intrapersonal to interpersonal redistribution spending, the UK is closer to Scandinavian than to so-called 'Anglo-Saxon' systems (ibid.), so the larger part of welfare spending merely replaces functions that could readily be provided by private financial intermediaries. At the same time, the weight of transfer payments that bear a strong relationship to the recipient's past contribution record is very small (see Brewer, 2009). To all intents and purposes, national insurance contributions are little else but a second income tax.

The present coalition has thus far not announced anything to rectify this situation. Of the £7 billion welfare savings that have been announced in the CSR, £2 billion will come from time-limiting the receipt of contributory Employment and Support Allowance (ESA). This will further erode the contributory principle, but without facilitating an expansion of private insurance-based alternatives.

High spending, poor outcomes

Welfare provision has long ceased to be a 'safety net'. For at least a third of the population, the state has become the main financial provider, and it continues to be an important income source even for middle- and high-income strata. It should be noted that the figures in Table 18 substantially understate the role of government welfare provision in most people's economic lives. ONS figures rely on large-scale surveys, and it is well known that benefits are significantly under-reported in survey responses. For example, grossing up the ONS's 2008/09 figures for Housing Benefit, it would appear that UK households have received a total of £13.1 billion in Housing Benefit payments (Department for Work and Pensions and Office for National Statistics, 2010). However, judging from Department for Work and Pensions (DWP) data, around £17.1 billion must have been paid out during 2008/09 (DWP Statistics, 2011).

Table 18 **Benefits by income decile, £, 2008/09**

Decile	Non-contributory benefits	Contributory benefits	Benefits in kind
1st	3,200	2,300	6,600
2nd	4,000	3,400	6,100
3rd	3,900	4,000	6,800
4th	3,600	3,700	6,000
5th	3,100	3,400	6,000
6th	2,400	2,700	6,000
7th	1,900	2,500	5,200
8th	1,000	1,900	4,800
9th	700	1,200	4,200
10th	500	1,200	3,600

Source: Office for National Statistics (2010)

Why is it a problem if the state becomes a key breadwinner and service provider for large segments of society? Apart from problems of dependency, from a 'Hayekian' or classical liberal perspective, the main objection to an omnipresent transfer state is that it crowds out alternative, potentially superior, ways of making provision against risks, and smoothing consumption over the life cycle. As with most goods and services, no single institution can know in advance which way of delivering these things works best, in which setting and for which people. Removing the state from large areas of welfare provision is not just about 'cutting benefits', but about enabling competition at various levels: non-profit versus for-profit organisations; specialised versus integrated providers; small independent providers versus large chains, etc. Historically, many of the functions that are performed by the welfare state today have been fully or partially privately provided (Seldon, 1996). But competition is not possible when one provider can rely on coercive funding and deliver 'free' services. If a discovery process in welfare provision is to be unleashed, with consumers as sovereigns, then the role of

Figure 7   **Workless households – UK and EU**

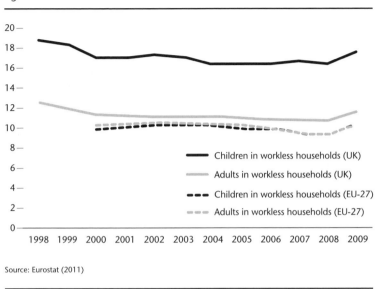

Source: Eurostat (2011)

the state must be diminished to that of a provider of last resort.

These considerations apply most clearly to areas like healthcare and old-age provision, which are very complex products that could be provided in many different ways. But to some extent, they are also applicable to the more conventional areas of welfare such as unemployment insurance, income replacement and poverty prevention. The British welfare state does not appear to fulfil these tasks well. In 2010, there were 5.45 million recipients of out-of-work benefits, 2.84 million of whom were long-term (>2 years) recipients (New Policy Institute, 2011). Yet what sets the UK apart from other European countries is not the overall *level* of economic inactivity, but its cross-household distribution. The UK has an above-average proportion of workless *households*, or working-age households with no member in gainful employment. Above all, no other European country has such a large share of children living in workless households (Eurostat, 2009a). It is remarkable that even the decade of strong labour market performance up to 2008, coupled with expensive employment policies, has not come anywhere near over-coming this situation: see Figure 7.

Alongside concentrated long-term worklessness, chronic under-employment is also widespread, often affecting the same population subgroups. In 37 per cent of all households with children receiving Working Tax Credit (WTC), the main breadwinner works fewer than 24 hours per week. Among single-parent recipient households, that share is 50 per cent (Office for National Statistics & HM Revenue and Customs, 2010). Underemployment is the main explanation for the often-heard claim that the number of the 'working poor' is increasing.

In its present structure, the welfare system creates worklessness, underemployment and dependency. The group that the present system fails worst is single parents and their children. In most European countries, the share of children living in single-parent families is between 10 and 15 per cent (UNICEF, 2007) and employment rates of single parents are between 70 and 80 per cent (Eurostat, 2009b; HM Treasury & Department for Work and Pensions, 2010). Countries outside this range fall into two categories: countries where single parenthood is very prevalent and almost all of them are employed (e.g. the Scandinavian and Baltic countries), or countries where the employment rate among single parents is low but there are few of them (e.g. Belgium). The situation of the UK is exceptional in Europe insofar as it combines one of the highest shares of single-parent households, and by far the lowest employment rate among them. We have a welfare system that encourages single parenthood and discourages single parents from working. In the UK, around 17 per cent of all children live with a single parent (UNICEF, 2007), and only 56 per cent of these parents are in some form of employment (Eurostat, 2009b).

The coalition's welfare reforms: so far so good

The coalition has announced a series of welfare measures in the Budget 2010, the CSR, the DWP's White Paper and the Welfare Reform Bill.

They contain elements which are likely to rectify some of the problems identified above, especially with the introduction of the Universal Credit (UC). The UC's main achievement is that it will greatly reduce the uncertainty and risk associated with both moving into work, and lengthening the working week. In the present system, taking up work means replacing a secure form of income with an insecure one. Out-of-work benefits, once an application has been granted, are open-ended, while income from a job is not. If the job turns out to be short-lived, people have to go through the lengthy benefits application process again. For people in minor employment faced with the decision to lengthen their working week, the variability of EMTRs can make it difficult to predict what the pay-off will be. The common response to uncertainty is inertia. The Universal Credit, with its single application process and single taper rate, will largely put an end to this aspect of the poverty trap. The introduction of sanctions in the event of failure to comply with job search requirements will also make welfare spending more focused.

Nevertheless, the government's claim that, under the UC, it will always pay to work has to be rejected. Since the UC will bridge the current system's gap between out-of-work benefits and in-work benefits, it will always pay – somewhat – to work *for a small number of hours*. But as Table 17 shows, the pay-off from moving on from there will remain weak.

As far as the magnitude of the fiscal savings in welfare is concerned, the projected total annual savings of £18 billion by 2014/15 look impressive at first sight. But it must be noted that about half of these savings will come from changes to uprating and so on. This chapter suggests a more radical approach.

Changes to the benefit system
Curtailing middle-class benefits

So far, the coalition has proposed limiting child benefit in an incoherent way while making few fiscal savings. Here it is proposed that all universal benefits cease. Table 19 summarises the fiscal cost of non-contributory benefits paid to people in the upper half of the income distribution. It provides an absolute lower bound for the fiscal savings that could be achieved by making transfer spending more focused. It is *not* the purpose of this chapter to present numerical values for parameters such as taper rates and thresholds of an alternative tax and benefit system. Therefore, Table 19 ignores the income range over which benefits would be tapered. Nor does it account for the substantial degree of benefit under-reporting, which cannot be allocated to specific ranges of the income distribution.

Table 19 **Non-contributory transfer payments to people in the upper half of the distribution of equivalised incomes, 2008/09**

	Annual amount received by the upper half of the income distribution (£bn)
Benefits in cash	
Income support and pension credit	2.2
Child benefit	4.7
Income-based Jobseeker's Allowance	0.1
Student support	0.4
Non-contributory incapacity-related benefits (except for severe disability)	4.3
Other non-contributory cash benefits	1.1
Benefits in kind	
Housing subsidy	0.2
Rail travel subsidy	1.1
Bus travel subsidy	1.1
Total cash and kind	15.2

Source: Office for National Statistics (2010)

However, we cannot curtail middle-class benefits alone. Some have evolved for good reason. For example, when the tax credit taper rate was lowered, the – entirely sensible – motivation was to improve work incentives for low earners. Technically, the easiest way to constrict benefit entitlement to those on the lowest incomes would be to steepen taper rates severely. But since this would be tantamount to a drastic increase in EMTRs for many, this mechanism would almost certainly create adverse dynamic effects. Curtailing middle-class benefits remains a valuable aim, but the devil is in the *mechanism* by which they are being curtailed: this will be discussed later.

Flat-rate housing benefits

It has been mentioned that while standard rates of income replacement benefits are not particularly generous, replacement ratios can nevertheless be very high, weakening financial incentives to take up work. The gap is largely explained by Housing Benefit (HB) and exacerbated by Council Tax Benefit. Recipients do not have command over these earmarked benefits, but they are withdrawn with net income, and therefore drive up replacement ratios and EMTRs. Their fiscal costs are also huge. In 2010/11, the government spent £21.5 billion on HB (DWP Statistics, 2011). That represents a real-term increase of 49 per cent compared with a decade earlier.

The CSR and the Budget 2010 contained a series of measures aimed at limiting Housing Benefit payments. Hitherto, HB rates have been set equal to local median rents, so that, in theory, half of all available homes in every locality were accessible to HB recipients without a rent co-payment. This is now being lowered to local rents at the 30th percentile of the distribution of rents, so that the share of homes available to HB recipients without a rent co-payment falls to three out of ten. Also, HB payments are being lowered by some arbitrary ceilings on payments and the size of property for which a claim can be made. Taken together, these measures are expected to lead to major fiscal savings. But they do not address the underlying dynamics that have led to the cost explosion in Housing Benefit in the first place. These underlying dynamics include very high UK house prices arising from the land use planning system and the very poor incentive structure that exists within the HB system.

The amount of HB a recipient is entitled to is pegged to market rent levels in a specified area: the so-called 'Broad Rental Market Area' (BRMA). While it is clear that HB rates must take account of local variations in housing costs, the net of BRMAs is so tight that it makes the HB system effectively operate like a full-cost reimbursement scheme. Great Britain is divided into 193 BRMAs and Greater London alone accounts for twelve (Local Housing Allowance Direct, 2010).[2] Cost reimbursement systems provide no incentive for recipients to economise on housing costs. Moving from an average-priced one-bedroom flat in Inner North London to one in Outer Northeast London would cut rental costs by almost £5,000 per year, for example. But it would cut a recipient's HB entitlement by exactly the same amount. As a result of this, Housing Benefit recipients tend to be highly over-represented in high-rent areas.

The government's measures leave this defective payment structure in place, and essentially ignore the importance of economic incentives. The Universal Credit will not address the shortcomings of HB either; it will merely unite HB under a common roof with other transfers without changing its structure. A better alternative would consist of moving away from quasi-reimbursement, and converting Housing Benefit into flat-rate payments. This could be achieved by slashing the number of BRMAs to twelve. Within each BRMA, the benefit would be paid out as a lump sum depending on household type only.

Recipients would then begin to make trade-offs between housing and other goods, just as those who do not receive housing benefit do. If they saved rental costs by relocating, they would be able to keep the full amount. If they incurred additional rental costs, they would have to pay in full. This would give policymakers an effective tool to control costs. Recipients would be encouraged to become cost-conscious; they could respond by gradually moving to cheaper areas, moving to cheaper accommodation within a given area, and/or increasing work search efforts. In some areas, there would also be a downward pressure on rent levels.

---

2   That is 152 BRMAs for England, twelve for Wales and eighteen for Scotland, with Northern Ireland running a separate system.

Further savings are possible. The British safety net for housing consists of a mix of cash payments of housing benefit to households and state-subsidised houses (object subsidies). The latter occurs in the form of subsidised and regulated social housing. Economic arguments for object subsidies are generally weak. State-sponsored 'social housing' as a distinct tenure, separate from the regular housing market, should be ended. Object subsidies should be converted into subject subsidies, and subjected to across-the-board spending cuts of the type described above. All the lettable housing stock would move to the private sector, with all landlords and housing associations being subject to the same regulatory framework. All landlords would then have to compete for tenants, instead of fulfilling governmental targets (see King, 2006: 113–23). This would mean genuine choice and empowerment for tenants.

Bringing HB spending back to its level of just a decade earlier (£14.4 billion in 2010/11 prices) would be a modest benchmark. HB spending would then be £5.5 billion below the level envisaged for 2014/15 (£6 billion in 2014/15 prices). This should be considered an absolute lower bound for the savings that can be achieved in the area of housing provision for the poor. It does not even consider the savings that could be made in the areas of social housing or Council Tax Benefit.

Full-time work conditionality for in-work benefits

There are three main ways to limit expenditure on transfer programmes: lowering the maximum payout to the poorest people; steepening the taper rate at which the transfer is withdrawn; or tightening eligibility criteria to qualify for the transfer.

So far, the coalition has used a combination of these methods but avoided the most important approach to tightening the conditions for receiving benefits: that of placing work expectations on recipients as a precondition for transfer entitlement. This can apply to both out-of-work and in-work benefits. The basic logic here is to make receipt of a benefit conditional on a course of action which reduces that very benefit's own necessity. In other words, transfers should be designed in such a way that instead of crowding out recipients' self-help efforts, they would 'crowd them in', by making self-help the very condition of entitlement.

There is one measure in the coalition's welfare savings package which is indeed compatible with this logic: the increase in the minimum working hours requirement to qualify for Working Tax Credit (WTC). WTC is a work-contingent means-tested benefit; adults with children currently have to work at least sixteen hours per week to qualify. For two-parent families, this threshold is now being raised to twenty-four hours per week. The rationale behind this measure is clear: WTC payments fall with hours worked, making those who work for sixteen hours a week or just above the most 'expensive' recipients. Raising the minimum work requirement does not mean striking them from the rolls, but incentivising them to increase their workload to at least twenty-four hours. This would not decrease their income but change its composition, with the share of earned income increasing and the share of transfer income decreasing. Their earned income would increase to a level where they can no longer claim the full amount of WTC – this is where the savings come from. Ideally, this will create a 'double dividend' of higher incomes for low earners *and* lower government spending.

The very opposite is true for the coalition's above-indexation increases in Child Tax Credit (CTC), which have been motivated by the desire to mitigate the short-term impact of other welfare changes on child poverty (HM Treasury, 2010a: 34, 69). It is difficult to argue against a policy aimed at keeping child poverty low, but the government's measures of child poverty are so misleading that this aim is not as laudable as it sounds (see Niemietz, 2011). The costs, in any case, are substantial: spending on CTC will rise by nearly £2.6 billion in 2014/15. Perhaps more importantly, since CTC is not work-contingent, increases in CTC raise replacement ratios. This is especially true for groups with the weakest labour market attachment, for whom the impact is largest since CTC represents a large share of their total household income. These are precisely the 'targeted' policies encouraged by income-based poverty measures, but they create adverse dynamic effects. Applying the do-no-harm principle to budgetary policies would have implied raising CTC only in line with inflation. As one of the most promising elements of the savings package, the coalition should have taken its approach to WTC a lot farther. In the short term, this could mean applying the higher work requirement to *all* WTC recipients, not just two-parent families. Of the 0.7 million WTC recipient households working between sixteen and twenty-four hours, 0.5 million are single-parent households (Office for National Statistics & HM Revenue and Customs, 2010). Subsequently, the minimum working hours requirement should be applied to other in-work benefits (in the course of merging them into a single transfer). The number of working hours required should then be raised to a workload close to full-time employment. If this happens alongside labour market liberalisation facilitating job creation, increasing the likelihood that those seeking work can actually find work, the above-described double dividend could be reaped many times over. Indeed, if £0.4 billion can be saved by expecting a higher workload from just 0.2 million households, then surely at least the same amount could be realised by expecting a higher workload from another 0.5 million households.

In the long run, making in-work benefits contingent on full-time employment for the vast majority of working-age recipients could be the way to square the circle of simultaneously achieving well-targeted, tightly focused transfer spending *and* low EMTRs. Since in-work support would no longer have to replace the pay of entire workdays, the maximum amount could be much lower to begin with, which would make a low withdrawal rate feasible without in-work support turning into a middle-class benefit.

There are two options for treating part-time employment in this system of conditionality. One is to introduce a time limit for the receipt of in-work benefits for part-time employees. After the expiry of the time limit, part-time employees would have to switch to full-time employment, or cease to receive any transfer payments. A second option is to assess entitlement to in-work support on the basis of full-time equivalent earnings – that is, not on part-time employees' face-value income, but on the income they would receive if they were in full-time employment. Transfer income of part-time employees would then not fall (rise) if they increased (decreased) their working hours. In isolation, raising the bar for the receipt of in-work support would, of course, only push part-time employees receiving tax credits into worklessness. The above must go in tandem with a wholesale reform of out-of-work support for working-age households.

A Negative Income Tax as an alternative to the Universal Credit

As mentioned above, a longer-lasting approach to restoring the public finances would consist of uncovering the fiscal illusions that feed the demand for ever-increasing volumes of income transfers. In the UK's transfer system, this applies especially to the large amount of 'churning', which occurs when people pay direct taxes and receive cash transfers at the same time (so that they effectively pay for their own transfers). The volume of churning could be substantially reduced in a fiscally neutral way. The first step would be to convert transfers that can be received while in work into a Friedmanite 'Negative Income Tax' (NIT). The basic idea of a NIT is simple: suppose the tax-free allowance is 150 gold coins and the tax rate is 20 per cent. A household earning 200 gold coins would then pay 20 per cent of (200 – 150) = 10 coins in 'positive income tax', while a household earning 100 gold coins would pay 20 per cent of (100 – 150) = –10 coins. That is, the latter household would *receive* 10 gold coins in NIT. A NIT can, of course, have multiple rates, just like the positive income tax.

At present, most recipients of tax credits are also taxpayers and NIC payers, just as most recipients of UC will be. In crude aggregate terms, only the bottom three deciles of the income distribution are net beneficiaries of tax credits plus child benefit, receiving more in the form of these transfers than they pay in income tax and NIC. But even for the bottom decile, the aggregate amount of 'churning' is considerable, with about one third of the payments received in tax credits and child benefit being clawed back in the form of income tax and NIC (based on data from the Office for National Statistics, 2010). This situation would be impossible under a NIT, where the amounts to which recipients are entitled would depend on the distance between their income and the tax-free allowance. By definition, a household receiving payments through the NIT system would be a household the income of which falls below the allowance.

In the present tax and benefit system, there is also a nonsensical duality regarding the unit of account: tax liability is assessed at the individual level, while benefit entitlement is assessed at the household level. This produces several anomalies, including heavy penalties on the formation of joint households. Such anomalies would be eliminated in a NIT system, where positive and negative taxes have to deal with the same unit of account. In other words, a NIT would require that tax allowances are allocated to *households* instead of to individuals, with the size of the allowance depending on the number of adults and children. Ideally, tax-free allowances should be set in such a way that *equivalised* tax-free allowances are broadly the same across all household types. This would make the tax system neutral with regard to household composition and family structure, neither discouraging nor encouraging any particular one.

The long-term dynamics created in this way will be beneficial in various ways. There is evidence that the tax and benefit system does affect patterns of household formation and childbearing (Morgan, 2007; Brewer et al., 2008), even though the magnitude of the effects is disputed and need not be huge. However, it is safe to say that under a more neutral tax and benefit system, more people would be inclined to defer childbearing until they have formed a financially independent household than otherwise.

In effect, this reform would hugely increase tax allowances and decrease benefit payments. It would slash both the number of income tax payers and the number of cash transfer recipients, by eliminating the overlap between the groups.

The resulting restoration of fiscal transparency would also ease long-term upward pressure on public spending. Undoubtedly, there would be losers too. The radical simplification and standardisation implied by this reform would inevitably make some recipients worse off. The present tax and benefit system contains a host of different rates, special rules and differential treatments which could not be translated into a NIT system. But even for the net losers there would be net gains. A highly desirable side effect of the above-described reforms is that they would, at one stroke, slash high EMTRs. Even in the short term, the dynamics created by removing obstacles to progressing in the labour market could not be other than positive.

Old-age provision

In the very long term, the largest fiscal savings can be achieved by removing some key tasks in welfare from the political sphere in their entirety. In particular, the implicit debt incurred in the form of unfunded pension liabilities has been estimated at 273 per cent of GDP (Silver, 2010). Non-means-tested benefits in old age are dealt with in a different chapter; in this chapter we will limit ourselves to old-age *assistance* benefits.

Regardless of whether the regular income source in old age consists of entitlements built up through previous contributions (in a pay-as-you-go system) or of assets built up through previous savings (in a funded system), there will be an auxiliary pillar for those whose entitlements or assets are insufficient. The system of non-contributory old-age benefits in the UK reflects all the deficiencies of the benefit system for working-age households and should be reformed along the same lines. There is no reason for running two separate benefit systems, one for people of working age and one for older people. The integrated system of negative and positive income taxation described above should be the same for all households, regardless of age and regardless of the composition of income. 'Age' would remain a relevant variable only insofar as the full-time work requirement would be dropped above a certain age threshold. In practical terms, this would mean abolishing the Guarantee Credit, the Savings Credit and other age-related benefits, cash and kind. Low-income pensioners would receive the same NIT payments as low-income working-age households. The goal should be a unified system of positive and negative taxation, neutral with regard to age and income composition, in which saving and working always pay and political vote-buying cannot be hidden from the sight of taxpayers.

Full-time work conditionality for out-of-work benefits

It was argued above that spending on middle-class benefits should be severely constrained, but without raising the taper rates that give rise to adverse dynamic effects. There need not be a contradiction between these two aims, because entitlement to benefits can be limited in ways other than through the use of taper rates. Making the receipt of the NIT conditional on a workload close to full-time work would 'crowd in' rather than crowd out recipients' work effort. A household with at least one earner working for 35 hours per week at the minimum wage would already obtain a monthly gross income of £900. Topping up an income of this magnitude, and then withdrawing the income supplement at a low rate, is both affordable and compatible with the aim of tightly focused transfer spending. Problems arise when the government transfers cease to be an income supplement and begin to be a long-term income replacement.

Implemented in isolation, however, a tightening of the eligibility criteria for in-work benefits would simply make part-time employment less attractive than not working at all. The part-time worker would not receive a Negative Income Tax payment, yet the person who was unemployed would receive some form of benefit payment. The result would be to push many part-time employees into worklessness. Indeed, an empirical labour market model by Brewer et al. (2006: 710–14) suggests the employment rate of single parents would be more than ten percentage points lower if there were no tax credits at all.

A way out of this predicament consists of attaching work requirements to the receipt of out-of-work benefits as well, in the form of a localised 'workfare' scheme. Perhaps the most successful scheme (in terms of moving recipients back into work) that has been tested over the last few decades is the one in Wisconsin. In this system, there is no automatic entitlement to benefits. Instead, entitlement is conditional on participation in a work capability assessment and, provided the results are positive, in activities such as supervised job search, work placements or working for the local council. Work requirements as such are nothing exotic, and with the mixture of sanctions and mandatory work placements set out in the DWP's White Paper (Department for Work and Pensions, 2010), elements of them will be introduced in the UK as well. What distinguishes Wisconsin, not least compared with many other US states, is that they are actually enforced on the ground in the vast majority of cases (Mead, 2004: 6, 71). People would, of course, be perfectly entitled to work part-time. But this would be a choice. Only households whose adult members worked full-time or who submitted themselves to the 'workfare' scheme would receive Negative Income Tax payments.

This model turns the incentive structure of welfare upside down. Engaging in a structured daily routine and receiving the full amount of benefits becomes the baseline scenario. Non-participation in the requested activities, or turning down job offers, then leads to deductions from the benefit. Workfare is commonly associated with 'penalising the poor' or 'blaming the victim', which is a misunderstanding. Basically, 'workfare' is simply a welfare system in which the daily life of a working-age benefit recipient who is not employed is not that different from the daily life of their working peers.

After the enactment of the key work requirement reform, welfare caseloads in Wisconsin fell by 82 per cent in just over half a decade (ibid.: 5). Labour market models (Mead, 1999) and surveys among senior welfare administrators (Mead, 2004: 197–202) suggest that work requirements were the main contributory factor. If a similar system were adopted in the UK and if it was only half as successful as the prototype – that is, if caseloads were cut by 40 per cent – this would save around £4.7 billion in Income Support and Job Seeker's Allowance (based on data from DWP Statistics, 2011). This corresponds to £5.1 billion in 2014/15 prices.

But the benefits of workfare go far beyond fiscal savings. A very likely and highly desirable side effect would be the removal of the social stigma from welfare recipients as well as the rooting out of fraudulent claims (by people who are working in the black market and receiving benefits). These issues are particularly relevant in the UK, where attitudes towards welfare recipients are much more negative than elsewhere in Europe (see Sefton, 2009: 237–42, on survey data). The improvement in the recipients' social standing is an upside which could appeal even to critics of workfare schemes.

Is the Wisconsin experience transferable to the UK context? What is important to note in this regard is that workfare in Wisconsin did not emerge as a uniform model, but through local variation and mutual learning (Mead, 2004: 79–106). This stands in sharp contrast to the UK's centralised approach to welfare policy. When imposed from above, a workfare model would almost certainly be doomed to failure. There are at least two reasons why a workfare system requires a high degree of local autonomy in order to be able to function.

First, administering a work requirement system is highly challenging (see ibid.: 63–9). It places complex demands on the responsible institutions and therefore has to evolve through experimentation, trial and error and learning from best practice. For example, a workfare system consists of different components, and it is not clear at all what the 'right mix' of these is. If the work activity component occupies too much of claimants' time, it may well distract them from their actual job search.

Yet if work activity requirements become too sporadic, workfare loses much of its effect. Similar trade-offs exist between the aims of providing training, and placing recipients into jobs fast. It is easy to get the mix wrong, which critics will then present as a failure of workfare as such (see Crisp and Fletcher, 2008).

Secondly, a workfare system must reflect local labour market conditions. In a region where the primary problem is high youth unemployment, localised workfare would presumably take a very different form than in, say, a former factory town suffering from a skill mismatch.

Instead of the traditional UK top-down approach we could grant local governments a high degree of autonomy in the administration of the new regime – coupled, of course, with a high degree of fiscal responsibility. This could be administered in various ways. But the local authority would become financially responsible for the lax enforcement of work requirements.

The interaction of benefits and tax allowances

What would this new system actually mean for somebody on low income, somebody on no income and the middle classes? The tax allowances within this system would depend on the total amount of public spending that had to be financed from income tax. If we started with a single person's tax allowance of £12,000, however, then the tax allowance for a couple household would be about £19,000 and, for a couple household with one child, about £23,000. Those earning below the allowance would receive a Negative Income Tax payment which, feasibly, could be about 30 pence for every pound earned below the tax allowance. We would return to the situation of a generation ago when a household on average earnings with two children paid no income tax. There would be a much higher household tax allowance – partially financed by the welfare savings – but nobody would both pay tax and receive benefits. Those a little below the tax allowance would pay no tax and receive a small amount in benefits. Middle-class families would receive no benefits but would have a very high tax allowance. Other savings suggested in this monograph would also allow other taxes to be reduced.

Benefits for those on workfare programmes could be similar to the level of benefits being received by those who do not work under current arrangements. Some thought would have to be given to whether the benefits on the workfare programme were integrated with the benefits received under the negative income tax system. In fact, EMTRs could be higher on the workfare programme than in the Negative Income Tax system because work incentives would arise from the fact that those who were not working full-time in paid work would have to work on the workfare programme.

Conclusions and companion reforms

The UK welfare system often combines the worst features of the various systems that exist elsewhere in the developed world. Short-term income replacement devices are not particularly generous, but high replacement ratios arise nevertheless. Withdrawal rates are generally high, and yet benefits are poorly targeted. Most redistribution is intrapersonal, crowding out private savings and insurance; at the same time, in most transfer programmes, the link between contribution and entitlement is rather weak. As a whole, the system discourages work, family formation and saving. Even a decade of robust labour market performance and extensive work promotion programmes has done little to curb concentrated, entrenched dependency.

The fact that the transfer state could grow so large despite performing so poorly suggests that fiscal illusions are at work, creating permanent electoral pressure for further rounds of expansion. Any lasting reform would have to address these underlying dynamics. An important element of ending fiscal illusions is the strict separation of tax liability and transfer entitlement, which, in turn, requires a drastic simplification and standardisation of the benefit system (and ideally the tax system as well). As a highly desirable side effect, this would immediately cut the highest EMTRs, creating beneficial dynamics.

This chapter should reduce transfer spending by around £31 billion in 2014/15 prices. The total fiscal savings from the proposals in this chapter are listed in Table 20. Part of the savings would be recycled into higher household tax allowances.

Table 20 **Summary of fiscal savings**

Reform area	Approximate fiscal savings (in 2014/15 prices, £bn)
Curtailing middle-class benefits	17.3
Standardising HB rates	6
Extending the 24h/week working hours requirement to all WTC recipients, and waiving the above-indexation increase in CTC	3
Limiting receipt of IS, JSA and ESA through 'Wisconsin-style' work tests and work requirements	5.1
Total	≈31

The reforms proposed here would be more effective, and easier to implement when coupled with reforms in other areas. These are beyond the scope of this paper, but suffice it to name two areas. The beneficial effects of improved work incentives will, of course, best unfold in a flourishing labour market. Indeed, introducing the work requirement system proposed above will lead to fiscal savings only if it succeeds in moving many recipients into the regular labour market eventually. Welfare reform would increase labour supply; we also need liberalisation of labour market regulation, where the UK lags behind not just the USA but countries such as Australia, Switzerland and Denmark. Another important companion reform would be a wholesale liberalisation of the land use planning system, enabling a drastic increase in the supply of housing, and a plummeting of its cost. The remit of the welfare state could be substantially reduced if basic requirements like housing were easily affordable across the income distribution. Planning liberalisation should also help labour mobility. One might expect the development of a more vibrant market in unemployment insurance for those who did not wish to submit to work requirements if they became unemployed. Similarly, though the topic is not covered in this chapter, there would seem to be a strong case for replacing incapacity benefits with disability insurance. The work requirement might not apply in the same way to those who are disabled but income additional to the Negative Income Tax payment would require private insurance.

The logic of the proposals in this chapter is simple. Topping up the incomes of low-earning full-time workers requires much less input from the state than substituting the pay of several workdays. If people wish to receive income supplements then they should be prepared to work a full week. If they cannot find work, we should ensure that the pattern of their week is not dramatically different from that of people who do work full-time. Full-time work requirements are by no means 'tough on the poor'. They are the very prerequisite for low EMTRs, which, in turn, are the key to breaking up the poverty trap. Benefits for those on workfare programmes could be similar to the level of benefits being received by those who do not work under current arrangements. This level of benefits would be withdrawn relatively slowly as household income increased. There would be a much higher household tax allowance – partly financed by the welfare savings – but nobody would both pay tax and receive benefits. Those a little below the tax allowance would pay no tax and receive a small amount in benefits. Middle-class families would receive no benefits but would have a very high tax allowance.

References

Adam, S. and J. Browne (2010), 'Redistribution, work incentives and thirty years of UK tax and benefit reform', IFS Working Paper 10/24, London: Institute of Fiscal Studies.

Adam, S., M. Brewer and A. Shephard (2006), 'Financial work incentives in Britain: comparisons over time and between family types', Working Paper 06/2006, Institute for Fiscal Studies.

Blundell, R., A. Duncan and C. Meghir (1998), 'Estimating labor supply responses using tax reforms', *Econometrica*, 66(4): 827–61.

Booth, P. (2011), 'Sharing the burden – how the older generation should suffer its share from the cuts', IEA Discussion Paper no. 34, London: Institute of Economic Affairs.

Brewer, M. (2009), 'How do income support systems in the UK affect labour force participation?', Working Paper 2009: 27, Institute for Labour Market Policy Evaluation.

Brewer, M. and A. Shephard (2004), 'Has Labour made work pay?', London: Institute for Fiscal Studies and Joseph Rowntree Foundation.

Brewer, M., E. Saez and A. Shephard (2008), 'Means-testing and tax rates on earnings', paper prepared for the Report of a Commission on Reforming the Tax System for the 21st century ('Mirrlees Review'), Institute for Fiscal Studies.

Brewer, M., A. Duncan, A. Shephard, M. Suarez and M. Jose (2006), 'Did Working Families' Tax Credit work? The impact of in-work support on labour supply in Great Britain', *Labour Economics*, 13: 699–720.

British Social Attitudes Survey (2010), 'Has welfare made us lazy? Employment commitment in different welfare states', BSA, 25th Report, London: Sage.

Buchanan, J. (1999 [1967]), *Public Finance in Democratic Process: Fiscal Institutions and Individual Choice*, Indianapolis: Liberty Fund.

Cawston, T., A. Haldenby and P. Nolan (2009), 'The end of entitlement', London: Reform.

Crisp, R. and D. R. Fletcher (2008), 'A comparative review of workfare programmes in the United States, Canada and Australia', Research Report no. 533, Department for Work and Pensions.

Department for Work and Pensions (2010), *21st Century Welfare*, London: DWP.

Department for Work and Pensions (2011), 'Housing Benefit – uprating local housing allowance by CPI from April 2013', Impact Assessment, Department for Work and Pensions.

Department for Work and Pensions & Office for National Statistics (2010), 'Housing Benefit and Council Tax Benefit, summary statistics', Dataset, campaigns.dwp.gov.uk/asd/asd1/hb_ctb/hbctb_release_feb10.xls.

DWP Statistics (2011), Benefit expenditure tables – medium term forecasts, dataset, statistics.dwp.gov.uk/asd/asd4/index.php?page=medium_term.

Dollary, B. and A. Worthington (1996), 'The empirical analysis of fiscal illusion', *Journal of Economic Surveys*, 10(3): 261–97.

Eurostat (2009a), 'Net expenditure on social protection benefits', *Statistics in Focus*, 102/2009.

Eurostat (2009b), *Labour Market Statistics*, Eurostat Pocket Books, Luxembourg: Publication Office of the European Union.

Eurostat (2011), Statistics database, overarching indicators, available at epp.eurostat.ec.europa.eu/portal/page/portal/employment_social_policy_equality/omc_social_inclusion_and_social_protection/overarching.

HM Treasury (2010a), *Budget 2010*, London: HM Treasury.

HM Treasury (2010b), 'Budget 2010, Press Notice 2: Rates and allowances'.

HM Treasury & Department for Work and Pensions (2010), 'Ending child poverty: mapping the route to 2020', Companion document to the 2010/11 Budget.

Horton, T. and J. Gregory (2009), *The Solidarity Society: Why we can afford to end poverty, and how to do it with public support*, London: Fabian Society and Webb Memorial Trust.

Institute for Fiscal Studies (2010a), *Inequality and Poverty Spreadsheet*, online spreadsheet accompanying 'Poverty and inequality in the UK: 2010', IFS Commentary no. 116.

Institute for Fiscal Studies (2010b), 'Conservatives and Liberal Democrats would extend Labour's tax credit cuts for middle-income families', Observations: Reflections on current events, by Mike Brewer.

Joseph Rowntree Foundation & New Policy Institute (2007), *Monitoring Poverty and Social Exclusion 2007*, Oxford: Alden Press.

King, P. (2006), *Choice and the End of Social Housing*, Hobart Paper 155, London: Institute of Economic Affairs.

Korpi, W. and J. Palme (1998), 'The paradox of redistribution and the paradox of equality: welfare state institutions, inequality and poverty in the Western countries', *American Sociological Review*, 63(5): 661–87.

Local Housing Allowance Direct (2010), LHA Direct website, https://lha-direct.voa.gov.uk/Secure/Default.aspx.

Martin, D. (2009), 'Benefit simplification: how, and why, it must be done', Centre for Policy Studies.

Mead, L. (1999) 'The decline of welfare in Wisconsin', *Journal of Public Administration Research and Theory* (J-PART), 9(4): 597–622.

Mead, L. (2004), *Government Matters. Welfare reform in Wisconsin*, Princeton, NJ: Princeton University Press.

Meghir, C. and D. Phillips (2008), 'Labour supply and taxes', Working Paper 08/04, London: Institute for Fiscal Studies.

Morgan, P. (2007), *The War between the State and the Family*, London: Institute of Economic Affairs.

New Policy Institute (2011), The Poverty Site, www.poverty.org.uk/.

Niemietz, K. (2011), 'An analysis of the welfare cuts in the Comprehensive Spending Review and the Budget 2010', *Economic Affairs*, 31(1): 80–85.

Office for National Statistics (2008), *Family Spending, 2007 edition*, Basingstoke: Palgrave Macmillan.

Office for National Statistics (2010), 'Data: the effects of taxes and benefits on household income, 2008/09', Dataset, http://www. statistics.gov.uk/downloads/theme_social/Taxes-Benefits/All_ fig_&_tabs_0809.xls.

Office for National Statistics & HM Revenue and Customs (2010), 'Child and Working Tax Credits statistics', London: ONS & HMRC.

Puviani, A. (1960), *Die Illusionen in der öffentlichen Finanzwirtschaft*, Berlin: Duncker & Humblot; originally (1903) *Teoria dell'Illusione finanziara*, Milan/Palermo/Naples: Remo Sandron Editore Libraio.

Sefton, T. (2009), 'Moving in the right direction? Public attitudes to poverty, inequality and redistribution', in J. Hills, T. Sefton and K. Stewart (eds), *Towards a More Equal Society? Poverty, inequality and policy since 1997*, Bristol: Policy Press.

Seldon, A. (ed.) (1996), *Re-privatising Welfare: After the lost century*, IEA Readings 45, London: Institute of Economic Affairs.

Silver, N. (2010), 'A bankruptcy foretold 2010: post-financial-crisis update', IEA Discussion Paper no. 28, London: Institute of Economic Affairs.

Snowdon, C. (2010), *The Spirit Level Delusion: Fact-checking the left's new theory of everything*, Trinity Farm/Ripon: Little Dice.

Sørensen, P. and A. Bovenberg (2007), *Working to Account? Social security without dependency*, London: Politeia.

UNICEF (2007), 'Child poverty in perspective: an overview of child wellbeing in rich countries', Report Card 7, UNICEF Innocenti Research Centre.

PART FIVE: THE INFRASTRUCTURE STATE

10 COMPREHENSIVE TRANSPORT REFORM
Richard Wellings

The government spent £22 billion on transport in 2010/11, just 3.2 per cent of total spending (HM Treasury, 2010: 5). The Comprehensive Spending Review suggests this figure may fall to around £20 billion in 2014/15 (2.7 per cent of total spending), representing a real-terms cut of over 15 per cent.[1] The small proportion of public expenditure devoted to transport belies the sector's economic importance. After housing, transport receives the largest share of household expenditure (ONS, 2010) and it is also a major business cost. Moreover, private road transport is an important source of tax revenues: road fuel duty, for example, currently raises about £30 billion per annum,[2] while Vehicle Excise Duty raises about £5.5 billion (DfT, 2010a).

The efficiency of the transport sector has a significant impact on the wider economy and thus on the magnitude of general tax receipts. Lower transport costs translate into productivity gains by facilitating a more specialised division of labour, together with economies of scale, increased competition and improved labour mobility. The market mechanisms that drive transport improvements, however, have been severely hampered in recent decades by state intervention. Patterns of investment have tended to reflect political priorities rather than consumer demand, and resources have been misdirected into uneconomic projects. Pricing has also been politicised and has been severely distorted by discriminatory taxes and heavy regulation. As a result, the big economic gains from lower transport costs seen in the past have generally not been

---

1   The exact figure will depend on the expenditure of various local and regional authorities, so cannot be determined precisely.
2   Including the value added tax charged on the duty.

evident in the last fifteen years or so.[3] Indeed, in many locations costs have increased significantly as a result of rising traffic congestion.

This chapter argues that improved efficiency in the transport sector can be combined with significant reductions in government spending. It is feasible to reduce taxpayer subsidies by perhaps three-quarters by 2014/15, making an annual saving in excess of £15 billion. Cuts in transport spending therefore have the potential to make a significant direct contribution to a programme of deficit reduction, as well as a large indirect contribution through the positive effects of more efficient transport on the wider economy.

For convenience, the chapter is organised by mode. The main focus is on land transport, state spending on air and shipping being negligible. The discussion begins with public transport, which, as the largest recipient of taxpayer subsidies (totalling over £12 billion), must be a major target for cuts.

Rail

The railways (not including London Underground) officially cost taxpayers £5.3 billion in 2009/10. If increases to Network Rail's debt are included, as well as support channelled through other agencies, the total probably exceeds £7 billion – a figure that will be held broadly constant until 2014/15 (thus representing a small real-terms cut). While this total amounts to almost one third of the total transport budget (see Table 21), rail accounts for a very small proportion of the market for mobility – 7 per cent of passenger travel (see Table 22) and 10 per cent of freight (DfT, 2010a). Total taxpayer support may now exceed the £6 billion collected annually in fare revenues (ibid.). By 2014/15, the planned above-inflation ticket increases should bring down the ratio of subsidies to fares.

---

3   Air and shipping may be exceptions to this statement. Their international nature has constrained efforts at political control. In terms of land transport, a step change in policy took place in the mid-1990s, which made environmentalism a central consideration (see Wellings, 2006a).

Table 21 **Estimated government expenditure on transport by mode (£bn), 2010/11 and 2014/15[4]**

	2010/11	*2014/15*
Roads	9.5	7.5
Rail	7.0	7.0
Buses	4.0	4.0
London Underground	1.5	1.5

Table 22 **Passenger travel by mode (%), 2009**

Cars, vans, taxis and motorcycles	85
Rail	7
Buses and coaches	6
London Underground	1

Source: DfT (2010a)

Reducing operating subsidies

An examination of the detailed patterns of subsidy reveals further disproportionality in government spending. Although the complex structure of the rail industry makes it problematic to ascertain levels of support, it is nevertheless apparent that London commuter and inter-city routes are close to self-supporting through fare revenues (at least in terms of operating costs), whereas 'regional railways' routes are very heavily subsidised (see Table 23).

There is little economic justification for such taxpayer support, and arguments based on equity or environmentalism are weak. The proportion of journeys made by rail in areas of low population density such as rural Wales is so low that the mode is largely irrelevant in terms of its impact on mobility and pollution. There is therefore a strong case for

---

4   Estimated from DfT (2010a) and (HM Treasury, 2010); see also http://www.publica-tions.parliament.uk/pa/cm201011/cmselect/cmtran/473/47306.htm; transport funding has become so complex and opaque that only rough estimates can be given.

Table 23 **Subsidies to train-operating companies (TOCs), 2008/09**

TOC	Passenger km (millions)	Subsidy (£ millions)	Subsidy per passenger km (pence)
Arriva Trains Wales	1,014	115	11.3
C2C Rail	919	1	0.1
The Chiltern Railway Company	968	11	1.1
Cross Country Trains	1,841	119	6.5
East Midland Trains	1,972	46	2.3
First Capital Connect	3261	–112	–3.4
First Great Western	5,229	–71	–1.4
First/Keolis Transpennine	1,278	83	3.2
First ScotRail	2,601	222	8.6
Gatwick Express	–	–4	–
National Express East Coast	4,695	–185	–3.9
London and Birmingham Rly	1,575	114	7.3
London and South Eastern Rly	3,896	36	0.9
London Eastern Railway Company	3,968	–98	–2.5
New Southern Rly	3,793	12	0.3
Northern Rail	1,970	79	4.0
Stagecoach South Western Trains	5,346	–42	–0.8
West Coast Trains	4,452	–72	–1.6

Source: ORR (2010: 64)

phasing out these subsidies as quickly as possible.[5, 6]

Passenger traffic on the great majority of regional railway services would almost certainly be insufficient to enable them to survive without operating subsidies. Accordingly, services would cease operation. Under such circumstances, it is imperative that the government removes legal obstacles to the closure of railway lines. The sale of routes for alternative uses (such as property development and/or toll roads) would enable at least some money to be returned to taxpayers in compensation for many decades of support.

While some London commuter routes currently receive relatively

---

5   It is a moot point whether train-operating companies and rolling-stock companies should be compensated under such circumstances.

6   In a much more decentralised fiscal system a case could perhaps be made for leaving decisions about subsidising regional railways entirely to local government.

small operating subsidies, this could be addressed by the simple removal of price controls. Rail companies would be free to set fares in order to maximise profits but would not receive taxpayer support.[7] In a deregulated environment they would also be free to fund infrastructure improvements through land development. Rail companies could then harness for commercial gain their ability to determine the siting of and pricing at commuter stations. Fares on south-east commuter routes are well below what the market could bear. Market-based fares would not just cover the costs of operation and capital costs but the high imputed rental value of the land used to run railways operations in London and the south-east together with the high value commuters put on the ability to reach London quickly. Appropriate costs should, in turn, be passed on to the railways operators by Network Rail – thus raising the value of those assets in a potential privatisation. If market-based fares were to reflect all the costs of commuting in the south-east it is possible that the incentive for firms to locate in London would be considerably reduced, congestion would be eased, and other costs of living and working in London would fall.

Cancelling uneconomic projects

The figures in Table 21 might suggest that taxpayers are making a profit from the major intercity rail operators, who are paying fees for their franchises. Such an interpretation is only possible, however, if infrastructure costs are ignored. For example, the West Coast Main Line was recently upgraded for £9.5 billion in today's prices (see National Audit Office, 2006) and it is clear that the train operators' franchise payments are only a tiny fraction of what would constitute a commercial return on the capital invested.

Large-scale rail infrastructure projects are heavily loss-making for the

---

7   Commuter rail services are not monopolies. Travellers are free to use alternative modes such as buses, cars and motorcycles. They may also relocate to locations with cheaper fares or locations close to work.

taxpayer. Accordingly, cancelling such schemes – in particular, Crossrail and High Speed 2 (HS2) – promises to make a significant contribution to cuts in overall transport spending. Crossrail is a £16 billion scheme to build an east–west rail link across London linking Heathrow, the West End, the City and Canary Wharf (Butcher, 2010). Scheduled for completion in 2018, it is likely that the annual bill will be approximately £2 billion over the next few years. While preparatory construction work for Crossrail is already under way, HS2 is unlikely to be started until 2017 at the earliest, although significant preparatory costs will be incurred over the next few years. HS2 is a proposed high-speed line from London to Birmingham and eventually on to the north of England and Scotland. The cost of the first stage to the West Midlands has been estimated at about £17 billion (High Speed Two Ltd, 2009) but the total for the entire route is likely to be in the region of £40–£60 billion.

It is clear that both projects are uneconomic on a conventional commercial basis. As with the Channel Tunnel Rail Link (see Myddelton, 2007), now known as High Speed 1, fare revenues are unlikely even to cover operating and maintenance costs, let alone the enormous capital costs. The history of big government projects suggests they tend to be subject to large cost overruns and delays (ibid.: 203–204). Accordingly, Crossrail could end up costing, say, £25 billion and HS2 perhaps £70-billion-plus for the whole route. Clearly such outcomes would be highly detrimental to the public finances. Any economic analysis should also factor in the 'deadweight' losses resulting from the additional taxation required to fund these projects (see Harrison, 2006). Another consideration should be alternative ways of investing these sums. For the same cost as Crossrail, for example, it might be possible to construct over a thousand miles of six-lane motorway, adding 45 per cent to the length of the UK network.[8] This is not to advocate taxpayer funding of

---

8   Archer and Glaister (2006) estimated average construction costs for a six-lane motor-way at £6.46 million per kilometre in 2003 prices (equating to about £13 million per mile in 2011, based on cost-increase estimates from the road construction tender price index (DfT, 2010a)).

such road schemes, but rather to question the value for money of big rail projects vis-à-vis other transport projects.

Both rail projects have been justified in terms of relieving congestion and increasing capacity. A more rational way to address congestion is to raise fares at peak times – a strategy that reduces taxpayer subsidies, unlike new infrastructure. Yet many rail fares are regulated by the government, making comprehensive congestion pricing impossible. Another consideration is that increasing rail capacity can mean more taxpayer subsidies for more uneconomic services.

The productivity gains from the big projects are also likely to be small. The busiest section of the Crossrail route is already served by the underground Central Line. Heathrow is already served by the Heathrow Express and the Piccadilly Line. This means time savings are likely to be minimal. Alternative ways of improving travel times for journeys across London include introducing tolls on the M25 (see the roads section) and introducing express services on tube lines that bypass poorly used stations. Moreover, for high-value business travellers the limited time savings offered at huge cost by Crossrail are likely to be eclipsed by the delay and inconvenience engendered by the government's decision to prevent the privately funded expansion of Heathrow.

The time savings from HS2 will also be limited. Both the West Coast Main Line and the East Coast Main Line already offer 125 mph travel. The faster services reach Yorkshire in 90 minutes. English cities are relatively close together and high-speed trains are likely to spend a significant proportion of their journeys accelerating or braking. Of course, the productivity gains from these time savings will have wider economic benefits, and this ostensibly enhances the economic case for HS2. But such arguments tend to ignore the hidden opportunity costs and deadweight losses associated with taxpayer funding. There is also a real danger that HS2 will act as a stimulus to expensive state-funded regeneration schemes in centres along the route, designed to create the illusion that the project has brought about economic revival. St Pancras and Stratford City are examples of this policy along the route of HS1 (the Channel Tunnel Rail

Link). It should also be noted that the environmental case for high-speed rail is very weak (see Kemp, 2004; Booz Allen Hamilton, 2007).

High-speed rail is being promoted as an alternative to Heathrow expansion, the idea being that domestic air passengers will transfer to rail. Plans for a third runway at Heathrow were stopped by the incoming coalition government in 2010. This has serious implications for fiscal policy. Heathrow expansion was to be privately funded, whereas the expansion of rail capacity will require substantial public subsidies as detailed above. Moreover, the decision to prohibit increases in airport capacity threatens the relative position of Heathrow (and other London airports) as international hubs, with implications for the attractiveness of the UK as a business location. This could have a negative effect on tax revenues in the medium to long term.

Enabling vertical integration

The previous two sections have demonstrated that significant savings can be achieved by phasing out operating subsidies to the railways and cancelling big rail infrastructure projects. The final way to cut rail spending (while removing regulatory barriers to commercial viability) involves allowing the industry to reorganise along more efficient lines.

When rail industries grow up spontaneously in the private sector, they tend to exhibit a high degree of vertical integration. The explanation lies in transaction cost economics (see Williamson, 2008). The privatisation model deployed in the 1990s imposed a complex artificial structure on the industry with separate ownership of track and train. The resulting transaction costs partly explain the explosion of subsidy levels in the decade following privatisation (see Tyrrall, 2004). Significant savings could be obtained by allowing the different parts of the railways to reintegrate. One mechanism would be to distribute shares in Network Rail to the train-operating companies. The latter would also be free to merge. It seems likely that economies of scale would favour the 'BR plc' structure, in which one owner controlled nearly the entire network, though the government should not attempt to predetermine an 'ideal' outcome.

Buses

After the railways, buses are the largest recipient of public-transport subsidies. Annual taxpayer support for bus services totals about £4 billion per year, including concessionary fares and fuel duty rebates, a figure likely to remain broadly constant in nominal terms until 2014/15.[9] In addition there are indirect subsidies such as the use of scarce road space as bus lanes and various other bus priority schemes.

Bus subsidies are often justified by the socialist-egalitarian argument that bus services constitute an essential public service for the elderly and relatively poor (Smith, 1984; Prescott, 1992; Torrance, 1992). Such transfers can be challenged on economic grounds, however, because they redistribute resources from productive individuals to non-productive individuals, thereby hampering the creation of wealth. But even if public policy should be driven by equality concerns, it is by no means clear that subsidising bus services is an efficient way to help the less well off: paying a portion of everybody's bus fares is a much less effective way of helping the less well off than funding less-well-off people and providing income transfers. Accordingly, there is a strong economic case for phasing out bus subsidies, starting with one of the largest interventions – the taxpayer funding of concessionary fares.

Abolishing concessionary fares

The annual cost of concessionary fares for the over-sixties exceeds £1 billion (DfT, 2010b). There are plans to save money by raising the age to 65. A better policy, however, would be to abolish them completely. Free bus passes undermine the price signals that tell providers of transport

---

9   The precise figure will depend on spending decisions by local authorities, etc.

.

services where and how to allocate their resources, leading to inefficiencies. They also represent a further bureaucratic intrusion into the transport market, effectively turning operators into subcontractors (Hibbs, 2005: 109) and encouraging rent-seeking behaviour. To the extent that concessionary fare payments make otherwise loss-making services financially viable, they may sustain and/or trigger additional public transport subsidies as well as associated spending on anti-car measures (see below). Another regrettable impact is the crowding out of alternative travel options such as shared taxis, which may be more appropriate for many elderly travellers, who would benefit from a door-to-door service. If there were cases of particular hardship following the abolition of concessionary fares then it would make more sense to pay cash directly to the elderly people concerned rather than to interfere in the transport sector through introducing new entitlements. Transport for the elderly is also provided by charities, and it is plausible that voluntary provision in this area has been 'crowded out' by fare subsidies. The role of charities in transport could presumably expand to fill any perceived gaps left by the phasing out of taxpayer support. Furthermore, bus companies themselves are likely to offer lower fares at those times of day when buses are not full to capacity – or provide lower fares to pensioners in order to maximise profits by price discrimination.

Improving mobility for the less wealthy

Of course, it is not just the elderly who are disproportionately reliant on bus services. Working-age people on relatively low incomes are another group. Fortunately their mobility can be increased dramatically without taxpayer subsidies. The cost of taxis can be decreased and their availability increased through deregulation, as successfully carried out in Ireland (Barrett, 2010). Deregulation would also allow the development of low-cost shared taxi services, as seen in the developing world. The cost of private motoring could also be significantly reduced, bringing it within reach of those on the lowest incomes. This would involve removing protectionist non-tariff barriers that prevent free trade in motor vehicles and liberalising the controls that raise purchase and running costs. Accordingly, phasing out bus subsidies need not reduce the mobility of the less well off. A programme of deregulation would radically increase the availability of low-cost transport options.

Introducing VAT on public transport fares

Value added tax (VAT) destroys wealth by discouraging exchange and reducing the division of labour, competition and economies of scale that drive productivity growth. Nevertheless, under circumstances where VAT is widely levied there are economic efficiency gains from applying it equally to all activities and at a lower rate than if numerous exemptions had been included (see Bassett et al., 2010).

Public transport fares are currently exempt from VAT, while motorists pay VAT on petrol (including on the fuel duty). Thus the transport market is severely distorted by its fiscal regime. Phasing in VAT, alongside the subsidy reductions advocated, would help mitigate the price distortions. Based on current fare revenues, VAT at 20 per cent would raise around £1.2 billion from the railways; £300 million from London Underground; and £800 million from buses – a total of £2.3 billion.[10] In reality, however, the effect of higher prices on demand, together with the impact of abolishing concessionary fares (see above), would reduce this sum significantly, perhaps to under £2 billion. But there could be a large additional political dividend for taxpayers: by reducing passenger numbers and congestion on busy routes, VAT would help undermine the rationale for uneconomic infrastructure projects, thereby promoting further savings.

---

10   Revenue figures obtained from DfT (2010a). Additional revenue would be obtained from Eurostar services, Le Shuttle and ferry services. Air travel is already subject to Air Passenger Duty, so has not been included.

Roads

Roads expenditure is the largest single component of transport spending, at £9.5 billion in 2009/10. Roads will bear the brunt of the planned cuts, however – despite moving over 90 per cent of passenger traffic (see Table 22) – with this figure likely to fall to approximately £7.5 billion by 2014/15 (the precise total will depend on the spending decisions of local and regional authorities). Capital spending on national roads (trunk roads and motorways) faces particularly severe cuts of 40 per cent (DfT, 2010c).

As with public transport, the roads market is heavily distorted as a result of government intervention. Tax rates, in particular fuel duty, are high; costs are inflated by various regulations;[11] and at the same time, nearly all roads are free at the point of use. The provision of infrastructure is politicised and largely centrally directed, resulting in a severe mismatch between patterns of demand and supply. Endemic traffic congestion, said to cost businesses and individuals upwards of £10 billion per annum (see, for example, Eddington, 2006), is perhaps the most obvious consequence of government failure in transport. Other effects, still harder to quantify, include higher trade costs which hinder productivity growth.

A combination of cuts and reform certainly has the potential to deliver very substantial efficiency gains. But the fact that, for the best part of a century, the Treasury has soaked private road users for tax revenues (see Plowden, 1971) means there are great difficulties, both moral and economic, in ascribing to the road network a role in reducing the budget deficit. This tax take makes private road transport categorically different from public transport. For example, adding road-user charges and associated administration costs on top of fuel duty would potentially constitute a tax on top of a supertax, creating further economic distortions through still greater discrimination against

---

11   For example, the Renewable Transport Fuels Obligation (RTFO) forces fuel suppliers to use biofuels as a percentage of the road fuels they supply in the UK. Vehicle standards (safety and environmental) are another area of regulation.

road transport vis-à-vis other modes of transport and other economic activities.[12]

Rolling out road pricing

Nevertheless, the more widespread introduction of road pricing would be a key element of a more effective roads policy. Higher tolls at peak times would reduce congestion costs significantly. Pricing for road space would also enable investment in maintenance and new infrastructure to be allocated far more efficiently: profits from pricing over the rental value of land and the cost of capital provide signals indicating where road space is too scarce and incentives for new roads to be built.

If the roads concerned remained owned by the government or heavily regulated, however, pricing could be counterproductive. Toll rates would tend to be set for political reasons rather than economic ones; special interest groups could be exempted from the charges; transport bureaucracies and their corporate collaborators could inflate administration costs; arbitrary environmental levies could be imposed on top of the basic tolls; and finally, pricing revenues could be used for redistribution – for example, to subsidise buses or pay for uneconomic public transport links to 'deprived' areas (see Wellings and Lipson, 2008). Recent government road-pricing schemes in the UK, both operational and proposed, have been characterised by many of these deficiencies, a prime example being the London Congestion Charge (Wellings, 2009).

---

12   Some economists would use social cost arguments to justify motoring taxes, including the costs of environmental externalities, although it can be argued that such methodologies are not valid (see Wellings, 2006b). Nevertheless, estimates of the environmental costs of road use are typically far lower than current fuel duty and VED charges. Sansom et al. (2001) produce a figure of about £10 billion (adjusted to 2011 prices). Accident costs and capital charges might also be factored in, although once again this is a flawed approach as such estimates are contingent on current and historic government intervention.

Privatising motorways and trunk roads

The pitfalls of government pricing can be avoided by the private ownership of toll roads. The profit motive would incentivise owners to maximise revenues by using traffic management techniques to maximise traffic flow, paring down running costs and improving services to customers. Perhaps most importantly, they would have no commercial reason to use revenues to invest in loss-making public transport projects.

Compared with privatising local and residential roads, the privatisation of motorways and motorway-style trunk roads is relatively straightforward. In particular, property access issues are not generally a constraint. This leaves the question of whether to implement a 'big bang' approach by privatising much of the strategic network in one go or to adopt an incremental policy.

The former option could bring the benefits of privatisation far more rapidly than the latter – the network could be floated on the stock market. A sale of the assets would present problems, however. The process of valuing the network is fraught with difficulties, including political risks with the potential to affect toll revenues, which include tax rates (especially fuel duty), vehicle regulations and planning law (e.g. to what extent competition from new roads would be possible). Government could also subsidise competing routes, including railways. At the same time, there are incentives for the government to manipulate regulatory structures in order to maximise flotation receipts, in ways that do not necessarily promote economic efficiency.

In the context of the fuel duty supertax, there is also a danger that transport prices would be artificially inflated, leading to the misallocation of resources. In some locations the savings from reduced congestion could exceed the additional costs. Nevertheless, on the great majority of routes that are uncongested (and indeed on otherwise congested routes at off-peak times), costs would almost certainly increase without corresponding benefit if there were any form of pricing – even if only to cover administration costs. Consequently, in order to prevent road users on such routes paying more than existing fuel duty and vehicle excise duty (VED), these taxes would have to be cut substantially. The impact of wholesale privatisation on the budget deficit is therefore far from clear, although it is conceivable that a share of the spending cuts set out in this and other chapters could be used to reduce considerably fuel duty and perhaps abolish VED. There would be an initial capital sum that the government would receive followed by lost taxes which would be replaced by road-user charges accruing to the new owners. The complete privatisation of the motorways and trunk roads should therefore be a key long-term policy objective once these fiscal distortions have been removed.[13]

To achieve substantial savings and efficiency gains by 2014/15, however, a more incremental approach might be appropriate. This has the further advantage of facilitating the development of technologies, expertise and institutional forms without the same economic risks as a big-bang approach. An incremental approach to the privatisation of the strategic network would focus road pricing on the most congested locations, where the costs of delays to road users are most likely to exceed the costs of additional tolls to fund capacity enhancements and scheme administration.[14] The savings to the Treasury are also clear-cut and quickly realised. This is because the approach advocated is to remove the state from the construction and operation of *new* infrastructure with older infrastructure being privatised in the medium term.

Capital expenditure on the strategic road network is expected to be about £1 billion in 2014/15 (DfT, 2010c). Instead, private enterprise should fund and build new stretches of trunk road and motorway, and add extra lanes and active traffic management to existing routes, with ownership transferred to private firms and costs recouped by pricing. In this way the UK's inter-urban congestion hot spots could incrementally become subject to pricing. Indeed, many more projects could be

---

13   The detailed privatisation process is the subject of a forthcoming monograph (Knipping and Wellings, 2011).

14   Case studies demonstrating the economic viability of such schemes are provided in Wellings and Lipson (2008: 48–50).

undertaken than under the current state-funded plans, provided they were commercially viable.

Decommissioning minor roads

At the other extreme, there are (mostly) rural roads that may be uneconomic in the sense that their maintenance costs may exceed the tolls that might be received from users. These routes could be transferred to local residents, either individually or collectively. Indeed, a wide range of forms of ownership would be possible. Residents would gain the ability to restrict access to their properties, with large potential benefits for reducing crime. A major obstacle may be the current legal environment where private road owners would be liable for large compensation payments for accidents in which they were deemed negligent (i.e. for not filling in potholes, etc.) – even when the injured party is trespassing. Such legal rules could be changed. Alternatively, uneconomic rural roads could simply be 'de-owned' by local authorities and classified as common land or pedestrian rights of way. Residents might then become *de facto* maintainers of the roads, but not *de jure* owners.

The 'right to own' urban roads

Urban roads perhaps present still greater challenges. Yet the benefits of privatisation are likely to be much greater in cities, particularly given the opportunities for owners to exclude undesirables from their streets, as well as to implement safety and parking arrangements tailored to the specific preferences of residents. Many forms of antisocial behaviour could be eliminated with private residential roads.

A relatively simple, incremental way of rolling out private residential roads would be to end the process whereby house builders sign over communal space on new developments to the local authority. And residents of established streets could be given the right to obtain ownership (perhaps by unanimous agreement) and be given appropriate council tax discounts. This might be a similar process to the successful 'right-to-buy' scheme for council house tenants (see King, 2010), although in this instance there would be no charge (since property developers generally paid for the construction of the roads and taxpayers for their maintenance). The installation of gates and walls could be exempted from planning controls to maximise the potential benefits for residents, although established rights-of-way (through-routes) might have to be maintained. Local authorities are spending £3.5 billion a year maintaining roads (largely funded through central government grants), so the incremental privatisation of parts of the network could make considerable savings in the long term.

Liberalising state-owned local roads

Local government spending on roads also includes £2.5 billion per annum of capital expenditure (DfT, 2010a), although this is likely to fall significantly by 2014/15. Since the mid-1990s, various traffic control measures rather than road improvements have come to dominate council projects. These include 'traffic-calming' schemes such as constructing road humps and chicanes; narrowing roads and widening pavements; increasing the number of traffic lights; installing bus and cycle lanes, etc.

It is difficult to produce a precise estimate of annual spending on control measures. The DfT provided local authorities with a road safety grant of £110 million in 2008/09 (House of Commons, 2009). Part of the £600 million annual 'integrated transport block' given to councils is spent on controls, particularly those that favour socialised transport over private cars. Besides these funds, improvements to local roads typically come packaged with the kind of measures listed above.

There is some evidence that traffic-calming measures reduce the number of road casualties (DETR, 2000). But they may also slow down the emergency services, cause pain and discomfort to the infirm, damage vehicles, increase pollution and reduce travel times. On the first point, the London Ambulance Service has suggested that road humps and other measures, by slowing down their vehicles, may cause hundreds of deaths a year in London alone (LAS, 2003).

In an unhampered transport market, the costs and benefits of traffic control measures would be carefully weighed. But the transport planners at local authorities have arguably neglected the negative aspects, perhaps in part because central government grants have been available for anti-car schemes.

There is now a growing body of evidence that removing traffic controls actually improves road safety and promotes more civilised interaction between drivers and pedestrians (Cassini, 2010). Further economic benefits would include reduced travel times and lower vehicle maintenance costs. Paring down the command-and-control transport bureaucracies would be a highly effective method of achieving significant cuts. The process would be straightforward, involving ending associated central government grants. Reversing the expansion of traffic control measures could perhaps save over £1 billion per year, including savings in administration and maintenance costs.

Conclusion

This chapter has not examined every element of state transport expenditure. Nevertheless, it has demonstrated that substantial economies can be achieved by focusing on the railways, buses and roads. Cuts can also be combined with reforms to achieve significant efficiency gains, in particular by a programme of incremental road pricing through privatisation. In the medium term, the elimination of operating subsidies and capital spending on uneconomic projects could reduce rail expenditure by up to £7 billion per year. Phasing out bus subsidies and deregulating local transport markets to help the less well off could save perhaps £4 billion a year, while applying similar policies to London Underground might cut another £1 billion or so.[15] Introducing VAT on public

---

15   Unfortunately the opaque nature of London Underground's finances, including the fall-out from collapsed PFI projects, means an exact figure cannot be provided.

transport fares would perhaps raise £2 billion per year. On the roads, the suggested incremental privatisation of motorways and trunk roads could remove £1 billion of Highways Agency spending, as well as gradually reducing its £1.4-billion-a-year maintenance budget. The savings from part-privatising local roads could be substantial but are extremely difficult to estimate, though the estimated £1 billion from ending funding for councils' anti-car measures can reasonably be factored in. In addition, the extension of market-based pricing in the transport sector would produce dynamic benefits with a positive impact on general tax revenues. However, the difficulties of quantification mean that an estimate is not provided here. These measures may well lead to higher transport costs for public transport users in the south-east. This is as it should be. Artificially reduced transport costs distort decisions about where to locate businesses and personal decisions about where to live and encourage congestion in those parts of the country with the highest rents and living costs. They may also raise house prices.

In conclusion, the transport budget could plausibly be cut by about £15 billion per annum by 2014/15. A continuing programme of road privatisation would then lead directly to government capital receipts and hence lower debt interest costs together with reductions in vehicle excise duty and fuel duty. If this process were to commence in 2014/15 (assuming it is not feasible to proceed earlier), it is plausible that the government could raise approximately £10–20 billion in the first year based on recent estimates of the value of the strategic network.[16] Remaining state transport spending would be phased out in the longer term as government roads were gradually denationalised.

---

16 This estimate assumes that the network would be privatised in a series of tranches, starting with, say, 10–20 per cent of the network in the first year. The strategic roads network (i.e. motorways and trunk roads) has been valued at about £100 billion (Mulheirn and Furness, 2010: 15). The reforms proposed in this chapter would tend to raise this figure.

References

Archer, C. and S. Glaister (2006), *Investing in Roads: Pricing Costs and New Capacity*, London: Imperial College.

Barrett, S. (2010), 'The sustained impacts of taxi deregulation', *Economic Affairs*, 30(1): 61–5.

Bassett, D., A. Haldenby, P. Nolan and L. Parsons (2010), *Reality Check: Fixing the UK's Tax System*, London: Reform.

Booz Allen Hamilton (2007), *Estimated Carbon Impact of a New North–South Line*, London: Booz Allen Hamilton.

Butcher, L. (2010), *Railways: Crossrail*, Standard Note SN/BT/876, London: House of Commons Library.

Cassini, M. (2010), 'Traffic lights: weapons of mass distraction, danger and delay', *Economic Affairs*, 30(2): 79–80.

DETR (Department for the Environment, Transport and the Regions) (2000), *Tomorrow's Roads: Safer for Everyone*, London: DETR.

DfT (Department for Transport) (2010a), *Transport Statistics Great Britain*, London: The Stationery Office.

DfT (2010b), *Concessionary Fares: Cost and Impact of options for extending the current statutory minimum*, London: TSO.

DfT (2010c), 'Transport Spending Review Press Notice', 20 October, http://www.dft.gov.uk/about/spendingreview.

Eddington, R. (2006), *The Eddington Transport Study, the Case for Action*, London: The Stationery Office.

Harrison, F. (2006), *Wheels of Fortune*, London: Institute of Economic Affairs.

Hibbs, J. (2005), *The Dangers of Bus Re-regulation*, London: Institute of Economic Affairs.

High Speed Two Ltd (2009), *High Speed Rail: London to the West Midlands and Beyond. A Report to Government by High Speed Two Limited*, London: HS2 Ltd.

HM Treasury (2010), *Budget 2010* (June), London: The Stationery Office.

House of Commons (2009), *Improving Road Safety for Pedestrians and Cyclists in Great Britain*, Public Accounts Committee, 49th report of session, London: The Stationery Office.

Kemp, R. (2004), 'Transport energy consumption', Discussion Paper, University of Lancaster, http://www.lpdu.lancs.ac.uk/ research/download/Transport%20Energy%20Consumption%20 Discussion%20Paper.pdf.

King, P. (2010), *Housing Policy Transformed: The right to buy and the desire to own*, Bristol: Policy Press.

Knipping, O. and R. Wellings (2011), *Private Roads* (working title), London: Institute of Economic Affairs.

LAS (London Ambulance Service) (2003), 'Investigation into the impact of speed humps', Submission to London Assembly Transport Committee.

Mulheirn, I. and D. Furness (2010), *Roads to Recovery: Reducing congestion through shared ownership*, London: Social Market Foundation.

Myddelton, D. (2007), *They Meant Well: Government Project Disasters*, London: Institute of Economic Affairs.

National Audit Office (2006), *The Modernisation of the West Coast Main Line*, London: The Stationery Office.

ONS (2010), *Family Spending, 2010*, London: Office for National Statistics.

ORR (Office of Rail Regulation) (2010), *National Rail Trends 2009–10 Yearbook*, London: ORR.

Plowden, W. (1971), *The Motor Car and Politics, 1896–1970*, London: Bodley Head.

Prescott, J. (1992), 'Foreword', in J. Roberts, J. Cleary, K. Hamilton and J. Hanna (eds), *Travel Sickness: The need for a sustainable transport policy for Britain*, London: Lawrence and Wishart.

Sansom, T., C. Nash, P. Mackie, J. Shires and P. Watkiss (2001), *Surface Transport Costs and Charges: Great Britain 1998*, Leeds: Institute for Transport Studies.

Smith, G. (1984), *Getting Around: Transport today and tomorrow*, London: Pluto.

Torrance, H. (1992), 'Transport for all: equal opportunities in transport policy', in J. Roberts, J. Cleary, K. Hamilton and J. Hanna (eds), *Travel Sickness: The need for a sustainable transport policy for Britain*, London: Lawrence and Wishart.

Tyrrall, D. (2004), 'The UK railway privatisation: failing to succeed?', *Economic Affairs*, 24(3): 32–8.

Wellings, R. (2006a), 'Environmentalism, public choice and the railways', in J. Hibbs (ed.), *The Railways, the Market and the Government*, London: Institute of Economic Affairs.

Wellings, R. (2006b), 'Rail in a market economy', in J. Hibbs (ed.), *The Railways, the Market and the Government*, London: Institute of Economic Affairs.

Wellings, R. (2009), 'Economy and environment: tackling Britain's transport problem', in V. Uberoi, A. Coutts, I. Mclean and D. Halpern (eds), *Options for a New Britain*, Basingstoke: Palgrave Macmillan.

Wellings, R. and B. Lipson (2008), *Towards Better Transport*, London: Policy Exchange.

Williamson, O. (2008), 'Transaction cost economics: the precursors', *Economic Affairs*, 28(3): 7–14.

11 SELLING OFF THE FAMILY SILVER[1]
Nigel Hawkins

Introduction

Soon after being elected in 1979, the Conservative government initiated a wide-ranging programme of privatisation, which has subsequently been replicated around the world: privatisation had been strongly advocated in the 1960s and 1970s by the Institute of Economic Affairs (IEA) and by economists such as Milton Friedman. British Telecom (BT), British Airways (BA), the British Airports Authority (BAA) and British Steel were among the high-profile companies sold to the private sector. In the latter part of the 1980s, the process to privatise the English and Welsh water companies and virtually all of the UK electricity supply industry was launched.

Privatisation gave rise to many benefits, notably a substantial increase in investment. In many cases, too, it brought down retail prices as competition was introduced. Furthermore, it yielded substantial financial benefits to the government, both in terms of the actual privatisation proceeds and in enhanced tax revenues. In many cases, loss-making industries requiring government subsidies were turned into profit-making industries paying corporation tax. Given that the UK's public sector net debt (PSND) is close to £1 trillion, there is a compelling case for further privatisation initiatives to be pursued. This should not just be thought of as a way of selling assets to reduce government liabilities but also as a way of improving the efficiency in key economic sectors.

---

1   This chapter is based on *Privatisation Revisited*, published by the Adam Smith Institute in October 2010. It is published with kind permission of the Adam Smith Institute.

This chapter analyses privatisations that could raise around £112 billion. In summary, the main assets that the government holds and which it should sell are its banking assets, the Royal Mail, Network Rail and various other infrastructure, broadcasting, telecommunications and leisure assets.

Following the near-collapse of the UK banking system in 2008, the government, through UK Financial Investments (UKFI), now owns 83 per cent (including B shares) of Royal Bank of Scotland (RBS) and 41 per cent of Lloyds. These two shareholdings (assuming RBS's B shares are valued *pari passu*) are currently worth over £53 billion. Once market conditions are favourable, these stakes should be progressively sold – starting with the placement of a tranche of Lloyds shares. The government should also aim to return RBS – in its entirety – to the private sector.

The Royal Mail is also a privatisation candidate, despite its huge pension fund deficit. Its core Post Office division needs additional funds for expansion – it has trusted access to around 27 million UK addresses. EU mail delivery deregulation has boosted the overseas activities of both Germany's Deutsche Post and the Dutch-based TNT.

The efficiency of the UK rail network could be considerably improved and privatisation of Network Rail would help this process. Following the recent £2.1 billion High Speed One 30-year franchise sale, a restructured Network Rail – the successor to Railtrack – should return to the stock market, a sale which could raise up to £12 billion. With regard to other transport and logistics infrastructure, the government should also sell its 49 per cent stake in the UK air traffic control network, together with the larger Trust Ports, led by Dover Port.

So far, the Scottish and Northern Irish water industries have not been privatised yet water privatisation elsewhere in the UK has delivered an £85 billion investment programme since 1989. The case for replicating the 1989 sales of the English and Welsh water industry is strong, although privatising NI Water is not an immediate option. Within the energy sector, the government's 33 per cent stake in Urenco should also be sold.

In the media sector, Channel 4 and a demerged BBC Worldwide should be privatised. A high priority should also be accorded to ensuring that the timetable for the UK spectrum auction, planned for the first half of 2012, does not slip once again. Other potential privatisation candidates include the CDC Group, British Waterways, various support service businesses and those parts of the government property estate that do not need to remain publicly owned.

The remainder of this chapter discusses all these privatisation candidates in more detail. It does not discuss the privatisation of the road network, which is dealt with elsewhere in this monograph.

Reprivatising the banks

The government owns two particularly valuable stakes in UK banks through UKFI. Following the near-collapse of the UK banking system in 2008, the government injected over £65 billion of taxpayers' money into Royal Bank of Scotland (RBS) and Lloyds.

Royal Bank of Scotland (RBS)

Given RBS's shocking experience in 2008, as a result of which an unprecedented £45.5 billion of public money was invested in the bank, it will be no simple task to sell the government stake in its entirety. Furthermore, RBS placed £282 billion of its so-called toxic assets into the Asset Protection Scheme (APS).

Table 24 shows the vast scale of public funding that has been necessary to ensure the viability of RBS.

As part of its participation in the APS, the government acquired 51 billion B shares in RBS. Their status is slightly different from RBS's ordinary shares. The B shares rank *pari passu* in the event of a winding up or liquidation of RBS and are eligible for enhanced dividends over the ordinary shares: this latter benefit falls away if RBS's share price reaches 65p.

Table 24 **HM Treasury holdings in Royal Bank of Scotland**

Investment	Date	Shares (m)	Total Investment (m)	Investment per share (p)
Initial recapitalisation	12/2008	22,854	14,969	65.5
Preference share conversion	4/2009	16,791	5,058	31.75
APS B shares	12/2009	51,000	25,500	50.0
Total investment		90,645	45,527	50.2 (av.)

Source: UK Financial Investments Ltd

For valuation purposes, this chapter assumes RBS's B shares to be the equivalent of its ordinary shares. If these B shares are considered as part of RBS's total capitalisation, the government's shareholding equates to 83 per cent. If they are excluded, the percentage shareholding falls to 67 per cent.

Last year, the government set up the Independent Commission on Banking (ICB) whose interim report has just been published. The ICB, however, rejected proposals to split up any of the UK's four leading integrated banks. Clearly, the IBC recommendations will have an impact on the valuation of RBS, along with other more obvious trading metrics, including the level of bad debts. Consequently, the government will need to tread carefully in seeking to sell its stake.

Indeed, there is a strong case not to proceed with a sale at all until the market has been tested both by the planned initial public offer (IPO) of the Spanish-owned Santander UK, which is expected to take place later this year, and by at least a part-placing of the government's 41 per cent Lloyds stake. If both of these market operations attract sufficient investor interest, then placing an initial tranche of RBS stock would be a feasible option.

Partly for political reasons, the government will be keen to avoid crystallising any loss from its colossal RBS investment (although the economic case for not crystallising a loss is difficult to see). Its average entry price is 50.2p per share so – assuming the principle of avoiding a loss is upheld – it is unrealistic to expect any sale until a material premium is achieved over this average purchase price. The government should, however, set a long-term target of returning RBS – in its entirety – to the private sector by the time of the planned general election in 2015. Given the size of RBS, this is a very challenging task. The current market value of the government's 83 per cent stake in RBS is £38.4 billion – assuming the B shares are included on a *pari passu* basis. If a 10 per cent discount were applied to this valuation, however, the sale of the entire stake (including B shares) could be expected to yield £34.6 billion.

Lloyds

Lloyds, too, faced grave financial challenges in 2008 – and subsequently – following the highly controversial acquisition of Halifax Bank of Scotland (HBOS). In total, Lloyds received £20.3 billion of taxpayers' money to ensure its ongoing viability.

Table 25 lists the various cash injections into Lloyds since January 2009.

Table 25 **HM Treasury holdings in Lloyds Bank**

Investment	Date	Shares (m)	Total investment (m)	Investment per share (p)
Initial recapitalisation	1/2009	7,278	12,957	182.5
Preference share conversion	6/2009	4,521	1,506	38.43
Rights issue	12/2009	15,810	5,850	37.0
Total investment		27,609	20,313	73.6 (av.)

Source: UK Financial Investments Ltd

As a result of its successful December 2009 rights issue, for which the government subscribed, Lloyds did not need to sign up to the APS; originally, it had planned to do so. Following its acquisition of HBOS, whose finances were severely extended, Lloyds held around 32 per cent of the UK mortgage market – this percentage has fallen subsequently. Lloyds' future trading operations, however, which are heavily UK based, will be affected by the ICB's recent interim report; this recommended further UK branch divestments.

Given the government's minority status, Lloyds' non-participation in the APS and various other relevant factors, it should be relatively less difficult to place part of the Lloyds stake than that of RBS. It would be prudent, though, to assess market demand for the planned Santander UK initial public offer (IPO), especially as the latter business – notably in respect of its high UK mortgage exposure following the Abbey National acquisition – has many similarities to Lloyds' lending portfolio.

The current market value of the government's 41 per cent stake in Lloyds is £14.7 billion. If a 10 per cent discount were applied to this valuation, however, the sale of the entire stake could be expected to yield £13.3 billion.

Northern Rock

In 2007, the collapse of Northern Rock – the promoter of the notorious 'Together' mortgage that lent up to 125 per cent of the property's value – was the first obvious sign of the storm that was about to engulf the UK banking system.

Having taken Northern Rock into the public sector, the government has recently divided it into two separate elements. The 'good' bank, Northern Rock PLC, is well capitalised as a deposit-taking and mortgage-providing institution. It is now a viable candidate to be privatised once confidence returns to the banking sector. Alternatively, it could be sold directly to a competitor, possibly outside the existing high-street banks, especially if the government retains its stance on promoting competition among retail lenders.

Placing a valuation on Northern Rock plc is very difficult given the lack of financial data that is in the public domain. A central case estimate for 100 per cent of the business, however, is £1.5 billion.

Support services

In the support services sector, the most obvious candidate for privatisation is Royal Mail, which is facing testing challenges on many fronts.

Royal Mail/Post Office

The publicly owned Royal Mail Group (Royal Mail) operates the mail services and post office network in the UK. Successive governments have avoided, partly for political reasons, undertaking structural changes of the key businesses within Royal Mail. The publication of the Hooper Report, however, set out a near-unequivocal case for major reform of Royal Mail. Furthermore, the government has recently introduced the Postal Services Bill into Parliament. Within this bill, there are provisions for majority private sector ownership of Royal Mail.

Currently, Royal Mail has four core businesses – the key data, based on 2009/10 figures, are set out in Table 26 below:

Table 26 **Key Royal Mail data**

Business	Staff	Revenues (£m)	Op. Profit (£m)
Royal Mail (letters/packages)	155,312	6,564	121
GLS (pan-EU logistics)	12,885	1,487	112
Parcelforce Worldwide	4,434	399	17
Post Office (11,905 branches)	8,209	838	72

Source: Royal Mail Annual Report 2009/10

In recent years, Royal Mail has suffered fierce competition, especially from the rapid growth of e-mail, in its core business operations. In 2009/10, inland addressed mail volumes – of letters, packages and parcels – were down by 7.3 per cent on 2008/09. Average daily mail volumes in 2009/10 were 71 million against a peak in 2005/06 of 84 million.

Despite some efficiency gains, far more are possible, especially with greater use of machinery in sorting offices. In 2009/10, staff costs amounted to £5.7 billion, equivalent to 64 per cent of Royal Mail's overall costs. Hence, a rigorous focus on reducing the cost base is a top management priority. Royal Mail's finances are heavily influenced by regulation, which will be integrated into Ofcom once the Postal Services Bill is enacted. Undoubtedly, the permitted charges for first-class and second-class stamps remain crucial in determining Royal Mail's overall financial returns. Importantly, the long-standing pension fund deficit will remain in the public sector. At March 2010, the pension fund deficit had soared to over £8.0 billion.

With its unique level of customer contact, Royal Mail's potential for cross-selling is considerable. Furthermore, the scope for becoming the market leader for online deliveries, a rapidly growing segment of the retail market, is self-evident. In private hands, Royal Mail may thrive.

To ascertain Royal Mail's value, comparisons have been made with other quoted post office businesses, notably the Dutch-based TNT, and recent private equity valuations. Royal Mail's underlying value should be at a considerable premium to the £2.3 billion regulatory asset value (RAV) that had previously been applied to its core business. With the £8 billion (or more) pension fund deficit remaining in the public sector, Royal Mail's value is probably about £4 billion.

Other support services businesses

Within the support services sector, there are twelve other publicly owned businesses – categorised under other support services in Table 27 – that have undoubted attractions for private sector investment. They are:

- Covent Garden Market Authority;
- Export Credits Guarantee Department;
- Forensic Science Service;
- Land Registry;
- Met Office;
- Ordnance Survey;

- Partnerships UK;
- Royal Mint;
- Student Loan Book;
- Industry Training Boards (three).

These have been valued at £700 million to £1.5 billion.

Transport and logistics

In the transport and logistics sector, there are some valuable publicly owned businesses that should be privatised in addition to the 30-year franchise for operating High Speed One – the owner of the Channel Tunnel Rail Link – that was recently sold for £2.1 billion.

The possible privatisations of the road network and of London Underground, however, have been excluded from this chapter. In the former's case, a major extension of road charging would probably be needed – this is dealt with in Chapter 10. In the latter's case, the financial collapse of Metronet Rail and the transfer of Tube Lines to Transport for London (TfL) make privatisation difficult for the foreseeable future.

Network Rail

Network Rail, which was set up in 2002, is a not-for-profit company. Its predecessor was Railtrack, which had replaced the former publicly owned British Rail; Railtrack had been floated in 1993 and had subsequently prospered. Following abiding concerns about its ability to finance very large investment requirements, which soared in the wake of the Hatfield accident in 2002, Railtrack was effectively – and controversially – nationalised.

Network Rail itself runs, maintains and develops 20,000 miles of railway track in the UK, the signalling system, 40,000 bridges/tunnels and many level crossings; furthermore, it operates eighteen core stations. Network Rail is currently undertaking a £35 billion five-year investment programme, which is due to end in 2014. Despite the heavy investment over the last decade, notably the £9 billion West Coast Main Line project, much of its asset base remains in a poor condition, especially many of its railway bridges. Consequently, formidable investment levels seem inevitable for the foreseeable future. Nevertheless, the prodigious level of cash consumption in recent years, along with the bureaucratic governance structure, suggests that there is real scope for efficiency improvements that privatisation could, in time, deliver.

Clearly, prior to any privatisation initiative, Network Rail's finances would need some restructuring. At March 2010, Network Rail had net debt of £23.8 billion, compared with a regulatory asset value (RAV) of £37.2 billion, thereby giving a RAV gearing ratio of 64 per cent. In seeking to return Network Rail to the private sector as a conventional privatised company, which would undoubtedly be difficult politically, it would be preferable to undertake the process in tranches. An initial offer of shares to leading financial institutions, in order to judge the appetite of investors, would be a prudent first step.

On the above basis, Network Rail's implicit equity value – assuming it traded in line with its RAV – would be £13.4 billion. Given its very chequered past, its major investment programme and its dated asset base, a discount to RAV would be expected. Hence, a 5 per cent discount has been assumed, which would give rise to a valuation of between £11 billion and £12 billion.

National Air Traffic Services

The history of National Air Traffic Services (NATS) dates back to the early 1960s. Subsequently, its role – as a unified national air traffic control organisation – has becoming increasingly important. In recent years, major investment has been undertaken in order to modernise the air traffic control infrastructure, which has had to adjust to much-enhanced security criteria.

In 2001, NATS's ownership was transferred to a public/private partnership (PPP). The key investors in this PPP were the government, with a stake approaching 49 per cent, and the Airline Group – a consortium of seven airlines – with a 46 per cent stake. The remaining shares were allocated to NATS's Employee Share Trust. Post-9/11, BAA, currently owned by a consortium led by Spain's Ferrovial, took a 4 per cent stake in NATS, with the Airline Group's interest falling to just below 42 per cent.

Given the solidity of its long-term revenue flow, the level of which is principally determined by regulators at the Civil Aviation Authority (CAA), NATS would offer real attractions for infrastructure funds. The government could sell its stake either directly to the Airline Group and its shareholders or to a third party via a trade sale. Alternatively, it could offer its stake to outside investors through a public flotation. A more radical option would be to undertake a public flotation of the whole business, a policy that the Airline Group, whose seven shareholders are airlines, might welcome.

In its 2009/10 financial year, NATS reported revenues of £755 million. Its pre-tax profit, prior to exceptional items, was £101 million, while net debt at March 2010 amounted to £520 million. If substantive regulatory changes are imposed, NATS's finances may need fundamental reassessment. Ideally, regulatory reform should precede any sale of the government's 49 per cent stake in NATS. If, however, any major regulatory changes are deferred for some years, the government should offer its NATS stake for sale prior to their implementation.

Based on a 10 per cent premium over a RAV figure of about £1.1 billion, NATS's value, after deducting net debt of £520 million, is estimated at £700 million. Hence, any sale of the government's 49 per cent stake, after deducting an appropriate discount for its minority status, could be expected to realise around £300 million.

Trust Ports

Following several acquisitions in recent years, very few UK ports companies remain publicly quoted: the largest, Forth Ports, has recently recommended an offer from Arcus. Associated British Ports (ABP), P&O and Mersey Docks are now all owned by either sovereign or private equity funds. There are currently over 100 ports, some of which are no longer operational, that are classified as Trust Ports. Under this special legal status, they are run by independent statutory bodies, governed by their own local legislation and controlled by an independent board rather than by shareholders.

Between 1992 and 1997, seven former Trust Ports – Clyde, Dundee, Forth, Ipswich, Sheerness, Thamesport and Tilbury – were sold. Significantly, six of the remaining larger Trust Ports – Dover, Harwich, Milford Haven, Poole, Port of London Authority (PLA) and Tyne – were reclassified as public corporations in 2001.

The most high-profile of these Trust Ports, Dover, has annual revenues of around £60 million; many of the smaller Trust Ports have very modest revenues. By comparison, Forth Ports reported annual revenues of £182 million for 2010: its market value has been boosted by its property portfolio at Leith, near Edinburgh.

Undoubtedly, any ownership change affecting the Trust Ports would be a protracted legal process. Nonetheless, given the need for modernisation, any privatisation initiative should ultimately benefit the ports concerned.

By privatising the five Trust Ports identified above, along with the PLA, proceeds of around £1.0 billion are anticipated. This figure represents a discount to the multiples currently applicable to Forth Ports, but it could be boosted by property revaluations.

The utilities and energy sectors

In the utilities and energy sectors, there is still some unfinished business, especially with regard to UK water. Given its low commercial risk, investment in the regulated water sector has become increasingly popular for long-term investors.

Scottish Water

When the nine English water companies and Welsh Water – now Glas Cymru, a not-for-profit company – were floated in 1989, the owner-ship of the Scottish water industry was left in the public sector. North of the border, opposition to water privatisation had been particularly trenchant.

Scottish Water, which was formed from the consolidation of three regional water businesses, has undergone considerable reorganisation in recent years and efficiency has improved. Water charges in Scotland, however, are partly subsidised by loans from the Scottish government. Moreover, for many years Scotland has received a disproportionately high allocation of public funding via the much-debated 1970s Barnett formula.

There is a strong case to extend water privatisation to Scotland, an issue that would assuredly give rise to complex legal debates between the UK government and the devolved Scottish government. Signifi-cantly, too, there is some support within the Scottish Executive itself for Scottish Water to become a not-for-profit company on the Glas Cymru model.

Scottish Water had a regulatory asset value (RAV) of about £5.4 billion in March 2010. Clearly, any privatisation value to taxpayers would depend upon the level of debt in its restructured balance sheet. If unchanged from the latest net debt figure of £2.9 billion, the sale of Scottish Water should raise around £2.5 billion.

Northern Ireland Water

Fundamental changes are currently under way in the supply arrange-ments for water and sewerage services in Northern Ireland, which are under the control of the publicly owned Northern Ireland Water (NIW), which was set up in April 2007.

The issue of water charges is particularly sensitive in Northern Ireland, to such an extent that the NI Executive has decided to postpone the introduction of domestic water charging, which was originally due to start four years ago.

In common with the situation in Scotland, there is a formidable capital expenditure programme to be financed by NI Water as it seeks to achieve higher standards and to comply with EU Water Directives. As the shambolic operating performance over the 2010 Christmas period clearly demonstrated, investment levels have been inadequate for decades.

For various reasons, including the need for investment, there is a strong case for undertaking a public flotation of NIW once the charging regime issue and its many operating problems have been satisfactorily resolved. In time, given annual revenues of around £360 million and some balance sheet restructuring, NIW might command a value of around £400 million. This estimate is subject to substantial variance, partly depending on the debt structure that is eventually determined.

Urenco

While the government owns several small nuclear businesses, the most valuable nuclear energy asset still in the public sector is the government's 33 per cent stake in Urenco, the uranium enrichment business. Until the recent Fukushima disaster in Japan, Urenco's putative value had risen very appreciably due to plans for a large build-out of new nuclear plant worldwide and the increased fuel volumes that would eventually be consumed as a consequence. Urenco has a current order book worth around £18 billion.

Selling this 33 per cent stake, however, will not be straightforward as the Dutch government also retains a 33 per cent stake in Urenco: the remaining 33 per cent shareholding is owned by two German energy companies – E.ON and RWE. The approval of these three shareholders will be required for any disposal: they also have a first right of refusal.

Placing a value on both Urenco generally, and more specifically on the government's minority 33 per cent stake, is complex, especially given the first-refusal options held by the three other shareholders. Nonetheless, Urenco's total valuation should be at least £2.5 billion, with the government's stake, after allowing for its minority status, worth around £750 million.

Media

In the media sector, there are two clear candidates for some form of privatisation – Channel 4 and parts of the BBC.

Channel 4

Channel 4 was launched in 1981 and has always been owned by the government. Its public ownership has often been justified on the basis that it enabled Channel 4 to commission programmes that private sector businesses might not otherwise have commissioned.

Channel 4's finances are improving. Its 2010 revenues amounted to £935 million, most of which was from advertising. This revenue figure compares with £830 million in 2009; previously, revenues had shown no increase since 2005. Despite almost £580 million being spent on programme commissioning and other content costs in 2010, Channel 4's operating margins have recovered – the pre-tax profit in 2010 was £54 million.

Against that background, it is clear that a new injection of finance – through whatever means – would benefit Channel 4, especially in the run-up to the switch-over to digital broadcasting in 2012. In terms of privatising the business – most probably by a trade sale or possibly via a public flotation – decisions would have to be taken about both the due process and, more specifically, whether two companies with major media interests should be allowed to participate.

In particular, the acquisition of Channel 4 by ITV would increase the latter's share of the free-to-air broadcasting market. The position of News International is less clear cut – and especially controversial. As a

39 per cent shareholder in BSkyB – shortly due to rise to near 100 per cent ownership – News International would certainly be interested in acquiring Channel 4, which would nicely complement BSkyB's satellite TV operations.

Channel 4 is probably worth about £700 million, a figure boosted by the reported £152 million net cash balance at December 2010. This valuation is based on a comparative analysis with the much larger ITV, whose market value is now £2.7 billion.

The BBC

The BBC continues to face major change following its decision to freeze its licence fee at the current level until 2016/17 and thereby waive its right to the previously agreed increases. For the BBC to operate within this tighter financial formula will mean substantial cost reductions, a process that is currently under way: the BBC's large pension deficit is a particularly intractable problem.

Against this background, any privatisation of the BBC would be even more complex. Irrespective of the rest of its operations, however, the BBC Worldwide subsidiary is prospering and is well suited – subject to the imposition of various regulatory obligations – to be moved into the private sector. BBC Worldwide has reported impressive figures. Revenues rose to £888 million in 2009/10, from £704 million in 2008/09. The operating profit performance is particularly encouraging, with a return of £140 million compared with just £44 million in 2008/09.

More generally, the separation of the commercial operations of the BBC from its globally respected public service element is probably the best way forward. Such a scenario might well fit in with recent proposals to allow part of the licence fee revenue to be allocated to other organisations that undertake public service broadcasting activities on a competitive basis.

Partly because of its undoubted trophy asset status, the privatisation of BBC Worldwide would attract very strong interest both in the UK and overseas – and command a significant premium over other broadcasting media assets. Its sale should raise at least £2.0 billion.

Telecoms

Between 1980 and 2000, most of the UK's telecoms sector was privatised – Cable and Wireless, British Telecom and the Hull-based Kingston Communications were all publicly floated. Sector leader Vodafone, which emerged from Racal Electronics, has never been publicly owned. In recent years, the most important commercial initiative in the UK telecoms sector was the holding of the 3G auction in 2000, which raised an astonishing £22.5 billion.

A further auction of bandwidth has been planned for some time – and has been the subject of considerable delay. This spectrum auction is now scheduled to be held in the first half of 2012. Two slices of bandwidth will be offered. The 800 MHz segment has become available owing to the switch from analogue to digital TV. Secondly, the 2,600 MHz segment should be eagerly sought after, given its potential in urban environments.

In the lead-up to this auction, there have been disagreements on several fronts, especially regarding the dominant role of Everything Everywhere – the UK joint venture of the French-owned Orange and the German-owned T-Mobile – and the status of the existing 2G spectrum holders, the Spanish-owned O2 and Vodafone.

In any event, holding this auction should be a high priority. It is not possible, at present, to project with certainty the level of proceeds. They are most likely, though, to lie within a range of £1 billion to £3 billion. In Germany, a similar – though not identical – auction took place and raised around £3.5 billion. There is an allowance for the projected proceeds from this auction within the franchise grouping estimate of £3 billion in Table 27.

Leisure

In the leisure sector, there are two sizeable publicly owned businesses that seem suitable for privatisation – the Tote and British Waterways.

The Tote

After years of disagreement, the process of privatising the Tote is nearing completion. The north-west bookmaker Betfred has now been confirmed as the preferred bidder, at a price of £265 million.

British Waterways

As a public corporation, British Waterways manages some 2,200 miles of inland waterways, mainly navigable rivers and canals. Many canals have received little investment, however, and, in some cases, are in a very poor condition.

While British Waterways has gradually adopted more commercial techniques, there is still much to do. The 2009/10 accounts reported a small operating deficit after a near £28 million cost of capital charge. The revenue line was materially boosted by government grants of £70 million, which supplemented commercial income of £101 million. Significantly, property rents continue to be the largest single element of trading income, accounting for over £31 million.

Arguably, it is property which holds the key to the future of British Waterways. While the property market is still recovering from falling prices, many of British Waterways' sites offer an attractive water environment, with a low flooding risk. At March 2010, British Waterways reported investment assets of £377 million, of which £370 million was attributable to freehold land, building and other structures.

The government is currently reviewing the status of British Waterways but any short-term privatisation initiative seems unlikely. If British Waterways were to be sold, the proceeds would be very dependent upon its £377 million of investment assets. On this basis, the sale might be able to raise over £300 million, although the extent of legacy liabilities would also be very relevant to any valuation.

Investment trusts

In the investment trust sector, CDC Group (CDC) is an obvious candidate for a conventional privatisation. But the government should also consider selling its 40 per cent stake in Actis, which was sold out of CDC for a negligible amount via a management buyout in 2004: the government retains a 40 per cent stake – equivalent to an 80 per cent economic interest – in Actis until 2013.

CDC Group

CDC was formed in 1999 out of the Commonwealth Development Corporation. While it remains government-owned, it is now more financially oriented and runs a fund-of-funds. CDC manages equity funds, which invest in the emerging markets of Asia, Africa and Latin America – but with a pronounced emphasis on low-income countries in South Asia and sub-Saharan Africa.

Given the nature of CDC's business, a trade sale to a respected fund management company would seem to be the most obvious way to deliver value for the government – it might also give rise to a more active investment policy.

With a net asset value (NAV) of £2.8 billion at December 2010 – a substantial part of which is accounted for by cash – any sale of CDC should be able to raise proceeds of close to NAV.

Real estate

The government owns a vast portfolio of assets, which the National Asset Register of 2007 valued at over £337 billion. Even if just a small fraction of this asset base were sold, the one-off proceeds would be very considerable. Of course, property prices have moved quite sharply since this valuation in 2007, and putting an open-market value on government property is very difficult. There are also apparent anomalies within the asset register which make the author doubt some of the figures. Furthermore, some items on the register have already been included as privatisation candidates either in this chapter or in other chapters.

Nonetheless, every effort should be made to sell off surplus land and building assets, especially by the Ministry of Defence, which has argued in the past that there is relatively modest scope to dispose of part of its valuable property portfolio. A small percentage sale – 10 per cent, for example – of the National Asset Register's total asset base would result in very substantial one-off proceeds – of perhaps £30 billion. Indeed, the other proposals in this monograph would lead to a requirement for a much smaller government estate. Both the suggested extent of the sale and the suggested sale proceeds are somewhat arbitrary – they would seem, however, to be the minimum that should be possible. Some of the estate could be sold to private firms that would be providing education and health services under other proposals in this monograph.

Projected government proceeds

Aside from the many operational benefits that would accrue from undertaking the privatisation programme outlined in this chapter, the government's finances would also benefit very substantially from the receipt of the proceeds.

In total, estimated proceeds of around £112 billion could accrue if this programme were pursued in its entirety, although it is recognised that there may be compelling reasons why a particular privatisation cannot be undertaken: in some cases, major financial restructuring may be necessary. On various assumptions generally outlined above, however, Table 27 provides estimates of the projected proceeds if the various privatisation sales discussed in this chapter were completed.

Table 27 **Projected privatisation proceeds**

Organisation	Government stake (%)	Estimated sales proceeds (£m)	Methodology
Royal Bank of Scotland	83 (inc. B shares)	34,600	Market quote (+ B shares) – 10%
Lloyds	41	13,300	Market quote – 10%
Northern Rock	100	1,500	City projections
Royal Mail	100	4,000	TNT/CVC comparisons
Other support services	Various	1,100	Revenues/returns
Network Rail	Not-for-profit	11,500	RAV – 5%
NATS	49	300	RAV + 10%
Trust Ports	Various	1,000	Forth comparisons
Scottish Water	100	2,500	RAV
NI Water	100	400	Sector comparators
Urenco	33	750	PER analysis
Channel 4	100	700	ITV/Channel 5 sale comparisons
BBC Worldwide	100	2,000	Sector comparators
Tote	100	250	Reported bids
British Waterways	100	300	Net assets
CDC	100	2,800	Net assets
Franchises*	Various	3,000	Projected bids
Others	Various	2,000	N/A
Real estate	100	30,000	National Asset Register
Total		112,000	

Notes: * Dartford Crossing, East Coast Main Line and Spectrum auctions. Closing prices as at 27 May 2011 have been used.
Source: Nigel Hawkins Associates

Conclusion

If the programme set out in this chapter were implemented in full, many benefits would accrue, especially in terms of efficiencies. It should also yield proceeds for the government of around £112 billion, 30 per cent of which relate to the 83 per cent shareholding (including the B shares) in RBS. In embracing such an opportunity, it would not only raise very substantial proceeds – to the benefit of the UK's desperately stretched public finances – but also recreate the drive that lay behind the original privatisation policy that has been replicated worldwide.

12 SERIOUSLY SUBOPTIMAL: UK ENERGY AND CLIMATE CHANGE POLICY
Richard Wellings

At first sight, energy and climate change appear to account for a very small percentage of total government expenditure. The budget of the Department of Energy and Climate Change (DECC) will rise from £2.9 billion in 2010/11 to £3.7 billion in 2014/15, a real-terms increase of 15 per cent (HM Treasury, 2010), but even then it will represent just 0.5 per cent of total spending.[1] This impression is deceptive, however, because significant energy and climate change expenditure is planned by other departments. Indeed, the climate change agenda permeates almost every aspect of government.

The Department for International Development (DfID), for example, plans to contribute, along with DECC and DEFRA,[2] £2.9 billion to 'International Climate Finance' over the spending review period. Moreover, the Committee on Climate Change has estimated UK public research and development spending on climate-change-related projects to be £550 million for 2009/10 (DECC, 2010a). Less directly, transport, regeneration, housing and welfare budgets are all clearly affected by climate change policies. The strong support for public transport since the mid-1990s has been justified on environmental grounds (see Hibbs et al., 2006); planning and regeneration policies have focused on eco-friendly urban forms; improving energy efficiency has been a key component of recent housing expenditure;[3] and rises in benefits such as the Winter

---

1   A high proportion of DECC's budget is unrelated to climate change, being spent on nuclear decommissioning. See http://www.hm-treasury.gov.uk/d/wintersupps_decc_1011.pdf.
2   Department for Environment, Food and Rural Affairs.
3   For example, through the Decent Homes Initiative.

Fuel Allowance may be related to the impact of energy policies on electricity and gas prices. The Department for Education provides guidance to schools on 'carbon management strategies' and engages in consultations on 'sustainable schools'. Climate change is also likely to be covered in at least four of the subjects taught at schools.[4] Even the Department of Health (DH), like all other government departments, has been obliged to produce a climate change plan (DH, 2010), which sets out how the health and social care sector can reduce its greenhouse-gas emissions.

The direct energy costs of government are also significant. In 2007 the National Health Service (NHS), for example, spent about £400 million per annum on energy, and there are also significant transport and waste disposal costs (NHS Confederation, 2007). Schools are estimated to spend a similar sum on energy bills (Carbon Trust, 2009). Energy consumption figures suggest that central government departments spend around £500 million a year on electricity and heating alone (see NAO, 2007). Energy costs are particularly significant for the armed forces, which are estimated to account for 1 per cent of the UK's greenhouse gas emissions (MoD, 2010). The public sector in Scotland was estimated to spend £200 million on electricity in 2008,[5] suggesting a figure of around £2 billion for the UK as a whole. Across the wide range of government activity it seems likely that annual expenditure on energy, including transport fuel, exceeds £5 billion per year. And this sum is likely to rise significantly as a result of efforts to meet ambitious targets on greenhouse gas emissions and renewable energy.

Climate change targets

The Climate Change Act (2008) enabled the government to set legally binding targets for reducing UK greenhouse gas emissions. The current target is at least a 34 per cent cut by 2020 and an 80 per cent cut by 2050,

---

4   Citizenship, geography, religious education and science – see http://curriculum.qcda. gov.uk/key-stages-3-and-4/index.aspx.
5   See http://news.bbc.co.uk/1/hi/business/7566715.stm.

compared with the 1990 baseline (CCC, 2008). In addition, under the European Union's Renewable Energy Directive,[6] the UK is legally bound to generate 15 per cent[7] of its energy from renewable resources by 2020. Under DECC's 'lead scenario' this will mean obtaining 30 per cent of electricity, 12 per cent of heat and 10 per cent of transport energy from renewables, compared with figures of 5.5 per cent, close to zero and 2.6 per cent respectively in 2009 (DECC, 2009).

The Renewables Obligation

Several strategies will be employed to meet this target. Incentives for the development of renewable energy supplies will be increased. For example, under the Renewables Obligation (RO), electricity suppliers will be required to obtain an increasing share of their electricity from renewable sources. Renewable Obligation Certificates (ROCs) are issued to accredited generators of renewable electricity, and suppliers must meet their obligations by presenting sufficient certificates to the regulator. Those suppliers that fail to produce sufficient ROCs must make payments into a 'buyout' fund to compensate for the shortfall. The fund is then redistributed to the suppliers in proportion to the number of ROCs submitted, thereby providing incentives to increase renewable generation. It is estimated that in 2009/10, the Renewables Obligation provided a subsidy to renewables of £1.1 billion (OFGEM, 2011).

The RO is defined by the Office for National Statistics (ONS) as a form of tax and spend (HM Treasury, 2010: 83) and this interpretation can clearly be applied to other interventions in energy markets. Consumers are forced to pay a levy which is then used to fund expenditure directed by government. Such expenditure can arguably be counted as government spending on climate change.

---

6   Available at: http://eur-lex.europa.eu/LexUriServ/LexUriServ.do?uri=OJ:L:2009:140:0
     016:0062:EN:PDF.
7   The 15 per cent figure is a proportion of gross final consumption of energy.

The EU ETS

As well as the RO, the UK energy sector is forced to participate in the European Union Emissions Trading System (EU ETS). Launched in 2005, this is a cap and trade scheme which aims to restrict greenhouse gas emissions. Companies receive allowances which they can then trade with each other. But the number of allowances is reduced over time as the cap is reduced. By 2020, a cut of 21 per cent is planned from 2005 levels (EC, 2010). As well as power stations, the EU ETS covers heavy industries such as steel and oil refining, and will be gradually extended to other sectors. To date, a large majority of allowances have been allocated free of charge, but from 2013 the next phase of the scheme will require at least 50 per cent of allowances to be purchased at auction (DECC, n.d.). The Office for Budget Responsibility (OBR) forecasts that government ETS receipts will rise from £0.5 billion in 2010/11 to £2.2 billion in 2014/15 (OBR, 2010).

Environmental taxes

In addition to the EU ETS and the RO, the government has used climate change to justify the imposition of a number of environmental taxes. The Climate Change Levy, which is added to non-renewable electricity and gas, and applied to non-domestic users, raised £0.7 billion in 2009 (ONS, 2011). In theory businesses have been compensated by a 0.3 per cent reduction in employer national insurance contributions, making the measure revenue-neutral. Climate change policy is also an important justification for the following: the Landfill Tax (£0.8 billion), Aggregates Levy (£0.3 billion), Air Passenger Duty (£1.8 billion) and Road Fuel Duty (£28 billion) (ibid.).[8] The great bulk of this revenue is used for general expenditure rather than spending on climate change mitigation.

---

8   The latter clearly pre-dates modern environmental concerns.

The impact on the energy sector

The government estimates that climate change policies, primarily the RO and the EU ETS, will be adding 26 per cent to domestic electricity prices in real terms by 2015 and 10 per cent to domestic gas prices (DECC, 2010b: 6). The impact on commercial users will be similar (ibid.: 10). It is hoped various governmental price supports will stimulate an estimated £200 billion of capital investment in the energy sector by 2020 (House of Commons, 2011). Not all this investment is directly related to climate change policies. Many coal-fired power stations will be forced to close by 2015 by the EU Large Combustion Plant Directive (see Helm, 2008). Over half this investment, however, is likely to be dedicated to wind power, in particular to construct offshore wind farms and the grid to connect them. A further considerable share will be devoted to a new generation of nuclear stations. The market will be rigged to deter investment in relatively low-cost fossil-fuel plants, although additional gas-generated capacity is likely to be sanctioned to compensate for unreliable wind output. It is clear that a very high proportion of the £200 billion investment is related directly to climate change policies. Replacing ageing plant with conventional fossil-fuelled stations would require a far lower level of investment in both new generating capacity and the national grid.[9]

The impact on government spending

A huge investment programme is thus central to UK climate change policy. And the deployment of scarce economic resources on such a grand scale will inevitably 'crowd out' other economic activity. Accordingly, investment in productive, wealth-creating enterprises is likely to suffer as a result. In consequence, both growth and general tax revenues are likely to be significantly lower than would have been the case without

---

9   For illustration, Lodge (2007: 11) estimates construction costs for coal-fired stations at £0.7–0.9 million per MW. At £0.9 million per MW it would cost £29 billion to replace the UK's estimated 32 GW capacity shortfall for 2016 (ibid.: i).

such high levels of investment in green energy. Climate change policy is therefore likely to affect government spending and taxation in several ways:

- Direct spending on climate change initiatives by DECC, DfID and other departments may be in the region of £3.5 billion per annum by 2014/15 (taking a conservative approach, and ignoring, for example, public transport expenditure, which has egalitarian as well as environmental rationales and which is covered in another chapter).

- Annual spending on energy bills by government departments is likely to rise as energy prices increase as a result of climate change policies. Based on official estimates this may be costing around £750 million a year[10] by 2014/15, although improved efficiency could reduce this figure.

- The estimated 26 per cent added to electricity prices will cost consumers approximately £9.5 billion per annum in 2014/15;[11] the 10 per cent increment to gas prices will cost about £2 billion per annum. Since the extra revenue will be funding government-directed climate change programmes, there is a strong argument it should be treated as public spending. Currently, renewable support schemes such as the RO are defined as tax and spend (HM Treasury, 2010: 83), but not the EU ETS and other measures. The RO is estimated to add about £1.5 billion to electricity bills in 2015 (BERR, 2008: Annex C).

---

10 As stated above, the government estimates that climate change policies will add 26 per cent to domestic electricity prices in real terms by 2015 and 10 per cent to domestic gas prices (DECC, 2010b: 6). Heating oil and road fuel will also be affected. Total government spending on energy bills was estimated at at least £5 billion, so a 15 per cent real-terms rise of £750 million is probably a conservative estimate.

11 Annual UK electricity consumption in 2010 was about 380 TWh, with climate change measures estimated to be adding about £25/MWh in 2015. Gas consumption was about 650 TWh (not including electricity generation), with about £3.50/MWh added in 2015 (DECC, 2010c, 2011). These estimates are conservative because they assume no growth in consumption levels.

• The investment in 'green' energy infrastructure funded by these price rises will crowd out investment in wealth-creating projects with negative, but difficult to quantify, long-term impacts on growth and therefore general tax revenues.

Spending on climate change policies is therefore likely to reach at least £15 billion by 2014/15. In reality the total will be much higher if big projects such as offshore wind and nuclear power suffer cost overruns and delays (see Myddelton, 2006); if increased transport fuel costs and spending on various public transport schemes are included (see transport chapter); if account is taken of climate-change-related regulatory costs; and to the extent that government raises social security benefits that are linked to a measure of inflation that incorporates energy prices.

The next section assesses the effectiveness of current policy. Could the UK's climate change targets be met at lower cost through more efficient mechanisms, and should the targets be either amended or abandoned?

Meeting the targets at lower cost

An efficient approach to meeting the targets would provide incentives to reduce emissions at the minimum economic cost. The policy framework in the UK – a complex web of sometimes contradictory measures – is very far removed from this ideal. A major problem is that climate change policies are overlaid on existing state interventions. For example, different types of carbon emissions are taxed at very different rates. Road fuel is taxed at approximately 150 per cent, while domestic gas and electricity benefit from a reduced VAT rate of just 5 per cent (an implicit subsidy of around 15 per cent). Several carbon-producing activities receive substantial government subsidies, including public transport and agriculture. Any attempt to reduce emissions efficiently would also be hampered by the impact of the different costs imposed by the varied regulatory regimes applied to various sectors. Even policies designed to reduce emissions directly fail the consistency test. For example, the Renewables Obligation, described by Helm (2008: 29) as 'among the most expensive schemes in the world', favours renewable energy options over potentially cheaper low-carbon alternatives such as nuclear power. The climate change levy is also applied to nuclear.

The efficiency and effectiveness of the EU ETS are also doubtful. In Phase 1 (2005–08), emissions covered by the scheme actually rose. An over-allocation of permits meant that the price of carbon collapsed to close to zero (see Robinson and O'Brien, 2007). Some member countries also appear to have set tougher quotas than others within the EU ETS, which will have further undermined the efficiency of the scheme. The effectiveness of Phase 2 (2008–12) remains to be seen. It is certainly possible to identify several flaws. In particular, the system's essentially political nature makes it vulnerable to rent-seeking behaviour (Tullock, 1967) and raises the prospect that the regulatory process will be captured by the big firms that are affected by it (Stigler, 1971). The over-allocation of permits in Phase 1 may have resulted, at least partly, from such pressures – which may be exacerbated by competition for better terms among EU member states. Political risks also make the long-term future of the ETS uncertain. As a result, companies may be deterred from making long-term investments in low-carbon technologies, a problem that may be exacerbated by related uncertainties regarding carbon prices (Helm, 2008: 8–9). For example, one risk is that the EU could bow to political pressure – perhaps in the context of a continuing economic slowdown – and release too many permits in Phase 3. Emitters under the EU ETS are also free to import credits from outside the EU under the United Nations' Clean Development Mechanism (CDM). The CDM allows firms in the developed world to obtain emissions credits by funding carbon reduction projects in developing countries such as China and India. It has been argued that the CDM may in practice encourage increased emissions by funding industrial development that would not otherwise have taken place and by allowing higher emissions in rich countries (see Campbell and Klaes, 2011). More generally, policies such as the EU ETS that increase energy costs in some countries risk displacing emissions to jurisdictions not covered by the scheme, a phenomenon known as 'carbon leakage'. Heavy industry, for example, may be encouraged to move from the EU to countries such as China. Recent research suggests that on a carbon consumption basis (i.e. including the carbon emitted to produce goods consumed within the EU but manufactured elsewhere), EU emissions have risen by 47 per cent since 1990 and UK emissions by 30 per cent (Brinkley and Less, 2010: 1).

An efficient carbon tax

The main alternative to cap and trade is the imposition of a carbon tax. Supporters of this option (see, for example, Lawson, 2008; Nordhaus, 2009) argue that it is far more transparent than cap and trade schemes. It is clear to consumers why they are paying more. In addition, a carbon tax may be less susceptible to rent-seeking by special interests. This is because it can be imposed on very large numbers of individuals rather than being focused on concentrated groups with high incentives to engage in lobbying activities, such as electricity generating companies (see Olson, 1965, for a discussion of the general problem of interest groups). Furthermore, a carbon tax can rapidly be applied to every polluting sector rather than being phased in slowly like the EU ETS, and can even be used to tax goods imported from, say, China, which may partly address the problem of carbon leakage. Importantly, the carbon tax rate is likely to be far more stable and predictable than carbon prices in a cap and trade scheme. This may encourage long-term investment in low-carbon technology.

An efficient carbon tax approach to reducing UK emissions could proceed as follows. First, it would be necessary to remove distortions from existing taxes, subsidies and regulations to ensure that the tax-incentivised emissions reductions took place in the most cost-effective manner. For example, VAT at the full rate would be introduced on domestic fuel, public transport and food (agriculture being a major source of CO_2 and methane emissions). Associated subsidies would be removed, such as the Winter Fuel Allowance, grants to bus and train operators, and payments to farmers from the Common Agricultural Policy. Relevant regulations, such as insulation standards for new buildings, would be rescinded. Road fuel duty would be abolished and replaced by the carbon tax. In the energy sector, the UK would withdraw from the EU ETS and the CDM, and abolish the Renewables Obligation and the Climate Change Levy. Power companies would be free to use whichever fuel they desired and there would be no government controls on the kind of new power stations that were permitted. The carbon tax itself would be applied at a uniform rate, based on units of emissions, across the economy, with the rate adjusted over time to meet the UK's climate change targets. The tax would be revenue-neutral, meaning the revenue raised would be used to reduce taxes elsewhere.

A simple carbon tax would enable the Department of Energy and Climate Change to be abolished, saving perhaps £2 billion per annum by 2014/15.[12] The ending of the Renewables Obligation would perhaps save a further £1.5 billion.

Implementation problems

The implementation of an efficient carbon tax would, of course, present difficulties. The phasing out of farm subsidies, together with withdrawal from the EU ETS, would require the cooperation of the European Union. Moreover, an efficient carbon tax would lead to a significant realignment of taxation in the UK. Those spending a high proportion of their income on domestic heating, public transport and food could face much higher bills (though in the latter instance, reform of the Common Agricultural Policy (CAP) would mitigate this effect). At the same time, motorists could face much lower fuel costs owing to the replacement of fuel duty with a carbon tax applied consistently across all economic

---

12   This estimate of savings does not include nuclear decommissioning expenditure. Responsibility for this would be transferred to another department.

sectors.[13] There would be major economic benefits from such a realignment of the tax system – for example, through lower transport costs, greater economies of scale, increased labour mobility and so on. But the likely losers, which could include politically powerful groups such as the elderly (Booth, 2008), would strongly oppose such a reform. It would, of course, be possible to recycle carbon tax revenues into increased welfare benefits for groups negatively affected, although this would reduce the efficiency of the scheme.

One problem is that the impact of a carbon tax on overall emissions would initially be difficult to forecast. It depends in part on the price elasticity of the relevant goods. If the price elasticity of, say, domestic heating is low, then a large price rise as a result of the imposition of full-rate VAT and the carbon tax will not lead to a correspondingly large fall in consumption and therefore emissions. There is evidence, however, that the long-term price elasticity of domestic fuel, particularly electricity, is considerably higher than that of road fuel (OFGEM, 2009; Goodwin et al., 2004), suggesting that a rise in the price of the former combined with a fall in the price of the latter would, *ceteris paribus*, lead to considerable emissions reductions. The price elasticity of carbon-emitting activities would also be affected by which taxes were cut to obtain revenue neutrality following the introduction of a carbon tax. Nevertheless, the carbon tax rate could be adjusted through an iterative process until it produced the desired emissions reductions – although this would remove any pretence that the rate had been set according to some calculation of the 'social costs' of each unit of carbon.

While this chapter has set out some key requirements of an efficient carbon tax, in practice a combination of interest group politics and egalitarian ideology mean that such a tax is extremely unlikely to be implemented. Thus if a carbon tax were to be introduced it would overlay

---

13   Stern (2006) estimated the current 'social cost' of carbon at around $85 per tonne of CO_2 in 2000 prices. In 2011 prices this equates to approximately 13p per litre of petrol (see Spark, 2006). It is debatable to what extent other road-transport-related 'social costs' are genuine externalities (see Hibbs et al., 2006).

existing distortions and could create additional inefficiencies. Indeed, it is not impossible that it would be imposed selectively on certain sectors in order to appease various special interests (for example, public transport and domestic heating for the elderly could be exempted). But there are more fundamental problems with a carbon tax, and indeed any government-directed interventions to address global warming, that question the very basis of current policy.

The limitations of climate change policy

The first problem is the scientific uncertainty surrounding climate change. If forecasts of warming and its economic effects prove to be exaggerated then it is possible that mitigation policies will waste huge amounts of resources for little benefit. Secondly, policymakers face insurmountable knowledge problems in setting policy objectives. The value of environmental goods is *subjective* and known only to individuals (Hayek, 1945): some people may prefer higher temperatures and the benefits they bring (for example, lower heating bills; increased crop yields in some regions). Valuations are also constantly changing and difficult to quantify in monetary terms (in the absence of markets). Yet policymakers somehow have to aggregate all this information to determine objectives, such as a desired limit to the rise in global temperatures by 2100, and the emissions cuts needed to achieve this aim. Since central planners do not have access to the information required to set optimal objectives for climate change policies, or optimal means to achieve them, policy targets are likely to be arbitrary and politically motivated, while the measures implemented are likely to be inefficient and may well be counterproductive (as has been argued in the case of the CDM). There is therefore a serious risk that the costs of climate change policies will far exceed the benefits. Even if policies allow developing countries to increase their emissions, the policies may impede growth in developed countries by diverting resources from productive uses. In turn, this will reduce the opportunities for Third World countries to develop through trade with rich countries (higher transport costs, for example through aviation taxes, will further damage trade). Environmental 'improvements' related to climate change (i.e. lower temperatures, etc.) may be at the expense of prolonging poor environmental conditions associated with poverty – such as dirty water and indoor pollution from open fires. It should also be pointed out that economies subject to increased levels of state control as a result of climate change policies are likely to be far less innovative and flexible than unhampered free market economies – thus rendering them less able to adapt to future environmental changes and less capable of producing technological and institutional solutions.

A market-based approach to climate change

A realistic approach to climate change policy – at both domestic and international levels – would recognise that policymakers are faced by severe knowledge limitations, that government actions will inevitably be corrupted by special interests, and that increased state intervention is likely to be characterised by 'government failure', which risks significant economic damage, with particularly serious consequences for poor inhabitants of developing countries. Accordingly, an anti-interventionist approach would seek to identify and eliminate state activities that actively contribute to climate change. The following are examples of 'win-win' situations where removing inefficient economic distortions is likely to reduce emissions:

- Phasing out agricultural subsidies (livestock farming is said to be responsible for 18 per cent of greenhouse gas emissions globally (Steinfeld et al., 2006)).
- Recognising the property rights of forest-dwelling people, including when they engage in hunting and gathering and/or shifting cultivation (deforestation is thought to account for 25 to 30 per cent of global emissions (FAO, 2006)).

- Allowing electricity companies to replace old coal- or gas-fired power stations with far more efficient new coal- or gas-fired plant.
- Ending government subsidies to energy-intensive sectors (coal, steel, chemicals, public transport and so on – energy prices are also subsidised in many countries).
- Charging full-rate VAT on domestic fuel, public transport and food (but reducing taxes elsewhere to ensure revenue neutrality).

In addition it should be noted that individuals and firms are capable of reducing their contributions to climate change through voluntary action (see Robinson, 2008: 63–6). Many companies, for example, are aiming to reduce their 'carbon footprints'; and consumers may buy products from organisations that seek to preserve the rainforests and so on. If evidence grows that climate change is producing significant harm, more and more people may choose to change their consumption patterns, for example by eating less meat and making fewer journeys.

An alternative approach based on a combination of voluntary action and the removal of harmful policy distortions would avoid the risks of government failure described above. It would, of course, mean abandoning the centrally determined targets and layers of intervention that characterise current climate change policy. But this means the savings are considerable. Eliminating climate-change-related spending by DECC and other departments would save about £3.5 billion in 2014/15. The projected increase in energy bills produced by the Renewables Obligation and the EU ETS, etc., much of which will be used to fund the expansion of wind power, would be avoided, saving a further £11.5 billion a year by 2014/15 (of this, approximately £10 billion is not currently reflected in government public spending figures). On top of these savings, there would be significant economic benefits from the reallocation of investment resources to productive, commercially viable projects and the removal of numerous climate-change-inspired regulations. Phasing out agricultural subsidies would save a further £5 billion (Rotherham, 2009: 3) and public transport subsidies about £12 billion (see Chapter 10), while introducing full-rate VAT on domestic fuel, public transport and food could raise approximately £25 billion (HMRC, 2011). Assuming that any tax increases are matched by reductions elsewhere to ensure revenue neutrality, a market-based approach to climate change could save taxpayers and energy consumers about £20 billion per annum by 2014/15 (excluding the transport measures). Of this £20 billion, approximately £10 billion is currently recorded in ONS definitions of public spending. As a strictly second-best policy, if further action were deemed essential to deal with climate change concerns in the future – as more information becomes available about the magnitude of the problem – a straightforward carbon tax could be less economically damaging than alternative policy interventions.

References

BERR (Department for Business, Enterprise and Regulatory Reform) (2008), *Renewables Obligation Consultation: Updated Modelling for Government Response*, London: BERR.

Booth, P. (2008), 'The young held to ransom – a public choice analysis of the UK state pension system', *Economic Affairs*, 28(1): 2–5.

Brinkley, A. and S. Less (2010), 'Consumption-based accounting for international carbon emissions', research note, London: Policy Exchange.

Campbell, D. and M. Klaes (2011), 'Copenhagen, Cancun and the limits of global welfare economics', *Economic Affairs*, 31(2): 10–16.

Carbon Trust (2009), 'Head teachers urged to wipe £70m off school energy bills', Press release, 16 June, http://www.carbontrust.co.uk/news/news/press-centre/2009/Pages/schools-carbon-footprint.aspx.

CCC (Committee on Climate Change) (2008), *Building a Low-Carbon Economy – the UK's contribution to tackling climate change*, London: The Stationery Office.

DECC (Department of Energy and Climate Change) (2009), *The UK Renewable Energy Strategy*, London: The Stationery Office.

DECC (2010a), *Annual Energy Statement*, London: DECC.

DECC (2010b), *Estimated Impacts of Energy and Climate Change Policies on Bills*, London: DECC.

DECC (2010c), *Digest of United Kingdom Energy Statistics 2010*, London: The Stationery Office.

DECC (2011), 'Energy price statistics', http://www.decc.gov.uk/en/content/cms/statistics/prices/prices.aspx.

DECC (n.d.), 'EU ETS Phase III', http://www.decc.gov.uk/en/content/cms/what_we_do/change_energy/tackling_clima/emissions/eu_ets/phase_iii/phase_iii.aspx.

DH (Department of Health) (2010), *Climate Change Plan*, London: Department of Health, http://www.dh.gov.uk/en/Publicationsandstatistics/Publications/PublicationsPolicyAndGuidance/DH_114929.

EC (European Commission) (2010), 'Emissions Trading System (EU ETS)', http://ec.europa.eu/clima/policies/ets/index_en.htm.

FAO (Food and Agriculture Organization of the United Nations) (2006), 'Deforestation causes global warming', http://www.fao.org/newsroom/en/news/2006/1000385/index.html.

Goodwin, P., J. Dargay and M. Hanly (2004), 'Elasticities of road traffic and fuel consumption with respect to price and income: a review', *Transport Reviews*, 24(3): 275–92.

Hayek, F. A. (1945), 'The use of knowledge in society', *American Economic Review*, 35(5): 519–30.

Helm, D. (2008), *Credible Energy Policy: Meeting the challenges of security of supply and climate change*, London: Policy Exchange.

Hibbs, J., O. Knipping, R. Merkert, C. Nash, R. Roy, D. E. Tyrrall and R. Wellings (2006), *The Railways, the Market and the Government*, London: Institute of Economic Affairs.

HM Treasury (2010), *Spending Review 2010*, London: The Stationery Office.

HMRC (HM Revenue and Customs) (2011), 'Estimated costs of the principal tax expenditure and structural reliefs', http://www.hmrc. gov.uk/stats/tax_expenditures/table1–5.pdf.

House of Commons (2011), *Energy and Climate Change – Third Report: The revised draft National Policy Statements on energy*, London: Parliament.

Lawson, N. (2008), *An Appeal to Reason: A Cool Look at Global Warming*, London: Gerald Duckworth.

Lodge, T. (2007), *Clean Coal: A Clean, Secure and Affordable Alternative*, London: Centre for Policy Studies.

MoD (Ministry of Defence) (2010), *MOD Climate Change Strategy 2010*, London: Ministry of Defence UK.

Myddelton, D. R. (2006), *They Meant Well: Government Project Disasters*, London: Institute of Economic Affairs.

NAO (National Audit Office) (2007), *Energy Consumption and Carbon Emissions in Government Departments*, London: National Audit Office.

NHS Confederation (2007), *Taking the Temperature: Towards an NHS response to global warming*, London: NHS Confederation.

Nordhaus, W. D. (2009), 'Economic issues in designing a global agreement on global warming', Keynote address, 'Climate Change, Global Risks, Challenges and Decisions', Copenhagen, 10–12 March.

OBR (Office for Budget Responsibility) (2010), 'EU Emissions Trading Scheme (ETS) auction receipts', http://budgetresponsibility. independent.gov.uk/d/eu_ets_receipts_211210.pdf.

OFGEM (Office of Gas and Electricity Markets) (2009), 'Can energy charges encourage energy efficiency?', Working paper, http://www. ofgem.gov.uk/sustainability/Documents1/Final%20discussion%20 paper%2022%20July.pdf.

OFGEM (2011), *Renewables Obligation: Annual Report, 2009–10*, London: OFGEM, http://www.ofgem.gov.uk/Sustainability/Environment/ RenewablObl/Documents1/RO%20Annual%20Report%202009–10. pdf.

Olson, M. (1965), *The Logic of Collective Action: Public Goods and the Theory of Groups*, Cambridge, MA: Harvard University Press.

ONS (Office for National Statistics) (2011), 'Government revenues from environmental taxes', http://www.statistics.gov.uk/statbase/Expodata/Spreadsheets/D5688.xls.

Robinson, C. (2008), 'Climate change, centralised action and markets', in C. Robinson (ed.), *Climate Change Policy: Challenging the Activists*, London: Institute of Economic Affairs.

Robinson, H. and N. O'Brien (2007), *Europe's Dirty Secret: Why the EU Emissions Trading Scheme isn't working*, London: Open Europe.

Rotherham, L. (2009), *Food for Thought: How the Common Agricultural Policy costs families nearly £400 a year*, London: TaxPayers' Alliance.

Spark, P. (2006), 'Discussion of the Stern Review', www.cambridgeenergy.com/archive/2006–11–10/cef10Nov2006spark.pdf.

Steinfeld, H., P. Gerber, T. Wassenaar, V. Castel, M. Rosales and C. de Haan (2006), *Livestock's Long Shadow: Environmental Issues and Options*, Rome: FAO.

Stern, N. (2006), *Stern Review on the Economics of Climate Change*, London: The Stationery Office.

Stigler, G. (1971), 'The theory of economic regulation', *Bell Journal of Economics and Management Science*, 2(1): 3–18.

Tullock, G. (1967), 'The welfare costs of tariffs, monopolies, and theft', *Western Economic Journal*, 5(3): 224–32.

ABOUT THE IEA

The Institute is a research and educational charity (No. CC 235 351), limited by guarantee. Its mission is to improve understanding of the fundamental institutions of a free society by analysing and expounding the role of markets in solving economic and social problems.

The IEA achieves its mission by:

* a high-quality publishing programme
* conferences, seminars, lectures and other events
* outreach to school and college students
* brokering media introductions and appearances

The IEA, which was established in 1955 by the late Sir Antony Fisher, is an educational charity, not a political organisation. It is independent of any political party or group and does not carry on activities intended to affect support for any political party or candidate in any election or referendum, or at any other time. It is financed by sales of publications, conference fees and voluntary donations.

In addition to its main series of publications the IEA also publishes a termly journal, *Economic Affairs*.

The IEA is aided in its work by a distinguished international Academic Advisory Council and an eminent panel of Honorary Fellows. Together with other academics, they review prospective IEA publications, their comments being passed on anonymously to authors. All IEA papers are therefore subject to the same rigorous independent refereeing process as used by leading academic journals.

IEA publications enjoy widespread classroom use and course adoptions in schools and universities. They are also sold throughout the world and often translated/reprinted.

Since 1974 the IEA has helped to create a worldwide network of 100 similar institutions in over 70 countries. They are all independent but share the IEA's mission.

Views expressed in the IEA's publications are those of the authors, not those of the Institute (which has no corporate view), its Managing Trustees, Academic Advisory Council members or senior staff.

Members of the Institute's Academic Advisory Council, Honorary Fellows, Trustees and Staff are listed on the following page.

The Institute gratefully acknowledges financial support for its publications programme and other work from a generous benefaction by the late Alec and Beryl Warren.

Other papers recently published by the IEA include:

The Legal Foundations of Free Markets
Edited by Stephen F. Copp
Hobart Paperback 36; ISBN 978 0 255 36591 8; £15.00

Climate Change Policy: Challenging the Activists
Edited by Colin Robinson
Readings 62; ISBN 978 0 255 36595 6; £10.00

Should We Mind the Gap?
Gender Pay Differentials and Public Policy
J. R. Shackleton
Hobart Paper 164; ISBN 978 0 255 36604 5; £10.00

Pension Provision: Government Failure Around the World
Edited by Philip Booth et al.
Readings 63; ISBN 978 0 255 36602 1; £15.00

New Europe's Old Regions
Piotr Zientara
Hobart Paper 165; ISBN 978 0 255 36617 5; £12.50

Central Banking in a Free Society
Tim Congdon
Hobart Paper 166; ISBN 978 0 255 36623 6; £12.50

Verdict on the Crash: Causes and Policy Implications
Edited by Philip Booth
Hobart Paperback 37; ISBN 978 0 255 36635 9; £12.50

The European Institutions as an Interest Group
The Dynamics of Ever-Closer Union
Roland Vaubel
Hobart Paper 167; ISBN 978 0 255 36634 2; £10.00

An Adult Approach to Education
Alison Wolf
Hobart Paper 168; ISBN 978 0 255 36586 4; £10.00

Taxation and Red Tape
The Cost to British Business of Complying with the UK Tax System
Francis Chittenden, Hilary Foster & Brian Sloan
Research Monograph 64; ISBN 978 0 255 36612 0; £12.50

Ludwig von Mises – A Primer
Eamonn Butler
Occasional Paper 143; ISBN 978 0 255 36629 8; £7.50

Does Britain Need a Financial Regulator?
Statutory Regulation, Private Regulation and Financial Markets
Terry Arthur & Philip Booth
Hobart Paper 169; ISBN 978 0 255 36593 2; £12.50

Hayek's *The Constitution of Liberty*
An Account of Its Argument
Eugene F. Miller
Occasional Paper 144; ISBN 978 0 255 36637 3; £12.50

Fair Trade Without the Froth
A Dispassionate Economic Analysis of 'Fair Trade'
Sushil Mohan
Hobart Paper 170; ISBN 978 0 255 36645 8; £10.00

A New Understanding of Poverty
Poverty Measurement and Policy Implications
Kristian Niemietz
Research Monograph 65; ISBN 978 0 255 36638 0; £12.50

The Challenge of Immigration
A Radical Solution
Gary S. Becker
Occasional Paper 145; ISBN 978 0 255 36613 7; £7.50

Other IEA publications

Comprehensive information on other publications and the wider work of the IEA can be found at www.iea.org.uk. To order any publication please see below.

Personal customers

Orders from personal customers should be directed to the IEA:
Isha Kacker
IEA
2 Lord North Street
FREEPOST LON10168
London SW1P 3YZ
Tel: 020 7799 8907. Fax: 020 7799 2137
Email: ikacker@iea.org.uk

Trade customers

All orders from the book trade should be directed to the IEA's distributor:
Gazelle Book Services Ltd (IEA Orders)
FREEPOST RLYS-EAHU-YSCZ
White Cross Mills
Hightown
Lancaster LA1 4XS
Tel: 01524 68765. Fax: 01524 53232
Email: sales@gazellebooks.co.uk

IEA subscriptions

The IEA also offers a subscription service to its publications. For a single annual payment (currently £42.00 in the UK), subscribers receive every monograph the IEA publishes. For more information please contact:
Isha Kacker
Subscriptions
IEA
2 Lord North Street
FREEPOST LON10168
London SW1P 3YZ
Tel: 020 7799 8907. Fax: 020 7799 2137
Email: ikacker@iea.org.uk